ARBITRATION

PRINCIPLES
AND PRACTICE

ARBITRATION

PRINCIPLES AND PRACTICE

JOHN PARRIS
LLB(Hons), PhD

COLLINS
8 Grafton Street, London W1

Collins Professional and Technical Books
William Collins Sons & Co. Ltd
8 Grafton Street, London W1X 3LA

First published in Great Britain by
Granada Publishing Limited 1983
(Original ISBN 0 246 11899 7)
Reprinted with minor amendments by
Collins Professional and Technical Books 1985

British Library Cataloguing in Publication Data
Parris, John
Arbitration.
1. Arbitration and award
I. Title
344.207'9   KD7645

ISBN 0–00–383171–X

Typeset by V & M Graphics Ltd, Aylesbury, Bucks
Printed and bound in Great Britain by
Mackays of Chatham, Kent

Contents

Introduction

Long ago, when I was a young man, there was an elderly gentleman – even more elderly than I am now – who used to parade outside the law courts in the Strand wearing a battered top hat and a billboard bearing the words 'Don't litigate – Arbitrate'. He was regarded as a nutcase and avoided by members of the Bar, but I was curious enough as a young barrister to talk to him.

At that time, I knew nothing of arbitration. In honours degree courses in law, final Bar examinations and post graduate courses, the dirty word was never mentioned. There is still not one single university in the United Kingdom that teaches arbitration law.

His story was simple. He had been the beneficiary of a disputed will. He had been offered the chance of arbitration about it but, advised by his solicitor, he had declined. Before any decision had been arrived at in the courts, all litigation ground to a halt. The entire estate had been expended on lawyers' fees; neither he nor his opponents got anything. The lawyers carved it up between them.

This is not exactly a novel theme. There is a fifteenth century earthenware plaque in York Castle Museum termed 'The Law Suit' which shows two farmers disputing about a cow, one pulling at its head and the other at its tail. Underneath are two lawyers in wig and gown busy milking the cow.

When I spoke to this old man I was sceptical about his story. Later, two cases in which I was involved as counsel, were discontinued because we, the lawyers, solicitors and barristers, had eaten up the sums in dispute. And I was also involved in dozens of cases where the costs dwarfed the sums in dispute, so there was appeal after appeal, partly to postpone judgment, and partly on the principle of the gambler's last desperate throw before going on to the terrace outside the casino and blowing his brains out.

There must be a better way of settling disputes than this, I thought. There is. It's called arbitration.

'The English have always been more given to peaceableness and industry than other people and rather than go so far as London and be at so great charges with attorneys and lawyers, they will refer their difference to the Arbitration of their parish priests, or the Arbitration of Honest Neighbours' – Edward Chamberlayne: *Angliae Notitia*, 12th Edition, 1684.

The attitude of lawyers to arbitration has been one of unmitigated hostility for centuries, for the reasons admirably explained by Lord Campbell in the *Scott* v. *Avery* case [2.12].

Since then, the enemies of arbitration have become more subtle and sought to encroach on the simple arbitration procedure by ensuring that they get in on the act. As a result in the latest legal tome on the subject there are references to some 1200 leading court cases on the subject, most of them, needless to say, contradictory.

The technique whereby this has been achieved can be summarised chronologically:

(1) An arbitrator in England as late as the eighteenth century was entitled to decide on whatever appeared to him to be just and equitable [1.04]. From the early nineteenth century, however, the courts started insisting that they decide according to law – even though expressly authorised to the contrary by the parties.

(2) A statute of 1698 authorised the courts to set aside awards 'procured by corruption or undue means'. In the 1889 Act these words became 'where the arbitrator has misconducted himself or an arbitration or award has been improperly procured' – quite clearly intended still to mean conduct that was basically dishonest. The courts, to enlarge their authority, have interpreted the words 'misconducted himself' to mean trifling technical errors in procedure [6.13]. They now often express surprise that arbitrators resent being accused of 'misconduct', particularly since that was the euphemism at one time in use in the courts for adultery.

(3) In 1802, the judges invented [6.03] the theory that they were entitled to set aside an award on the grounds of error of fact or law on the face of the award. (The 1979 Act removed that jurisdiction from

them.) The curious may wonder how they ever acquired it [6.03]. As late as 1857 Mr Justice Williams had qualms of conscience about the propriety of all this.

(4)   By 1958, the judges were claiming [6.02] they had an inherent right at common law to set aside arbitrators' awards quite apart from statute. If that were so, it is surprising that the statutes were found necessary.

(5)   The 1889 and 1950 Acts indicate that the intention of Parliament was to allow an arbitrator to conduct a formal hearing in an inquisitorial manner and not the usual adversary procedure used in the courts [4.08]. This is clearly shown by the provision, now contained in section 12(1), that the parties shall submit *to be examined by* the arbitrator on oath [4.08]. It will be noted that the word used in both statutes is *by* and not *before*. The courts have however insisted that the adversarial system of the courts should be employed, notwithstanding that statutory provision to the contrary. The present Master of the Rolls has even gone so far as to say that if a full hearing is intended, the procedure of the High Court must be followed.

(6)   The judges refused to allow the parties to exclude by contract the case stated procedure [6.06] for appeal.

(7)   The 1979 Arbitration Act was the great triumph of the lawyers. It passed through both Houses of Parliament 'on the nod', without examination, as a result of the unexpected collapse of the Labour Government. It originated in a bill drafted by the Commercial Court Committee, consisting of twelve lawyers and three laymen, without a single representative from the construction industry or other big users of arbitration.
   The result has been what many, myself included, predicted – an enormous increase in appeals to the courts from arbitrators' awards. So much so that, in panic, the courts in *The Nema*, and subsequent cases [6.08] have had to stamp on the brakes. That case, the first to be heard under the Act, is illustrative of all its evils. After eight hearings in court, and including three in the House of Lords, at vast expense and delay, the original award of the arbitrator was restored.

(8)   The latest triumph of the lawyers also occurred in *The Nema* [6.08]. The 1979 Act allows appeals only on points of law. The House

of Lords extended that to include the same right to review findings of pure fact as in the case of subordinate tribunals: *Edwards* v. *Bairstow* (1956).

The result is that every party who is allowed to should exercise the right to contract out which is given by section 3 of the 1979 Act [6.17]. Those who are not allowed to contract out should go and hold their arbitrations in the Channel Islands. Those happy isles have no arbitration law.

John Parris
Oxford

Note

References in square brackets are to section headings of the book.
The index, table of cases and table of statutes have been prepared by Daniel Gerrans BA(Cantab), LLB, Barrister.

Chapter 1
The nature of arbitration

1.01 What is an arbitration?

'What is an arbitration?' and 'Who is an arbitrator?' are questions which, although of immense importance, are not capable of simple answers in English law. Although there have been statutes passed by Parliament in England to regulate arbitration since the reign of William III, not one has ever defined what is an arbitration.

To add to that difficulty, the word is currently misused to apply to two procedures which are not arbitration, in that they lack at least one essential element of true arbitration.

The first is the use of the word in relation to labour disputes. It is commonly used by politicians and the press to describe the reference to a third party by employers and trade unions of a labour dispute. That procedure is not true arbitration, since neither party intends that the so-called award by the so-called arbitrator should in any way be binding on them. In England, labour unions do not contract. The most they do is to enter into what are humorously termed a 'gentlemen's agreement' with employers; and, as one judge observed, 'a gentlemen's agreement is an agreement to which neither party is a gentleman and to which neither intends to be bound if it does not suit his convenience.'

Agreements, in the United Kingdom, between management and labour are not contracts, for the simple reason that neither party wishes them to be enforceable by the courts as contracts.

In England, an intention to create legally enforceable relationships is essential before there can be a contract. It is otherwise in countries, such as the majority elsewhere in Europe, which have the Roman law system; there, certain situations will create contractual obligations, irrespective of the wishes or intentions of the parties.

The English system regarding labour relations apparently enjoys the confidence of employers and unions and received the approval of the Royal Commission into Trade Unions presided over by Lord Donovan.

The United States law is different. There, the unions do enter into contracts with employers which are enforceable by the courts, so that the arbitration of a labour dispute in the United States may indeed be true arbitration, in that both parties will be bound by the award. The United Steel Workers of America have binding contracts with 2600 employers. Disputes with major employers, such as United Steel, are settled in permanent arbitration courts or, more recently, for minor disputes, by an instant arbitration procedure. Awards given in these proceedings are legally binding on both parties and are therefore true arbitration. In England, decisions in labour disputes by a third party are binding on neither party, cannot be registered as a judgment of the courts and are therefore not true arbitration.

The term 'arbitration' has also been purloined for a procedure in the British county courts which is in fact litigation.

It is not arbitration because the parties do not themselves select the one who shall decide the issues between them. The trial is before the Registrar of the County Court. It is an effort by the lawyers to provide a small claims court which is what, of course, the original British county courts were intended, but have long since ceased, to be.

It is to be regretted that the goodwill attached to the word 'arbitration' should have been misappropriated for ordinary litigation, when the parties are saddled with a judge they may not want and have to attend whenever he instructs them to, in a place that is certainly not of their own choice.

The question as to what is an arbitration is of great importance because the provisions of the Arbitration Acts of 1950, 1975 and 1979 do not apply to any other procedures.

The question of 'Who is an arbitrator' is also often of vital importance, because, in the present state of English law, an arbitrator cannot be sued for negligence [3.09].

1.02 The resolution of disputes

Disputes between men are inevitable, and productive of much good to society. We are all of us freer, whatever our religion and more especially if we have none, because Luther pinned his thesis to the door of Würzburg Cathedral.

How these inevitable disputes and differences are resolved is a criterion of civilisation.

The earliest method, dating back to Cain and Abel, is dignified by legal theorists with the title of 'self-help'. Basically, it consists of beating an opponent over a head with a club.

It is popular even among the pious; witness the great Council of the Church of Adie, whose members tried to resolve the *filiosque* controversy (as to whether the Holy Ghost proceeded from the Father, or from the Father *and* the Son) by beating each other over the head with stools. But it tends to be counter-productive: the Eastern and Western churches are still divided on this point. It is also lacking in finality – especially if the opponent has relatives and friends. Notwithstanding that, it is highly favoured today, especially in international affairs.

The second method is not greatly superior to the first. This consists of submitting the dispute to somebody who has a bigger club than either of the disputants and who is powerful enough to beat both over the head. Some might say that this is the principle of the English legal system which owes its origins, and many of its characteristics today, to the sale of a portion of the absolute power of an absolute monarch by his servants for their personal profit. As *The Times* newspaper remarked in an editorial: 'The English legal system is medieval, with Victorian trimmings.' There is no longer an absolute monarch but the judges, once described as 'lions under the throne' are now lions above the throne. They exercise the absolute powers of an absolute monarch with only public opinion to restrain them.

It is not perhaps surprising that the outstanding characteristic of the English legal system is that it leaves both parties feeling they have been beaten over the head. This is no new experience. As Richard Burton put it over three hundred years ago: 'He who goes to law takes a wolf by the ears.'

The third and most civilised method of settling disputes is for those concerned to submit their disagreement to a third party and agree to abide by his decision. 'Sometime in the Saxon or Old English, it was called a *Love-Day*, because of the Quiet and Tranquillity that should follow the ending of the Controversie': *Arbitrium redivivam* (1694). This is what Paul advocated when he called upon believers not to pursue their disputes before the courts of any state but to submit them to the brethren.

The original Roman concept of civil litigation in classical times was a submission to an arbitrator whom both parties had agreed upon. 'None would our ancestors permit to be a *judex*,' wrote Cicero, 'even in the most trifling money matter, unless the opposing parties were agreed upon him.'

The English courts only began enforcing contractual obligations not under seal in the sixteenth century, and then only as an action 'on the case' of the quasi-criminal writ of trespass – what we now term 'a tort'. Centuries before that, merchants in this country were enforcing amongst themselves oral and written contracts by arbitration.

1.03 Arbitrations and the legal system in England

Arbitrations were in fact well known in England long before there was any legal system which applied to the whole country. They have always been viewed with jealousy and suspicion by lawyers, who see themselves deprived of work thereby. As Lord Campbell frankly admitted in *Scott* v. *Avery & Ors* (1856):

> 'I know that there has been a very great inclination in the courts for a good many years to throw obstacles in the way of arbitration. I wish to speak with great respect of my predecessors the judges: but I must just let your lordships into the secret of that tendency.
>
> There is no disguising the fact that as formerly the emoluments of the judges depended mainly or almost entirely upon fees and they had no fixed salary, there was great competition to get as much as possible of litigation into Westminster Hall, and a great scramble in Westminster Hall for the division of the spoil, and hence the disputes between the different courts about the effect of a *latitat*, a *capias*, and a *quo minus* – the *latitat* bringing business into the court of Queen's Bench, the *capias* into the Common Pleas, and the *quo minus* into the Exchequer.
>
> They had great jealousy of arbitrations, whereby Westminster Hall was robbed of those cases which came neither into the Queen's Bench, nor the Common Pleas, nor the Exchequer.
>
> Therefore, they said that the courts ought not to be ousted of their jurisdiction, and that it was contrary to the policy of the law of Common Pleas.'

In spite of fixed salaries, that attitude, some might say, has not disappeared from judges and lawyers, notwithstanding protestations to the contrary, and it is fully reflected in the Arbitration Act 1979.

By contrast, in the United States the courts have positively encouraged arbitration. As long ago as 1854, the Supreme Court held that arbitration 'as a mode of settling disputes should receive every encouragement from the courts': *Burchell* v. *Marsh* (1854). More recently in *Prima Paint* v. *Flood and Conklin* (1967) the same court again emphasised that it was national policy to encourage arbitrations. It honoured, it said, 'the unmistakenly clear Congressional purpose that the arbitration procedure, when selected by the parties to a contract, be speedy and not subject to delay and obstruction in the courts'. In that case it upheld the right of an arbitrator to decide whether the contract under which he himself was appointed had been induced by fraud – something which would undoubtedly be outside the power of any English arbitrator.

1.04 The earlier English system

At the time of Lord Coke in the seventeenth century, if there was an agreement to go to arbitration, 'to go to neighbours', as he charmingly put it, no action in the courts would lie until a 'verdict of the neighbour being first had and obtained'. In other words, in those days in *all* arbitration agreements, arbitration was a condition precedent to an action in the courts, and not only where it is expressly so stated in the arbitration agreement, as in the *Scott* v. *Avery* cases [2.12].

Moreover, it is clear that at that time, and for the centuries before that, an arbitrator was not bound to decide a case by law, but by what he considered just and equitable:

'It is said to be called an Arbitrement ... because the judges elected thereon may determine the Controversie not according to the Law, but according to their opinion and judgment as honest men': *Arbitrium Redivivam* (1694).

Courts were only given power to interfere with an arbitrator's award by the Arbitration Act 1698 whereby if 'any arbitration or umpirage was procured by corruption' the award was to be 'judged and esteemed void and of none effect'. The history of arbitration in England is of the encroachment of the courts upon these fundamental common law and human rights.

1.05 Arbitrations in the United States

Interestingly enough, the view that arbitrators can decide without reference to the law is still taken in the United States. Unless the parties expressly or impliedly specify that the arbitration should be decided by law and if so, by what substantive law, arbitrators are free to resolve the dispute in accordance with their own sense of justice and equity. The rules of the American Arbitration Association, which govern large numbers of commercial arbitrations in that country, lay down no requirement that the arbitrator shall decide according to law. Nor is it a ground for setting aside the award that the arbitrator has not applied the law, or has misdirected himself as to what it is.

In disputes in the U.S.A., therefore, there would be no question of an arbitrator, for example, who found that a bill of lading was not a 'clean bill' under the Rules of the Refined Sugar Association, because it bore an endorsement that the cargo had been discharged *en route* after being damaged by fire and water, and because it was a worthless bit of paper as the buyer and two banks had refused to accept it, having his award set aside because 'the bill of lading, unusual though it was, passed the legal test of cleanliness': Donaldson J in *M. Golodets Inc.* v. *Czarnikow–Rionda Co. Inc.* (1978); whiter than white in law, but worthless to the holder who tried to negotiate it.

The United States has accepted, however, a modification of these rules in the United Nations Commission on International Trade Law (UNCITRAL Arbitration Rules). Article 33 requires the arbitrator to apply the law designated by the parties, failing which, 'the arbitral tribunal shall apply the law determined by the conflict of law rules which it considers applicable'. The next part is the material change:

> 'The arbitral tribunal shall decide as *amiable compositeur* or *ex aequo et bono* only if the parties have expressly authorised the tribunal to do so, and *if the law applicable to the arbitral procedure permits such arbitration*.' (author's italics)

Modern English Law will not permit such decisions.

An *amiable compositeur* is not, in England, an arbitrator. The role of a conciliator is to try to effect a reconciliation between the parties so that they make a settlement of their differences. In many jurisdictions, one appointed as an arbitrator is entitled also to perform the role of an *amiable compositeur* and seek to get the parties to resolve their differences themselves. If he were appointed for that purpose in England he would not be an arbitrator.

Further, in England an arbitrator is not entitled to disregard the law, even if the parties expressly authorise him to, nor can he apply his own idea of what is fair and just, *ex aequo et bono*. These are powerful reasons why UNCITRAL arbitrations should not be held in England.

1.06 Essentials of English arbitration

As a result of the lack of any statutory definition, there has been much litigation about what is and what is not an arbitration, and who is and who is not an arbitrator. Much of it has arisen because, as has been observed, for the present the law appears to be that an arbitrator is immune from actions brought against him by either party for negligence, want of skill, or breach of express or implied terms of a contract [3.09].

For an adjudication by a third party to be an arbitration, it appears from the cases that there are seven essential elements:

(1) There must at the commencement be a dispute or difference between the parties. It is not sufficient that the third party has been appointed to decide for the parties things they have not been able to decide themselves.

(2) That dispute or difference must be of matters which are justiciable. This follows from the fact that the only valid arbitration award is one that is capable of being registered and enforced as a judgment of the courts.

Again, this is different from United States law. The Uniform Arbitration Act, which has been adopted in a majority of the States, provides that 'a written contract to submit to arbitration *any controversy* thereafter arising between the parties is valid, enforceable and irrevocable' and the New York arbitration code expressly provides for the enforcement of any agreement *'without regard to the justiciable character of the controversy'*.

(3) The parties in dispute must agree 'not by compulsion or coercion of law but of their own accord' to submit their dispute for resolution by a third party. (But there are numerous statutory provisions which require resolution of disputes by arbitration.)

(4) The agreement to submit to arbitration must be a binding contractual obligation.

(5) It must provide for the settlement of the dispute or difference by a third person chosen by themselves or by somebody they have agreed should appoint the third party if they fail to agree upon one.

(6) There must be a *formal* reference of the dispute to the decision of the third party [1.01].

(7) That third party must expressly or impliedly be required to decide according to law [4.06] because 'if the parties choose to provide in their contract that their rights and obligations shall not be decided in accordance with law, there is no contract, as the parties do not intend that their legal relations shall be affected': *Orion Compania Espanola* v. *Belfort Maatschappij* (1962).

This is a non-sequitur, if there ever was one.

1.07 Domestic arbitrations

The 1975 Act distinguishes between domestic arbitration agreements and non-domestic ones. Domestic arbitration agreements can be defined as follows:

(1) Arbitrations which do not provide for arbitration, expressly or by implication, in any state outside the United Kingdom. Arbitrations in jurisdictions other than the English one, e.g. Scottish and the Channel Islands, are still domestic arbitrations, as are arbitrations where the parties subsequently by agreement decide to hold their arbitration outside England, for example, in one of the Channel Islands.

(2) Where *none* of the parties is an individual who is a national of or habitually resident in any state other than the U.K. It is a non-domestic arbitration if an individual resident in the United Kingdom is a foreign national. So that if a non-British person, including an immigrant, buys a house subject to the National House-Building Council scheme, the agreement to refer a dispute to arbitration will be a non-domestic one.

(3) The 1975 Act also applies where one of the parties is a corporate body 'incorporated in or whose central management and control is exercised in any state other than the United Kingdom'. It must therefore apply to British registered companies which are controlled by overseas investors, whether wholly owned or not, e.g. under United States management.

From the above it will be apparent that the statement in the

Commercial Court Committee Report on Arbitration (Cmnd 7284) para 40. : 'Non-domestic arbitration agreements are not defined but are necessarily foreign or international in character' is not merely erroneous, but is seriously misleading as to the effect of the 1975 statute.

For non-domestic arbitration agreements the court has no discretion as to whether or not to order a 'stay of litigation proceedings': section 1 of the 1975 Act provides that it *shall* do so, as distinct from the word *may* which is used in section 4 of the 1950 Act: *Lonrho* v. *Shell Petroleum & Ors* (1978).

Moreover, it would appear that clauses excluding the judicial review by the courts under the 1979 Act can effectively be entered into in non-domestic arbitration agreements as defined above, e.g. Pakistani nationals resident in the United Kingdom can ensure that in all their contracts there is a clause excluding judicial review of any arbitrations to which they are parties. So, too, can all British registered but overseas controlled companies. British subjects and British controlled companies can only exclude judicial review if the exclusion clause is made *after* the commencement of an arbitration: section 3 of 1979 Act.

1.08 What is a dispute?

This is important because, even if there is an appointment of a third party, if there is no dispute it will not be an arbitration and he will not be an arbitrator. If the parties agree to refer some matter upon which they have been unable to agree to a third party, he is not an arbitrator but an independent expert, a valuer or certifier called in to complete their contract for them, or under the terms of the contract, as in the case of a rent review.

But it is also essential that there should be a dispute because unless there is, the courts have no power under section 4 of the Arbitration Act 1950 to stay proceedings and refer the matter to arbitration.

The question has become of even greater importance since the Arbitration Act 1975, since under section 1 of that act the courts have an obligation to stay an action brought by non-domestic parties.

In the case of domestic arbitration, under section 4 of the 1950 Act, the courts have a discretion as to whether or not they allow proceedings in court to continue: in the case of 'non-domestic' agreements, as defined in the 1975 Act, they have no discretion. They '*shall*' stay the proceedings.

An interesting illustration of this was the action in which Lonhro wished to litigate in the courts, rather than arbitrate, its claim against several well-known petrol companies for conspiracy to defeat the sanctions imposed by the United Kingdom and the United Nations on Southern Rhodesia. Because of the arbitration clause and because some of the parties were 'non-domestic', the court held that it had no option but to stay the proceedings.

There is, however, the important proviso in the 1975 Act that a stay may be refused if 'there is not in fact any dispute between the parties with regard to the matter agreed to be referred': section 1(1).

1.09 No dispute if no defence

There is no dispute if English law does not allow a defence by way of set-off or counterclaim, and these are relied upon.

There are two situations where no defence is allowed by operation of law: the hire of ships and actions on bills of exchange or cheques.

For ships' hire, if the charterer alleges that there were substantial defects in the vessel chartered, he is not allowed by law to offset a counterclaim for damages against the hire. He must pay the hire and bring a separate action for damages. In those circumstances, if there is a court action for the hire, there is no dispute subject to arbitration: *The Alpha Nord* (1977). The situation will apparently be different, however, if the charterer raises a genuine defence to the claim as opposed to a counterclaim, such as that the contract has been frustrated by supervening impossibility of performance: *Kissavos Shipping* v. *Empress Cubana* (1982).

It is similarly English law that if a bill of exchange, including a cheque, is issued, there is no defence to it by way of a counterclaim.

These are the only two cases where, by operation of law, there can be no defence to monies due.

But it is possible by the express terms of a contract to make similar provision that sums certified or otherwise payable shall not be disputed or subject to set-off for counterclaims and where the only remedy is a separate action for damages.

1.10 Set-off and counterclaims no defence under the building forms

The case of *Dawnays Ltd* v. *F. G. Minter Ltd and Trollope & Colls Ltd* (1971) turned upon the meaning of clause 13 of the standard 'Green Form' for nominated sub-contractors issued under the auspices of the National Federation of Building Trades Employers (NFBTE) and the Federation of Associations of Specialists and Sub-contractors

(FASS), and approved by numerous other associations in the construction industry.

This clause read: 'The contractor shall notwithstanding anything in this sub-contract be entitled to deduct from or set-off against any money due from him to the sub-contractor ... any sum or sums which the sub-contractor *is liable to pay* to the sub-contractor under this sub-contract' (author's emphasis).

An architect's interim certificate included a sum of £27,870 due to the plaintiff sub-contractors and this was paid to the main contractors. The contractors refused to pay it to the sub-contractors, claiming that they were entitled to unquantified unliquidated damages for delay caused by the sub-contractors.

The plaintiffs brought proceedings under Order 14 for summary payment of this certified sum and the defendants claimed to be entitled to a stay of the action under section 4 of the Arbitration Act 1950 because there was an arbitration clause in the 'Green Form.'

The defendants succeeded before a Queen's Bench Master and a judge in being granted a stay of proceedings pending arbitration of the dispute, but a strong Court of Appeal (Lord Denning MR, Edmund Davies and Stamp LJJ) reversed this on the ground that there was no dispute as to the certified sum and the contract gave no right of set-off for an unquantified or other claims to unliquidated damages for delay.

Lord Denning said:

'It must be remembered that a disputed claim cannot be referred at once to arbitration. Unless all agree, the determination of a disputed claim has to wait until completion of the work. The arbitration clause makes that plain.

It follows that if the contention of [counsel for the defendants] is correct, his clients could hold this money indefinitely. They could hold on to it until the end of the main contract, that is, until the whole work is completed. They could then hold on to it still longer whilst the dispute was referred to arbitration. They would not have to pay it over until the arbitration was concluded, maybe after a case stated to this court.'

He later went on to say:

'An interim certificate is to be regarded virtually as cash, like a bill of exchange. It must be honoured. Payment must not be withheld on account of cross-claims, whether good or bad, except so far as the contract specifically provides. Otherwise any main-contractor could always get out of payment by making all sorts of unfounded cross-claims. All the more so in a case like the present, when the main contractors have actually received the money.'

Regrettably, Lord Denning's judgment did not specify expressly whether a stay was being refused because:

(a) under section 4 of the 1950 Act, the High Court has a discretion as to whether or not litigation should be allowed to proceed, or whether

(b) a stay was being refused because there was no defence to the plaintiffs' action.

On either ground, it is submitted with respect, the stay was correctly refused.

Where a contract provides for no immediate arbitration and provides that no arbitration shall take place until completion of the main contract, it is within the discretion of the courts to refuse a stay. As Lord Salmon said in *Gilbert-Ash Ltd* v. *Modern Engineering* (1973), if sub-contractors were to sue because 'the contractors were unwilling to go to arbitration until completion or abandonment of the main contract, I am sure the courts, in exercise of their discretion, would refuse a stay'.

But Lord Justice Edmund Davies, as he then was, in *Dawnays*' case was more specific: 'There was clearly no defence in this case.' And later in his judgment he said:

'The simple fact is that the defendants can assert no definite and liquidated sum as being unquestionably due to them from the plaintiffs. Unless and until they can do this, they cannot invoke clause 13 in the manner sought by the defendants.

Any other view would involve that the sub-contractor could be kept out of his money until the contract is completed, whereupon the main contractor would condescend to go to arbitration about the matter. In the result, a sub-contractor could be kept out of his money for an unconscionable period, with possibly disastrous financial results.'

This decision of the Court of Appeal was subjected to review by the House of Lords on an application for leave to appeal. There, Mr K. F.

Goodfellow QC for the petitioners, the defendants in the courts below, said: 'We approach this contract on the assumption that you can only deduct or set off those sums that it specifically provides.' The application for leave to appeal was refused.

The decision of the Court of Appeal in the *Dawnays* case was followed by the Court of Appeal in *Frederick Mark Ltd* v. *Schield* (1971), in which Lord Justice Roskill, as he then was, explained what Lord Denning had said.

'In the context in which the Master of the Rolls was referring to bills of exchange, it is plain that his lordship was only using a bill of exchange as a convenient analogy, as a type of instrument, a debt ... which cannot ... in general be made the subject of set-off and counterclaim so as to avoid immediate payment of the sum due.

Of course, in many respects an interim certificate is not analogous to a bill of exchange. For example, it is not a negotiable instrument ...

What the Master of the Rolls was saying was that the debt was of the class which, *by reason of the contractual provisions of the contract*, ought not to be allowed to be made the subject of a set-off or counterclaim as a reason for not paying the sum which the architect had duly certified as due from the building owner to the builder ... I agree with every word of the Master of the Rolls' judgment' (author's emphasis).

His lordship then went on to say that he disagreed with Mr Justice Donaldson, as he then was, sitting as a judge in chambers, who had decided not to follow *Dawnays* case 'on the ground that the cases on equitable set-off ... had not been brought to the attention of the Court of Appeal'.

'If it be the fact that he said this, I think he was plainly wrong,' said Lord Roskill. 'It seems plain that the Court of Appeal must have had all those cases well in mind.' With this, Lord Justice Davies, as he then was, and Lord Justice Karminski agreed.

Other cases in which this was followed were *GKN Foundations* v. *Wandsworth Borough Council* (1972); *Algrey Contractors Ltd* v. *Tenth Moat Housing Society Ltd* (1972); *Brightside Kilpatrick Engineering Services* v. *Mitchell Construction* (1975); and *Token Construction* v. *Charlton Estates* (1973).

However, in an article in the *Law Quarterly Review* (89 LQR 36) the learned editor of the tenth edition of *Hudson's Building and*

Engineering Contracts attacked all these decisions.

As a result, some of the law lords in the House of Lords in *Gilbert-Ash (Northern) Ltd* v. *Modern Engineering (Bristol) Ltd* (1973) appear to have adopted that author's views without having the matter argued before them in a case where it was entirely irrelevant because the main contractor's own form of sub-contract expressly authorised the contractor to withhold or deduct monies alleged to be due under that contract 'or any other contract'. The House resiled from that position in *Mottram Consultants Ltd* v. *Bernard Sunley & Sons Ltd* (1974) and held that the *Gilbert-Ash* case did no more than establish that each case should be construed according to the terms of the contract in question, without any *parti pris* in favour of or against the existence of a right of set-off or counterclaim.

The NFBTE and FASS speedily altered the wording of the 'Green Form' to make it plain that the meaning attributed to the words 'is liable' in *Dawnays'* case was what they in fact intended, which wording has been continued into the Joint Contracts Tribunal Nominated Sub-Contract forms NSC/4 and 4a. On numerous occasions up to his retirement in 1982, Lord Denning himself asserted that *Dawnays* case was good law and had not been over-ruled.

With respect, it is submitted that that indeed is so. If a sum has been certified by the architect under the Standard Form of Building Contract as being due to the sub-contractor, the main contractor is not entitled to withhold payment on account of any alleged right of counterclaim or set-off, and there is therefore no dispute which can be referred to arbitration, any more than there is in the case of a bill of exchange or ship's hire. Regrettably, the Queen's Bench Masters do not seem to have taken this point.

1.11 Failure to pay not a dispute

In *London North Western Railway* v. *Jones* (1915) the House of Lords held that a simple failure to pay a debt was not within the scope of an arbitration clause which covered 'disputes' between the parties. Importance was apparently attached to the fact that the defendant had not disputed his liability to pay.

'It follows that the courts can be resorted to without previous recourse to arbitration to enforce a claim which is not disputed but which the trader merely persists in not paying,' said Mr Justice Rowlett.

However, in *Ellerine Brothers (Proprietary) Ltd & Ano.* v. *Klinger*

(1979) there was a contractual duty under seal to account to the plaintiffs for net profits. It was held that the obligation was to do more than just pay over any net profits, in that the defendant had from time to time to account to the plaintiffs with written statements, and this he had failed to do. Judge John Newey QC held that the correct meaning to be attributed to 'account' and the difference between gross and net profits were matters involving the construction of the deed, and must therefore necessarily fall within the scope of an arbitration agreement which provided that 'all disputes or differences whatsoever... between the parties hereto ... touching or concerning the deed and its construction or effect or as to the rights, duties or liabilities of the parties hereto ... or by virtue of this deed' should be referred.

The case fell within section 1 of the Arbitration Act 1975 since the plaintiffs were a company incorporated outside the United Kingdom. The judge indicated that, had he had a discretion whether or not to stay under section 4 of the 1950 Act, he would have undoubtedly refused a stay since court proceedings would have provided, as he put it, 'a more expeditious and satisfactory remedy than arbitration'.

1.12 Reference for a decision

It would appear that, for there to be an arbitration in English law, it is necessary that there should be not only a formulated dispute but also a formal application to a third party for a decision.

Monmouthshire County Council v. *Costelloe & Kemple Ltd* (1965) may not be binding authority on this point since it turns on the construction of clause 66 of the Institution of Civil Engineers (ICE) conditions [2.17], but it is nevertheless highly relevant, even though the court declined to express an opinion as to whether the engineer was or was not an arbitrator under that clause.

The contractors in that case undertook to do certain road works under the ICE Contract 4th Edition. The bills of quantities provided that only 1000 cubic yards of rock would need to be excavated. In fact, some 25,000 cubic yards had to be.

The contract provided in clause 12(2) that 'If... during the execution of the works the contractor shall encounter physical conditions ... which ... could not have been reasonably foreseen ...' he should give notice to the engineer. The contract provided that extra payment should be made in that event. Work commenced in December 1958 and on 23 March 1959 the contractors gave such notice. On 8 March 1961 the contractors wrote to the engineer giving a quantification of their claim, with other matters, totalling £64,406.

Earlier, on 11 April 1960, they had written to the engineer, who was an employee of the other contracting party: 'We note that you do not consider we have any substantial claims on this contract, but ... we have been involved in a most considerable extra cost in dealing with unforeseen circumstances ...' They advised him that they were quantifying these claims and added: 'Upon receipt of these claims you can, of course, give your decision under the relevant claims of the contract and we, in due course, will have to notify you of our intention to go to arbitration.'

On 7 April 1961, a letter from the engineer repudiated the quantified claims made in the letter of 8 March 1961. It began: 'With reference to your letter of 8th March 1961, I enclose my observations and comments on your claims numbered 1 to 11.' He concluded, in respect of each claim: 'I cannot agree with or consider this claim.'

Subsequently, it was claimed by Monmouthshire County Council that the letter of 8 March 1961 amounted to a reference to the engineer of a dispute or difference under clause 66 and his decision thereon was by his letter of 7 April 1961. Mr Justice Mocatta so held, with the result that he also held that the contractors had no right to go to arbitration since they had not instituted it, as required, within three calendar months 'after receiving notice of such decision'.

The Court of Appeal reversed his decision.

Lord Denning said:

'The first point is this: was there any dispute or difference arising between the contractors and the engineer?

It is accepted that in order that a dispute or difference can arise on this contract, there must in the first place be a claim by the contractor. Until that claim is rejected you cannot say that there is a dispute or difference. There must be both a claim and a rejection of it in order to constitute a dispute or difference.

Applying that here, it is clear ... there was a dispute or difference long before April 1961. But in regard to the detailed claim for rock under the other clauses and for several other of the eleven items, there was no claim before the letter of 8 March and no dispute or difference until they were rejected in the letter of 7 April.

The next point is this: was there any dispute or difference referred to the engineer for decision within clause 66? When one looks at the document, the only letter that can be said to be a reference to him is the letter of 8 March itself. I cannot read that letter as a reference to

the engineer of any dispute or difference for his decision ... I
read that letter as a reference to the engineer for his decision (
matter. It is simply a request for his comments and for subse
discussion.

    I do not regard the letter of 7th April 1961 as a decision on a
dispute or difference, but merely as a rejection of claims.'

Lord Justice Winn, agreeing, added that in his view the clause should
be regarded as requiring a reference, in the sense of a submission, to the
engineer so as to give him seisin (that is, jurisdiction) as an arbitrator
and for that 'there must be some positive act of reference to him of that
dispute'.

    With respect, that seems to summarise the legal position admirably:
before there can be an arbitration and before a person can be
constituted an arbitrator 'there must be some positive act of reference to
him' of the dispute.

1.13 Arbitration or litigation?

The commercial community, the construction industry and landlords
have long preferred arbitration to litigation. Their reasons may be
summarised as follows:

(1) *Expertise*

An arbitrator is normally selected for his expert knowledge of a
particular trade whereas, apart from the Official Referees, High Court
judges deal with such a wide range of cases that they possess little
expertise except by accident. As Lord Salmon frankly admitted in one
case, 'I cannot help thinking that building contractors and sub-
contractors and architects ... know far more about the building trade
than I, or indeed any judge, can hope to'. And Mr Justice Mocatta,
discussing this aspect of the question in *Gunter Henck* v. *André et Cie
SA* (1970), said that one of the advantages of arbitration is that 'the
tribunal ... is usually chosen from gentlemen in the trade who may be
assumed to know very much more of its technicalities than any judge
could hope to know ...'

(2) *Privacy*

Cases in the courts are conducted in public and inquisitive journalists
or trade competitors cannot be excluded except in the most
exceptional circumstances. At an arbitration hearing nobody except
the parties is entitled to be present, and nobody else can be without the

consent of both parties and the arbitrator. As Mr Justice Mocatta said in the *Gunter* case *supra*: 'One of the major attractions indubitably is the lack of publicity in relation to the proceedings.'

(3) *Convenience*

An arbitrator normally arranges for a hearing, if one is necessary (and oral hearings may not be necessary), at a time and place to suit the convenience of the parties. In litigation, the case is listed to suit the convenience of the court primarily, and after that the convenience of counsel. Once a case comes into the 'warned list' it can be called upon at any time at short notice.

Moreover, High Court actions for the most part have to be set down and heard in London, although it is possible for them to be heard sometimes in the provinces, but usually only after long delays.

(4) *Expedition*

Whether the dispute is resolved without delay by arbitration depends entirely upon the quality of the arbitrator. Some arbitrators may prove dilatory, and allow one of the parties to be dilatory. But if the arbitrator is competent, he can bring matters to a hearing very quickly. What can only be described as the 'professional' arbitrators in the City of London, dealing with shipping and cargo disputes, deliver their awards with great despatch.

Generally in any dispute there is one party who wishes to have the dispute resolved as quickly as possible, and one (usually, but not always, the respondent) who will adopt every strategem possible to prevent the issues being actually resolved. The Rules of the Supreme Court provide wonderful opportunities for procrastination. 'The pangs of dispriz'd love, the law's delay' are as evident today as they were in Shakespeare's day.

The arbitrator has ample powers to speed up the proceedings [4.25] and the fact that these powers are infrequently used tends to reflect on the arbitrator and not on the arbitration process.

As Lord Justice Lawton said in *Ellis Mechanical Services Ltd*, v. *Wates Construction Ltd* (1976): 'The courts are aware what happens in these building disputes: cases go either to arbitration or before an Official Referee; they drag on and on. The cash flow is held up. In the majority of cases, because one party or the other cannot wait any longer for the money, there is some kind of compromise, very often not based on the justice of the case but on the financial situation of one of the parties.'

(5) *Cost*

'There is a saving of expense, but not always,' said Mr Justice Mocatta in the case of *Gunter* quoted above. It should not be forgotten that the parties to arbitration have to pay for the room in which the hearing takes place and the fees of the arbitrator whereas, apart from court fees, the parties do not pay for the court or the services of the judge.

(6) *Advocacy*

The right to appear for parties in the High Court is limited to barristers, who in turn have to be instructed by solicitors. At an arbitration anyone can appear for the parties.

(7) *Relationship of the parties*

It is generally possible with arbitration to resolve disputes between two parties who wish to go on doing business together in a friendly way; whereas, by the time the parties have resorted to their lawyers, writs have been issued, and the lawyers have engaged in the 'adversary' litigation which is standard in the United Kingdom, there is always bad blood between them and little prospect of a resumption of trading relations on a friendly basis.

The disadvantages of arbitration as opposed to litigation are few but can be summarised as:

(1) *Joinder of parties*

In spite of a clumsy attempt in the Joint Contracts Tribunal 1980 Standard Form of Building Contract [2.16] to bring in sub-contractors, an arbitration is normally restricted to the parties to the contract. (But for string contracts see [2.07].) There is no power to bring in other defendants or to join other persons as third parties, either for an indemnity or for a contribution under the Civil Liability (Contribution) Act 1978, or its predecessor the Law Reform (Married Women and Tortfeasors) Act 1935.

(2) *Legal aid*

Legal aid is not available for arbitrations, whereas it is for litigation. In *Smith* v. *Pearl Insurance* (1939) the Court of Appeal decided that the poverty of the defendant was no grounds on which it should refuse to stay an action and not refer it to arbitration. But times change, and in *Fakes* v. *Taylor Woodrow Construction Ltd* (1973) the Court of Appeal in their discretion refused to stay an action where a sub-contractor brought proceedings against the main contractor, on the ground that legal aid was available for litigation but not for arbitration. If it is sought to reconcile these two cases on any other basis than that the passage of time can moderate a judge's view, three things distinguish the two cases:

(a) the *Smith* case was a *Scott* v. *Avery* clause [2.12]

(b) the plaintiff there was suing under the Poor Persons Rules; the legal aid scheme is substantially different; and

(c) in the *Fakes* case, it was alleged that the inability of the plaintiff to provide for his own legal expenses had been caused by the defendants.

(3) *Points of law*

In cases where the dispute between the parties is in essence a point of law [4.06] — and the meaning of a standard contract is a point of law — it may well be more expedient and cheaper to take the case to the High Court, since it is likely to end up there anyway under the provisions of the Arbitration Act 1979. This was advanced as a reason for not staying an action where there was an arbitration clause in *Bristol Corporation* v. *John Aird Ltd* (1913): 'Everybody knows that, with regard to the construction of an agreement, it is absolutely useless to stay the action because it will only come back to the court on a case stated.'

Case stated has now been abolished [6.05] but it may sometimes be cheaper to obtain a declaratory judgment of the High Court on the construction of the contract than debate it before an arbitrator, with the possibility of a subsequent appeal to the High Court.

1.14 Potentiality for delays

An illustration of the potentiality of delays is to be found in the case of *F. & A. (Building Contractors) Ltd* v. *Lennelric Ltd* (1978). The claimants built three houses for the respondents under the 1963 edition of the JCT Standard Form of Building Contract (private edition without quantities) which contained an arbitration clause.

The builders withdrew from the site in 1974, as they were entitled to do under the contract, when two certificates issued by the architect were not paid, after earlier trouble in getting the money due. One cheque 'bounced' three times.

Various counter allegations were made by the respondents and an arbitrator was appointed by the President of the Royal Institute of

British Architects. Solicitors acting for the respondents only answered two letters from the arbitrator. The first, on 23 December 1975, said that the gentleman dealing with the matter was on holiday. The other, on 23 January 1976, acknowledged receipt of the points of claim and said they would let the arbitrator have the points of defence 'as soon as possible'.

'That was the last the arbitrator heard of the respondents' solicitor,' said Judge Fay QC in the High Court.

'Of course, he wished to have the respondents' assent to his terms, to have their agreement to his directions and to have their co-operation in fixing the hearing. Instead, he got silence. He sent various letters by recorded delivery.'

More than a year later, on 17 January 1977, he warned them that if points of defence were not delivered he would proceed with the hearing *ex parte*. He warned them again on 3 February 1977 that he proposed to proceed *ex parte*, and on 11 February he advised them he had fixed the hearing for 6 April 1977 at Stratford-on-Avon.

The hearing duly took place. Neither the respondents nor their solicitors attended but the respondents' own quantity surveyor's valuation was put before the arbitrator who also inspected the houses in question. The arbitrator gave an award in favour of the builders for £7326.

Proceedings to set aside the award were started on the last day of the six week period allowed by the Rules of the High Court.

'They were the first intimation to either claimant or arbitrator that Lennelric Ltd intended to challenge the decision which they had allowed to go by default,' said the judge.

It was claimed that the arbitrator had been guilty of misconduct because he:

(1) proceeded to the hearing of the reference before he duly accepted the appointment to act as arbitrator in the manner in which he himself had prescribed;
(2) failed to give any proper notice to Lennelric Ltd
(3) proceeded to a hearing *ex parte*,

and that the award should be set aside.

On the day of hearing in the High Court, counsel for the respondents was allowed to add a further ground that the award should be set aside and the case remitted to the arbitrator in the interests of justice.

Of the allegations of misconduct against the arbitrator Judge Fay said of (1) 'there is no misconduct here'; of (2) he commented: 'It would have been irregular and not consonant with professional practice to communicate with the lay client when he has asked that his solicitors be dealt with, and here again there can be no misconduct.'

Of (3), the allegation that the arbitrator had erred in proceeding *ex parte*, he said: 'I think that [the arbitrator]'s procedure was correct and cannot be faulted.'

So far as the late amendment to the pleading was concerned, Judge Fay concluded:

'I think that on facts similar to these the High Court would not set aside a default judgment and, in exercise of the similar jurisdiction which I have under section 22 of the Arbitration Act, 1950, I hold that Lennelric Ltd by reason of their delay are not entitled to the remission they seek.'

That was on 20 February 1978. The respondents appealed to the Court of Appeal. On 4 April 1979 it was listed in the warned list for that court but it subsequently disappeared from there. The reason was simple. The respondents had been ordered to be wound up on the petition of the Inland Revenue.

Five years after they had finished the building work, the builders had got nothing and had incurred the arbitrator's expenses and the costs of the arbitration, legal expenses in resisting the application to set aside and the pending Court of Appeal case.

Of the now abolished case stated procedure [6.05] the Commercial Court committee reported: 'The procedure is capable of being used by undeserving parties for the sole purpose of postponing the day when they have to meet their commitments.'

1.15 Arbitration in Scotland

In Scotland, the arbitrator is described as 'the arbiter', and his award is termed the 'decree arbitral'.

Scottish law is based on Roman Law principles but there was in 1695, after the union of the two kingdoms, a statutory enactment about arbitration called 'The Articles of Regulation'.

Currently legislation is still based on that, with a further short Arbitration (Scotland) Act 1894 and one clause in the Administration of Justice (Scotland) Act 1972, which introduced the case stated concept [6.05] into Scottish law but out of which it is open to the parties to contract.

In Scotland, the courts have no discretion to refuse to stay litigation commenced in breach of an arbitration agreement. The parties are forced to adhere to their contractual obligations and there is no discretion, as there is under section 4 of the English Arbitration Act 1950, to relieve one party of his obligation to go to arbitration.

The arbiter normally appoints a clerk, a solicitor, who is responsible for the administration of the proceedings and all communication between the parties. He can act as an *amiable compositeur*, as can the arbiter. The clerk can also be the recipient of 'with prejudice' offers or 'sealed offers' which he does not have to disclose to the arbiter, so that there is in effect a system whereby costs can be effectively determined on the basis of unconditional offers to settle, not dissimiliar to payments into court, of which the judge knows nothing [5.10].

Acceptance of appointment of the arbiter is by a 'minute of acceptance'.

Procedure at the hearing is at the exclusive description of the arbiter, and there is no obligation on him to follow the procedure of the courts. Preliminary meetings are not held except in the most complex of cases. Even if one party demands a formal hearing, with sworn evidence, representation by counsel, and legal submissions, the arbiter is under no obligation to comply.

Written pleadings commonly comprise not only averments of fact, but also written submissions as to the law applicable, known as 'pleas-in-law'. Further and better particulars of either may be ordered and are known as 'adjustments'. When the pleadings are closed, they are embodied in a document known as 'the closed record', though an arbiter has a discretion subsequently to allow 'a minute of amendment'.

At the end of the hearing the arbiter commonly issues, before his decree arbitral, a 'note of proposed findings' and he can listen to further argument on these if he so desires.

Appeals to the courts from his 'decree arbitral' are very limited: it cannot be challenged even if he makes errors of fact or law. Even since the 1972 Act, there can be no reference by way of case stated to the courts unless application for it is made *before* the decree arbitral.

The only other ground of judicial review is *ultra fines compromissi*, namely that the arbiter has acted *ultra vires* his appointment by deciding matters outside the reference to him, or possibly where his decree arbitral fails to deal with all the points at issue between the parties. If he is dilatory, the Court of Session, it would appear, can direct him to proceed with due diligence.

In all, Scottish procedure is generally regarded as more expeditious and cheaper than English and it clearly has numerous advantages over the English system, in particular the freedom from judicial interference [6.01].

1.16 Statutory arbitrations

A very large number of English statutes provide for arbitrations to take place in specified circumstances. In many cases the provisions of the Arbitration Act 1950 are expressly excluded and the procedure laid down by the statute has to be followed.

For example arbitration under the Agricultural Holdings Act 1923 is significantly different from that under the Agricultural Holdings Act 1948, and cases which are authority on one statute have no application to another: *Cooke-Bourne (Farms) Ltd* v. *Mellow & Ano.* (1982).

An arbitrator under some statutory arbitrations will apparently not be guilty of misconduct if he exercises his discretion regarding the award of costs [5.07] without following the practice of the High Court in relation to the judicial exercise of discretion; and an arbitration under some acts has characteristics which differentiate and distinguish it from arbitrations to which the Arbitration Act 1950 applies: *Gray* v. *Ashburton (Lord)* (1917).

However, section 31 of the Arbitration Act 1950 provides that the provisions of sections 1–34 of that Act shall apply 'to every arbitration under any other Act ... as if the arbitration were pursuant to an arbitration agreement and as if that Act were an arbitration agreement'.

But that is qualified by the words 'except in so far as this Act is inconsistent with that other Act or with any rules or procedure authorised or recognised thereby'. An arbitrator and the parties in a statutory arbitration must therefore pay close attention to the words of the statute and any authorities on it.

Section 31 has been extended to apply the Arbitration Act 1979 to statutory arbitrations.

The 1979 Act provides in section 3(5): 'an exclusion agreement shall have no effect in relation to an award made on, or a question of law arising in the course of a reference, under a statutory arbitration'. This means that the parties to a statutory arbitration cannot by agreement prevent a judicial review of the award [6.08] by the court.

All the Arbitration Acts are applicable to the Public Utilities Street Works Act 1950 where section 31 reads that: 'any matter which under this Act is to be determined by arbitration shall be referred to the arbitrator appointed by agreement between the parties concerned or, in default of agreement, by the President of the Institution of Civil Engineers.'

Chapter 2
Arbitration agreements

2.01 Types of agreement

There are in essence three kinds of arbitration agreements:

The parties in dispute may agree, *after* the dispute has arisen, to refer it to a third party for his decision. This is commonly called an *ad hoc* arbitration.

By contrast, the parties may commit themselves, as they do specifically in most of the standard building and engineering contracts, to submit any dispute which may occur in the future to arbitration.

Apart from that, there is what may be termed 'institutional arbitrations', whereby members of a trade body agree, as a term of membership, to submit disputes as they arise to a formalised process of tribunals instituted by that body. Not infrequently, these bodies have a two-tier system, with an appeal to a review board.

2.02 A binding contractual obligation to arbitrate

For a valid agreement, there must be a contractual obligation to submit the dispute to arbitration. Mere aspirations or sentiments are insufficient.

Article 44 of the Canadian Standard Form of Construction Contract read:

'*Article 44. Arbitration*
In the case of any dispute arising between the owner (or the architect acting on his behalf) and the contractor as to their respective rights and obligations under the contract, *either party hereto shall be entitled to give to the other notice of such dispute and to request arbitration thereof*; and the parties *may* with respect to the

particular matters then in dispute agree to submit the same to arbitration in accordance with the applicable law of the place of building.

Arbitration proceedings shall not take place until after the completion or alleged completion of the work except (a) on a question of certificate for payment or (b) in a case where either party can show that the matter in dispute is of such nature as to require immediate consideration while evidence is available.' (Author's emphasis)

It was held in *McNamara Construction of Ontario Ltd* v. *Brock University* (1970) that this did not constitute an arbitration agreement which bound the university to submit a dispute to arbitration. The trial judge, Mr Justice Wright, whose judgment was upheld by the Ontario Court of Appeal, said:

'My view was and still is that on its face the article read by itself is not "an agreement to submit present or future differences to arbitration".

In terms it confers a right to give notice and contemplates that the parties may then agree to submit the matter to arbitration.

I think its function is merely to set the stage for the one-act play of arbitration for those who unite to prefer the homely intimacy of the private room and the "friendly neighbourhood arbitrator" to the dignity of the open court and the detached judge.

Nor do I believe that these particular signatories gave, each to the other, an irrevocable right to arbitration by that *section and that language. All they sought to provide was a pathway to arbitration if both wanted it.*' (Author's italics)

He then referred to section 16(1) of the relevant Ontario Arbitrations Act 1960 and other provisions by which an arbitral award was to be final and binding and not subject to any appeal.

'I do not believe that these parties, and still less do I believe that most of the contractors and clients in Canada, have bound or are binding themselves blindly by a contract to determine all their disputes by arbitration not subject to appeal, before they know what those disputes are.'

However, he did not refer to section 33 of the same Act, which provides that an arbitrator can state, and can be directed by the court to state, a special case; so that there was as much right for an appeal by way of case stated as there was under English law at that time.

It was argued that the words up to the semi-colon amounted to a binding obligation to go to arbitration, and those words following merely allowed the parties to subsequently agree on how they should submit to local law, having regard to the fact that Canada is a federation of ten provinces and two federal territories, and that arbitration is, under the British North America Act 1867, regarded as in the exclusive jurisdiction of the provinces. Until 1973, for example, Quebec province held all arbitration agreements, known there as *clauses compromissoires*, as being void as contrary to public order.

The one dissenting judge in the Ontario Court of Appeal thought that '... the use of the words "request" and "may" in art. 44 is nothing more than a polite way of indicating the steps to be taken ...' With respect, the present author entirely agrees with him. If this clause of the contract was to be given any commercial effectiveness at all, it should have been construed as an obligation to submit future disputes to arbitration. Of course, anybody can *request* an arbitration; and anybody may agree to anything they like *in futuro*: there is no need to write such existing rights as a specific term of a formal contract. However ill-expressed, it must have been intended to alter the relationship of the parties contractually by imposing obligations. Moreover, it was clearly intended to specify that the law applicable should be, not the proper law of the contract, or the law of the place where the arbitration should be held, but the law of 'the place of the building'. The courts should have construed it so as to give commercial effect to the obvious intention of the parties: see [2.08].

However, it is a salutary warning of the perils of sloppy draughtsmanship.

2.03 Do both parties have to have the right to refer?

Another difficulty has arisen out of the terms of the standard Indian civil engineering contract which read:

'In the event of any dispute or difference between the parties ... the contractor, after 90 days of him presenting his final claim ... may demand in writing that the dispute or difference be referred to arbitration.'

In the *Union of India* v. *Bharat Engineering Corporation* (1977) it was held that that was not an arbitration agreement because only the contractor had the right to refer disputes. In that, the court appears to have followed observations made *obiter* by Lord Justice Davies in *Baron* v. *Sunderland Corporation* (1966): 'It is necessary in an arbitration clause that each party shall agree to refer disputes to arbitration ... the clause must give bilateral rights to reference.'

The same question might well have been raised in connection with the Standard Form of Building Contract 1963 and earlier versions. Before amendments made in July 1973 following the case of *Hosier and Dickinson* v. *Kay* (1972), under the clause 30 (7), relating to the final certificate, only the contractor was entitled to go to arbitration to dispute it.

However, there seems no good reason why a contract should not specifically confer the right to go to arbitration on one party only, especially where, as under this Indian contract, the employer is given extensive powers to enforce his rights by other methods, throwing the onus of making the claim upon the contractor. Both parties, of course, must agree that there shall be recourse to arbitration, but both parties can also agree that only claims made by one should be referred: *Ronaasen* v. *Metsanomistajain* (1931); *Barni* v. *London General Insurance* (1933).

2.04 Mutual obligations
Nevertheless, unlike litigants in court proceedings, parties to an arbitration agreement owe duties to one another, arising out of their contractual agreement.

This is apparent from the two House of Lords' decisions, *Bremer Vulkan* v. *South India Shipping* (1981) and *Paal Wilson & Co.* v. *Partenreederei Hannah Blumenthal* (1982).

As Lord Diplock explained the position in the second case:

'An arbitration clause is collateral to the main contract in which it is incorporated and it gives rise to collateral primary and secondary obligations of its own. These collateral obligations survive the termination (whether by fundamental breach, breach of condition or frustration) of all primary obligations assumed by the parties under the other clauses in the main contract ....'

His lordship then went on to explain that the primary obligations created by an arbitration clause were subject to conditions subsequent.

The primary obligations only arose with:

(1) the coming into existence of a dispute between the parties as to their primary or secondary obligations under the main contract
(2) the invoking of the arbitration clause by a party to the contract, 'the claimant'.

In the earlier case he had said: 'The contractual obligation which the parties assume to one another in relation to the procedure to be followed in the arbitration, unless a contrary intention is expressed in the arbitration agreement, is that stated in section 12(1) of the 1950 Act.' He quoted the section verbatim and emphasised the concluding words *'and to do all other things which during the proceedings on the reference the arbitrator ... may require'*.

Later he said, 'a necessary implication ... [is] ... that both parties, respondent as well as claimant, are under a mutual obligation to one another to join in applying to the arbitrator for appropriate directions to put an end to delay .... Respondents in private arbitrations are not entitled to let sleeping dogs lie and then complain that they did not bark.'

The consequence of this reasoning was that where the claimant had procrastinated, the respondent was not entitled to an injunction from the court restraining him from pursuing his claim. As Lord Diplock put it in *Bremer Vulkan*: 'For failure to apply for such directions before so much time had elapsed that there was a risk that a fair trial of the dispute would not be possible, both claimant and respondent were ... in breach of their contractual obligations to one another; and neither can rely upon the other's breach as giving him a right to treat the primary obligation of each to continue with the reference as brought to an end.'

As a result, neither the court nor an arbitrator has the power to dismiss a claim for want of prosecution as the courts can, and do, in striking out an action for want of prosecution upon the principles laid down in *Allen* v. *Sir Alfred McAlpine* (1968).

But it is possible for the parties expressly or by implication to rescind their agreement by abandonment: *The Splendid Sun* (1981). These two decisions of the House of Lords are to be welcomed, although they were said to have created consternation in the City and Temple, as emphasising the essentially consensual nature of arbitration. It may, however, be difficult for a respondent to know when the sleeping dogs of *Bremer Vulkan* become abandoned strays under *The Splendid Sun*.

2.05 'Suitable' arbitration clause

If there is a binding obligation to arbitrate, it matters not that the parties have failed to specify in detail how the arbitration should take place.

It is apparently thought enough if their agreement simply includes the words 'arbitration clause'.

In one case it was argued that because the agreement said 'suitable arbitration clause' it was an inchoate agreement incapable of being enforced by the courts. This argument was rejected.

'It seems to me quite impossible to say that there can be no suitable arbitration clause. It may be that in the trade concerned with the sale and purchase of reinforcing steel bars there are no "usual conditions of acceptance", but it certainly cannot be suggested, in a contract such as this, that there can be no suitable arbitration clause; nor, in my view, that it would make any business sense of the contract to strike out that clause.

If ever there was a type of contract in which businessmen would want to include an arbitration clause, this must be a prototype of such a contract. Here is a dispute between what are, in effect, partners in a reinsurance broker's business who decided to split and go their divers ways.

Should there be any dispute in future concerning the meaning of the contract which effected this divorce, I should have thought it very unlikely that ordinary businessmen would want that ventilated in public and their business affairs perhaps exposed to the eyes of their competitors.

It seems to me that "suitable arbitration clause" means that these parties have agreed that, if any dispute arises between them under the contract, including any dispute as to the meaning of the contract, that dispute should be referred to arbitration rather than to the courts.

If the parties cannot agree upon an arbitrator, then they can invoke the terms of the Arbitration Act 1950, and an arbitrator will be appointed by the court.

The parties, by clause 16, have made it quite clear that their intention is that their differences should be arbitrated. I do not think that the word "suitable" adds to or detracts from the meaning of the clause.

If the clause had read "arbitration clause' there could have been no doubt that it would have been sufficiently precise to be given the meaning which, to my mind, any ordinary man would consider that it obviously bears. I do not think that we should be so pedantic as to suggest that the addition of the word "suitable" makes its meaning uncertain.'

The judge held that the word 'suitable' means any arbitration that businessmen in the insurance market would regard as 'suitable': *Hobbs Padgett & Co.* v. *L. C. Kirkland Ltd & Ano* (1969).

2.06 'London arbitration'

The courts have given effect to clauses which read 'Arbitration to be settled in London': *Tritonia Shipping Inc.* v. *South Nelson Forest Products Corporation* (1966).

An arbitration clause 'In London ... in the customary manner' means that each side will appoint an arbitrator who will appoint an umpire if they fail to agree, with liberty for the arbitrators to appear before him as advocates for the parties appointing them: *Laertis Shipping* v. *Exportadora* (1982).

For further details see [4.02].

2.07 Contracts in a string

One of the fundamental principles of English (but not Scottish) law is that those who are not parties to a contract cannot have obligations imposed on them by it, nor can they take a benefit under the contract even if it expressly purports to confer right on them: *McGruther* v. *Pitcher* (1904); *Tweddle* v. *Atkinson* (1861). This principle is fully applicable to arbitration agreements. In the case of *The Margery* (1902) the masters and crew of a ship were not bound by an arbitration agreement to which the owner was party.

But if each and every individual contract in a chain contains provision for arbitration by reference to a common procedure, such as that established by a commodity association, it is possible for the parties to be bound by that, just as members of a club can be bound by its rules. For example, the procedures for arbitration under the Arbitration Rules of the Grain and Feed Trade Association laid down that 'in the event of a contract forming part of a string of contracts which are in all material points identical in terms, except as to price, any arbitration for quality and/or condition shall be held between the first seller and the last buyer in the string as if they were contracting parties', provided that every party against whom arbitration is claimed and who claims to be in a string shall have supplied his contracts and all relevant information to the arbitrators.

Under this, even though there is in fact no contract between the first seller and the last buyer, these are deemed to have contracted for the purposes of the arbitration.

As to costs on 'string' arbitrations see [5.11].

2.08 Incorporation by reference

An agreement may incorporate an arbitration clause by reference to some other document. In *Modern Buildings Wales Ltd* v. *Limmer & Trinidad Ltd* (1975), a sub-contract was placed by a letter which read:

'To supply adequate labour, plant and machinery to carry out and complete ventilated and non-ventilated ceilings at the above contract, within the period stipulated in the programme of work and in full accordance with the appropriate form for nominated sub-contractors (RIBA 1965 Edition). All work to be carried out to the complete satisfaction of the Architect and in full accordance with our detailed programme which can be inspected on site or at this office. All as your quotation'.

There was, at that time, no RIBA (or JCT) form of contract between contractor and sub-contractor and no 1965 edition of any RIBA or JCT form. Both parties accepted that there was in fact a contract between them for the execution of the work.

The Court of Appeal held that the words 'the appropriate form for nominated sub-contractors' identified the NFBTE/FASS 'Green Form'. Lord Justice Buckley said:

'What follows in brackets is inappropriate to fit with identification of the "Green Form". It is not language which ought to be read as intended to cut down and restrict the identifying operation of the preceding words. It is just an added description which on investigation turns out to be factually inaccurate.

In those circumstances, in accordance with the ordinary practice of the courts in cases where there is some misdescription of this character, the court disregards what is inaccurate and inapplicable and proceeds on that which is appropriate and intelligible and what are evidently intended to be the governing words of definition.

Accordingly, I think the right way to construe this order form is to ignore the words in brackets altogether as being a *falsa demonstratio*, and to accept that the reference to the appropriate form for sub-contractors is a reference to the "Green Form", that being the only form to which it is suggested that those words could apply and the form to which it is said that anybody in the trade would understand them as applying.

Where parties by an agreement import the terms of some other document as part of their agreement those terms must be imported in their entirety, in my judgment, but subject to this: that if any of the imported terms in any way conflicts with the expressly agreed terms, the latter must prevail over what would otherwise be imported.

Here it is not disputed that the written contract between the parties, consisting of the quotation, and the order, contains all the essential terms of the contract, and, in my judgment, the "Green Form" of contract must be treated as forming part of the written contract, subject to any modifications that may be necessary to make the clauses in the "Green Form" accord in all respects with the express terms agreed between the parties.

For these reasons, I reach the conclusion that this is a case in which there is a written arbitration agreement between the parties which is applicable to any dispute or difference in regard to any matter or thing of whatever nature arising out of the sub-contract or in connection with it ... in my judgment, this is a case in which the action ought to be stayed under the section.'

2.09 'Condition' in bill of lading does not annex arbitration clause by reference

By contrast, where bills of lading contain a provision incorporating 'all conditions' of a charterparty, the most recent decision of the High Court has been that these words exclude the arbitration clause in the charterparty. Mr Justice Staughton held in the *Astro Valienti* (1982) that the words were sufficient to incorporate by reference an arbitration clause in the charterparty into the bills of lading. He said: 'Specific words in a charterparty will suffice, provided the bill of lading has once directed the reader to look at the charterparty.' But both counsel in *Skips A/S Nordhein* v. *Syrian Petroleum & Petrofina SA* later the same year agreed this was wrong and Mr Justice Hobhouse declined to follow it. He said that none of the four cases relied upon by Mr Justice Staughton supported his conclusion. They were *The Northumbria* (1906); *The Merak* (1964); *The Annefield* (1971); and *The Rena K* (1979). He said:

'In each of these cases ... the words of incorporation were wider than a reference simply to "conditions." The court's primary task is to construe the bill of lading ... The use of "conditions" in a bill of lading's charterparty incorporation clauses has a long history going back to at least the middle of the last century. It has consistently been interpreted as meaning the conditions which have to be performed on a ship's arrival by a consignee in asserting his right to take delivery of the goods. Even some 150 years, the question whether "conditions", should be construed as a synonym for "terms" or "clauses" has been before the courts on many occasions and on every occasion the wider construction has been rejected ... There can be no doubt that the narrower construction of "conditions" as opposed to "terms" ... represents the established meaning in the context of bills of lading and charterparties.

In recognition of that, the words "terms" or "clauses" are used by parties when they wish to effect a wider incorporation.'

He therefore held that the arbitration clause contained in a charterparty in the Finavoy form was not incorporated in a bill of lading for the carriage of a cargo of crude oil and therefore an application for a stay of proceedings, which he would have been obliged to grant under section 1 of the 1975 Act, should be refused. This was in spite of the fact that the charterparty, by clause 44, provides that all bills of lading issued should incorporate 'all terms and conditions of this charter including the ... arbitration clause'. The application for a stay was by the second defendants, Petrofina SA, but since the bills of lading only incorporated the 'conditions' of the charterparty and they were not parties to the charterparty itself, they could not rely upon that clause.

It is a fundamental principle of English law that those who are not parties to a contract cannot take advantage of the terms of that contract even though it expressly purports to confirm benefits or protection upon them: see [2.07].

2.10 Oral and written agreements

The 1950 Act contains the definition of an arbitration agreement under 'Meaning of "arbitration agreement"'.

> '32.   In this Part of this Act, unless the context otherwise requires, the expression "arbitration agreement" means a written agreement to submit present or future differences to arbitration, whether an arbitrator is named therein or not.'

It is interesting to notice that in the common law provinces of Canada, the same definition is given by their acts for the word 'submission', as it was in England under the 1889 Act.

The English acts therefore only apply to *written* agreements, but an oral agreement can constitute a valid agreement for arbitration at common law.

2.11 Is a signature necessary?

To be subject to the provisions of the Arbitration Act 1950, the agreement to arbitrate must be in writing; but does it have to be signed by both parties?

In *Hickman* v. *Kent and Romney Marsh Sheep-Breeders' Association* (1915) the articles of a limited liability company, an association not for profit, provided for the reference of disputes to arbitration. It was claimed that since the parties had not signed the articles there was no sufficient submission to arbitration within the meaning of section 4 of the Arbitration Act 1889 (in all respects similar to section 4 of the Arbitration Act 1950 except that, instead of the words 'an arbitration agreement', the words 'a submission' were used).

In *Baker* v. *Yorkshire Fire and Life Assurance Co.* (1892) an action was brought on a fire policy which was executed in the usual way by the company but not by the assured, and it was held that the policy, though not signed by the plaintiff, amounted to a submission to arbitration within the meaning of the Act.

Lord Coleridge CJ said:

> 'The plaintiff sues on the policy, and by so suing affirms it to be his contract; he cannot disaffirm a part of the very contract on which he is suing. He contends that, in order to bring into operation the arbitration clause contained in the policy, the policy must be signed

by both parties; but the Act of Parliament says nothing of the kind.

If the submission is in writing and is binding on both parties as their agreement, or as the equivalent in law to an agreement between them, the statute is satisfied: *per* Astbury J. in *Hickman* v. *Kent and Romney Marsh Sheep-Breeders' Association* (1915).'

2.12 The *Scott* v. *Avery* clause

Rarely seen in arbitration clauses in construction industry contracts these days (though usual in insurance contracts and some shipping contracts) is what is known as the *Scott* v. *Avery* clause.

In that case the plaintiff brought an action on a shipping insurance policy which included the words:

'Provided always, and it is hereby expressly declared to be part of the contract of insurance between the members of the association, that no member who refuses to accept the amount of any loss as settled by the committee in manner hereinbefore specified, in full satisfaction of such loss, shall be entitled to maintain any action at law or suit in equity on his policy, until the matters in dispute shall have been referred to and decided by arbitrators appointed as hereinbefore specified, and then only for such sum as the said arbitrators shall award; and the obtaining of the decision of such arbitrators on the matters and claims in dispute is hereby declared to be a condition precedent to the right of any member to maintain any such action or suit.'

The Court of Exchequer found for the plaintiff but the Court of Exchequer Chamber reversed this by a four to three majority. The plaintiff appealed to the House of Lords, on the grounds that the clause was contrary to public policy as being an ouster of the jurisdiction of the court. Lord Campbell said:

'Unless there be some illegality in the contract, the courts are bound to give it effect. There is no statute against such a contract. Then on what ground is it to be declared to be illegal?

It is contended that it is contrary to public policy ... what pretence can there be for saying that there is anything contrary to public policy in allowing parties to contract that they shall not be liable to any action until their liability has been ascertained by a domestic and private tribunal upon which they themselves agree? Can the public be injured by it?'

Having since been repeatedly upheld, the clause now generally appears in two forms:

(a) provision in the contract that 'arbitration shall be a condition precedent to the commencement of any action at law' *or*
(b) provision that 'the obligation shall be to pay a sum as may be awarded upon arbitration pursuant to this clause'.

But other words may have the same effect i.e. of making no sum payable until after an arbitration award.

The object is to prevent the court interfering with arbitration agreements by allowing one party to bring an action in the courts, in spite of the arbitration agreement.

One result is that a *Scott* v. *Avery* clause forms a defence to an action at law.

The court has however power, under section 25(4) of the 1950 Act, where it revokes the appointment of an arbitrator under section 25(2) to declare that the arbitration clause be no longer binding, and it has power under section 24(2), where the question is whether any party has been guilty of fraud, to order that the agreement shall cease to have effect.

Otherwise a defendant who is party to a *Scott* v. *Avery* type clause is entitled as of right to a stay of the proceedings, unless he has waived that or so conducted himself as to forfeit it: 'It is familiar law that a party who has prevented fulfilment of a condition precedent cannot set up the fact of its non-fulfilment.'

2.13 The *Atlantic Shipping* clause

A further development of the *Scott* v. *Avery* clause was the one known as the *Atlantic Shipping* clause from the case of *Atlantic Shipping* v. *Dreyfus* (1922). This includes provision that, unless arbitration is begun within a specified time, any claim shall be ended completely.

The usual words are:

'and it is further agreed that any claim hereunder must be in writing and the claimant's arbitrator must be appointed within *x* weeks of [a certain event] and that any claim not so made shall be deemed to be waived and absolutely barred.'

The *Centrocon* clause, which appears in several judgments, has similar wording, with a three or nine month period from final discharge of the ship.

The court has power under section 27 of the 1950 Act to extend the time if 'undue hardship would otherwise be caused'. But this is limited to clauses which bar any claims unless an arbitrator is appointed in time.

Where a contract provides that a claim should be made within a specified period or not at all, there is no power under section 27 to extend the time. In one case with a charterparty in a standard form, with an additional clause that provided that the charterers should be discharged from any liability unless the claim was presented to them 'in writing with all available supporting documents within 90 days from the completion of discharge of the cargo', and the 90 days expired on 16 March 1981 and a writ was issued on 17 March 1981 and subsequently the dispute was referred to arbitration, it was held that the court had no power to extend the time: *Babanaft International Co SA* v. *Avant Petroleum* (1982). The clause, said Lord Justice Donaldson, 'has no apparent connection with the commencement of arbitration procee-dings within 90 days or any other time. It relates solely to making a claim in a particular form within a fixed period.' The Court of Appeal expressly overruled the decision in *Nestlé Co Ltd* v. *E. Biggins & Co. Ltd* (1958) where the words used were 'any claim on quality or conditions of the goods must be made not later than 14 days from final day of weighing and for discharge of goods at port of final destination'.

'Section 27 empowers the court to extend the time fixed for giving notice to appoint an arbitrator ... it does not empower the court to extend any other time limits,' said Lord Justice Donaldson.

But it is possible that clauses of this nature may in some circumstances be unreasonable, with the result set out in sections 3 and 7 of the Unfair Contract Terms Act 1977.

It would appear that the nomination of an arbitrator is not the same thing as his appointment for this purpose.

The case of *Tradax Export SA* v. *Volkswagenwerk AG* (1970) was concerned with an arbitration between owners and charterers in the standard *Centrocon* clause:

'Any claim must be made in writing and the claimants' arbitrator appointed within three months of final discharge and where this provision is not complied with the claim shall be deemed to be waived and absolutely barred.'

One party notified the other side on 27 January of the nomination of their arbitrator, but they failed to notify the arbitrator himself until 24 July, when they were out of time.

The section was first included in the 1934 Act and was initially given a strict interpretation. However in *Liberian Shipping Corporation* v. *A. King* (1967), a more lenient view was adopted by the Court of Appeal. According to Lord Denning 'undue' simply means excessive. 'Even if a claimant has been at fault himself, there is undue hardship if the consequences are out of proportion to the fault,' he said. In that case, the sum at stake was £33,000 and the applicant was only nine days out of time. There are, however, a vast number of reported cases on this section, many of them inconsistent. It is primarily a matter for the discretion of the court, although the Court of Appeal will review the decision on the usual principles applicable to the exercise of judicial discretion.

2.14 The HB5 Agreement and successive arbitrations

A house purchaser, who goes to arbitration under the supplementary contract HB5 which he has entered into with the National House-Building Council (NHBC) and loses, cannot subsequently sue the builder under his original contract in respect of the same defects he has alleged in the arbitration, even though he has a different cause of action. That was decided by the Court of Appeal in the unreported case of *Willday* v. *Taylor* (1977). But there were so many curious observations made by their lordships in this case that it would appear that their lordships misunderstood the HB5 contract completely.

On the other hand, if there are a succession of different defects which appear, there can be a succession of arbitrations under the NHBC guarantee about these. This was decided by Mr Justice Forbes in *Purser and Co (Hillingdon) Ltd* v. *Jackson* (1977).

That applies in spite of the decision of the Queen's Bench Division Court in *Conquer* v. *Boot* (1928) that, if there has been an action for breach of contract in failing to complete a building in a good and workmanlike manner, there cannot be a second action of the same nature in which different defects are alleged.

Mr Justice Forbes said that the basis of that case was:

'It is in the public interest that there shall be an end to litigation. I doubt whether that maxim has any application to private arbitration. It is clear from the terms of the NHBC contract that the parties intended serial arbitrations.'

His lordship clearly took the view not only that the contract specifically contemplates successive arbitrations but that the rule in *Conquer* v. *Boot*, if still applicable to litigation (and it is habitually disregarded in construction industry litigation) had no application at all to arbitrations. It is of course patently unjust that a building owner who brings an action in respect of some defects he has discovered should be barred by this rule from instituting further proceedings when other defects manifest themselves years later. Indeed the case may well be limited to actions for breach of contract, leaving the owner free to sue in tort for negligence when he has learned of other defects.

Moreover, the reasoning the courts applied to the word 'fraud' in section 26(b) of the Limitation Act 1939 (now repealed and replaced by section 32 of the 1980 Act) may be applicable to most building work: see *Clark* v. *Woor* (1965); *Applegate* v. *Moss* (1971); *King* v. *Victor Parsons* (1973). Support for the view that equity can relieve the plaintiff in these circumstances can be found in the cases of *Spencer* v. *Spencer* (1828) and *Charter* v. *Trevelyan* (1844).

Arbitrators in all construction cases, it is submitted, should reject any submissions based on *Conquer* v. *Boot* on the authority of Mr Justice Forbes. If it is still applicable to litigation, that is another good reason for preferring arbitration to litigation.

2.15 JCT Standard Form of Building Contract: 1963 edition

From 1903 the Standard Form of Building Contract, already then in existence, became known as the RIBA contract. It bore this title until 1977 when the Royal Institute of British Architects withdrew its name from the document. On 5 August 1977, judges and other court officials were instructed by *Court Business* to refer in future to it as 'the JCT Form' (Joint Contracts Tribunal) or 'the Standard Form of Building Contract' and not the RIBA Form. It was an injunction which has been ignored.

Versions of this contract in current use are those based on the major rewritings which took place in 1963 and 1980.

In the 1963 edition the arbitration clause was clause 35 (see Appendix B of this book). Any difference between the employer and the contractor is to be referred to arbitration except, by a footnote, disputes arising out of value added tax.

There is also a curious provision in the local authorities' version in clause 17A dealing with the 1946 Fair Wages Resolution of the House of Commons. Clause 17A(3) provides that 'notwithstanding anything in Clause 35 ... (the provisions of which shall not apply to this Condition),' yet failure to comply with clause 17A is ground under clause 25(1) (d) for the employer determining the contractor's employment, and clause 35(1) provides that the rights and liabilities of the parties under clause 25 are to be subject to arbitration. This is now obsolete in view of the Government's repudiation of their obligations under the International Labour Convention.

Also apparently excluded from review or arbitration unless notice is given at the time, under clause 2(7), are all instructions issued by the architect, which 'shall be deemed for all the purposes of this contract to have been empowered by the provisions of these conditions specified by the Architect in answer to the Contractor's request'.

Dealing with fluctuations, clause 31D(3) authorises the quantity surveyor and the contractor to agree sums payable which 'shall be deemed for all the purposes of this contract to be the net amount payable'. In *John Laing Construction Ltd* v. *County & District Properties Ltd* (1982) it was held that the role of the quantity surveyor was restricted to agreeing quantum but not liability; still less had he power under the contract to waive the notice which the contractor was required to give as a condition precedent. It would appear therefore that an arbitrator will be bound to accept the agreed sum but has jurisdiction to decide whether or not it is payable. Neither the court nor an arbitrator has power in equity or law to vary the terms of the contract so as to dispense with a notice which is expressly made a condition precedent for payment: *Scandinavian Trading Tanker Co.* v. *Flota Petrolera Ecuatorlana* (1982).

The powers of the arbitrator are further circumscribed by clause 30(7) which (until the July 1976 revision) made the final certificate of the architect, unless a written request has been made within 14 days of its issue, 'conclusive evidence in any proceedings that the works have been properly carried out and completed in accordance with the contract', subject to three specific exceptions.

Any arbitrator appointed under the JCT 63 contract should be alert to the fact that the wording of this clause was changed in July 1973 following the House of Lords case of *Hosier and Dickinson* v. *Kaye* (1972). Contracts used before this date made the final certificate conclusive evidence as to defects, even if there was a High Court writ already issued at the time in respect of defects; and only the contractor had a right to challenge the final certificate within 14 days. The clause was also substantially changed again in July 1976.

In its final wording, thereafter, it is conclusive only as to matters which have to be to the architect's satisfaction – which normally are few.

But in the earlier versions, it means that, subject to the three exceptions, the arbitrator cannot allow either party to lead evidence to contradict what is in the final certificate. He and they are bound by it as 'conclusive evidence'.

However, it would appear that a final certificate not issued in strict accordance with the provisions of the contract, particularly as to time, may be void and of no effect. In *The London Borough of Merton* v. *Lowe & Pickford* (1979), the JCT 63 contract was entered into on 8 February 1965 which contained clause 30(7) in the original inflexible version. Judge Stabb held that 'the final certificate was defective by reason of being out of time and because it did not include the sums required'. It was therefore a nullity. This decision was subsequently approved by the Court of Appeal.

Subject to these considerations, the arbitrator has the power under the express terms of clause 35 to decide whether the architect has been right to withhold any certificate, even though such a certificate is a condition precedent to the contractor being paid: *Prestige* v. *Brethell* (1938).

One outstanding feature of the JCT 63 contract is that arbitration 'shall not be opened until after Practical Completion or alleged Practical Completion or termination or abandonment of the works', except for certain matters. There are similar provisions in the sub-contracts.

One result of this may be that the court may exercise its discretion under section 4(1) of the 1950 Act to refuse to stay litigation if a writ has been taken out by one of the parties. Lord Salmon in *Gilbert-Ash Ltd* v. *Modern Engineering* (1973) said that if a sub-contractor were to sue 'because the contractors were unwilling to go to arbitration until completion or abandonment of the main contract, I am sure the courts, in exercise of their discretion, would refuse a stay'.

Matters which can be dealt with, without the written consent of both parties, before completion are:

(1) Matters arising out of Articles 3 and 4 relating to the appointment of architect and quantity surveyor.
(2) 'On the questions whether or not the issue of an instruction is empowered by these conditions.'
(3) 'Whether or not a certificate has been improperly withheld or is

not in accordance with these conditions.'
(4) Disputes arising out of clause 32 dealing with hostilities and
    clause 33 war damage.

The words 'whether a certificate is not in accordance with these
Conditions' were said by Mr I. N. Duncan Wallace in his *Building and
Civil Engineering Standard Forms* (1973) to open 'the door to disputes
on all matters which should be dealt with on an interim certificate and,
as has been seen, these are very numerous'. He also suggested in
Hudson's Building Law (9th Edition) that 'the words are wide enough
to include even simple disputes of valuation on an interim certificate'.

With respect, that view is untenable. The question is whether the
certificate is in accordance with the conditions not with the work done.
It was held by the Court of Appeal in *Killby & Gayford Ltd* v.
Selincourt Ltd (1973), where Lord Denning said, dealing specifically
with JCT 63 clause 35(2): 'So long as a certificate is good on the face of
it and is within the authority given by the contract, then it is "in
accordance with the Conditions".' Lord Justice Megaw said in the same
case: 'There is no evidence ... that the certificate is not in accordance
with the contract.'

2.16 JCT Standard Form of Building Contract: 1980 edition

Article 5.5 of JCT 80 (see Appendix B) raises the question as to
whether the parties can by contract decide the law which should be
applicable to the conduct of the arbitration:

'Whatever the nationality, residence or domicile of the Employer,
the Contractor, any sub-contractor or supplier or the Arbitrator,
and wherever the Works or any part thereof are situated, the law of
England shall be the proper law of this Contract and in particular
(but not so as to derogate from the generality of the foregoing) the
provisions of the Arbitration Acts 1950 (notwithstanding anything
in s.34 thereof) to 1979 shall apply to any arbitration under this
Contract wherever the same, or any part of it, shall be conducted.'

Can the parties, for example, decide by contract that although the
arbitration takes place in England, the procedure shall be governed by
Scottish law? Can they decide by their contract to avoid the provisions
of the Arbitration Act 1979 by providing that the arbitration,
although held in England, shall be governed by the arbitration law of

Jersey (which happy land has no arbitration law)?

This question, described by lawyers as whether the parties can choose the *lex fori* or 'the curial law', was discussed in *James Miller & Partners Ltd* v. *Whitworth Street Estates* (1970).

It is submitted that the parties cannot, by agreeing that the procedural law of Jersey should apply in the case of arbitrations held in England, remove themselves from the provisions for appeal under the Arbitration Act 1979. Otherwise, everybody would do it.

Conversely, they cannot by Article 5 provide that arbitrations under the JCT 80 contract held in the Channel Islands shall be subject to the Arbitration Acts 1950, 1975 and 1979 in so far as they deal with procedural matters, including appeals, even where the proper law of the contract is not English and the work is not done in England [4.06].

An inelegant attempt has been made in the 1980 version of the JCT Standard Form of Contract to cure one of the inherent defects of arbitration – the inability to join parties who are not party to the contract [1.13].

The parties to this contract between employer and main contractor have the option in the Appendix to choose between a simple party and party arbitration by deleting the words 'Articles 5.1.4 and 5.1.5 apply' in the Appendix.

If these words are not deleted by Article 5.1.6, the provisions of Article 5.1.4 apply. This provides for a dispute to be referred to arbitration under JCT 80 if it 'raises issues which are substantially the same *or connected with* issues raised in a related dispute' between:

- the employer and a nominated sub-contractor under NSC/2 and NSC/2a
- the contractor and a nominated sub-contractor under NSC/4 and 4a
- the contractor and any nominated supplier.

Nominated suppliers for these purposes are defined in clause 36.1 of this contract but there is a further qualification. They must be not only nominated suppliers but also ones whose contracts of sale, whether they are selling to the employer or the main contractor, contain the provisions of JCT 80 clause 36.4.8 which reads:

'that if any dispute or difference between the Contractor and the Nominated Supplier raises issues *which are substantially the same as or are connected with issues* raised in a related dispute between the

Employer and the Contractor under this Contract then, where articles 5.1.4 and 5.1.5 apply, such dispute or difference shall be referred to the Arbitrator appointed or to be appointed pursuant to article 5 who shall have power to make such directions and all necessary awards in the same way as if the procedure of the High Court as to joining one or more defendants or joining co-defendants or third parties was available to the parties and to him and in any case the award of such Arbitrator shall be final and binding on the parties.'

This is a well intentioned but inept attempt to confer on arbitrators some of the powers of the courts. Indeed Article 5.1.4 purports to confer on the arbitrator 'power to make such directions and all necessary awards in the same way as if the procedure of the High Court as to joining one or more defendants or joining co-defendants or third parties was available to the party and to him': a pious aspiration indeed.

To start with, the words italicised above are so vague as to invite litigation as to their meaning. But they are also ineffective to bind sub-contractors unless the relevant contracts between the employer and nominated sub-contractor in the form NSC/2 or NSC/2a or between the contractor and the sub-contractor in form NSC/4 or 4a also contain effective similar clauses.

So far as nominated suppliers are concerned, it is difficult to conceive any sensible, well-advised supplier of building materials renouncing his rights to litigate and entering into any arbitration agreement, let alone an onerous one, which prevents an arbitration until after 'Practical Completion or alleged Practical Completion or termination of the Contractor's employment or abandonment of the Works', any of which events may be light years away from the time when he supplies the materials.

There are, of course, exceptions to the rule that arbitration must await practical completion similar to those contained in JCT 63 and commented on in [2.15]: see Article 5.2.

Article 5 still unhappily makes use of the words 'such reference shall not ... be *opened*'. That introduces an immediate ambiguity. None of the statutes and no reported case appears to have decided when an arbitration is 'opened', and there are many possible interpretations of this expression.

It is perhaps not surprising in view of the ineptitude of the draughting of JCT 80 Article 5 that agreement on the form in the Joint

Contracts Tribunal was long delayed by the desire of the Association of Metropolitan Authorities to have no arbitration clause at all in the Standard Form of Building Contract.

It would be much better if the industry were to set up, as most other industries have done, its own arbitration procedure, with an appeal procedure. As it is, arbitrations under the construction contracts are always expensive and prolonged and invariably end up in the courts. For as Mr Owen Luder, Past President of the RIBA, has frequently remarked 'the signature of a JCT contract is usually the signal for battle to commence'.

2.17 Is the engineer an arbitrator under ICE clause 66?

As has been pointed out [1.12], the Court of Appeal in *Monmouthshire County Council* v. *Costelloe & Keple Ltd* (1965) declined to decide this point, finding it unnecessary for their decision. Most commentators on the Institution of Civil Engineers conditions conclude that he is not, proceeding on the assumption that, because the engineer is not infrequently the employee of the employer, he cannot be. This is a fallacious assumption [3.02]. No other good reason has been advanced why he should not be. The chief argument is that since the clause refers to arbitration subsequent to his decision, his decisions cannot be arbitral. This is, of course, a question of the construction of the contract as to the intention of the parties. But, it is submitted, it is by no means conclusive.

Since these provisions of the contract governing the decisions of the engineer contain all essential elements of arbitration [1.06], it is submitted that in law he is an arbitrator. If this be correct, the provisions of the Arbitration Act 1950 are as much applicable to his awards, called 'decisions', as to those of any other arbitrator. More important, perhaps, is that he is not entitled to reject the claims of the contractor without listening to any submissions he has to make.

The point is probably purely academic but might have relevance if the contractor chose to appeal (under the 1979 Act) against some decision rather than go to further arbitration as provided by section 66; because there is the provision that 'such reference shall not be opened until completion ... of the works', there may well be an advantage to the contractor in so doing. There appears to be no good reason why a contractor should not apply for leave to appeal against the engineer's decision long before completion on the ground that it is an arbitral award.

It is also possible that an action framed in negligence may be brought against an engineer who rejects a contractor's claim. If engineers are not arbitrators under the first part of clause 66 and protected as such, they clearly owe a duty to the contractor to exercise due care in admitting or rejecting claims. Some day, some engineer under the ICE conditions may have to choose whether he is an arbitrator under this clause, and possibly therefore immune from negligence actions, or whether he is not an arbitrator and subject to the ordinary law regarding the duty to exercise reasonable care. But logic and law rarely coincide and it is possible that the court would reject such an application. In the meantime, engineers under the ICE contract might well be advised to consider the jurisdiction conferred on them by section 66 as arbitral, in that they are clearly called upon by the contract to exercise a judicial function.

Under the 4th edition of the ICE contract no arbitration could be opened 'except as to the withholding by the engineer of any certificate' before completion of the works. In *A. E. Farr Ltd* v. *Ministry of Transport* (1960) the contractor did excavations not provided for by the bills of quantities and the engineer rejected the contractor's claim for these, alleging that he could refer it again after completion. It was held that in the true construction of the contract, this was a dispute as to the withholding of a certificate.

2.18 The FIDIC Contract

This contract is the one prepared by the Fédération Internationale des Ingénieurs-Conseils and the Fédération Internationale Européenne de la Construction. Now in its 3rd edition, with revision under consideration, it is based on the obsolete 4th edition of the English ICE contract. Intended originally for use for works of civil engineering construction, it is also widely used for building work, including that sponsored by the World Bank. It was the contract selected by the German government for the erection of a school in England.

It is not proposed to comment in detail on the provisions of condition 67 of the contract (see Appendix B) because the International Chamber of Commerce in Paris never provides that any disputes should be arbitrated in England since they regard with justified horror the excessive interference of the English courts.

Difficulty has arisen because the FIDIC contract provides that arbitration shall be under the Rules of Conciliation and Arbitration of the International Chamber of Commerce in Paris. Those rules provide, in Article 16, that 'the law of procedure chosen by the parties or, failing such choice, those of the law of the country in which the arbitrator holds the proceedings' shall prevail.

In *International Tank & Pipe SAK* v. *Kuwait Aviation Fuelling* (1975) Lord Denning MR, commenting on this, said: 'Thus the parties may choose that the arbitration procedure is to be governed by the law of some country other than England. If they do not so choose, the procedure will be governed by the law where the arbitrator sits.'

For that he relied upon the approval expressed by Lord Dilhorne and Lord Wilberforce of the observations in Dicey and Morris, *Conflict of Laws*, 8th edition, 1967, page 1048:

'It cannot be doubted that the courts would give effect to the choice of a [procedural] law other than the proper law of the contract. Thus, if the parties agree on an arbitration clause expressed to be governed by English law but providing for arbitration in Switzerland, it may be held that, whereas English law governs the validity, interpretation and effect of the arbitration clause as such (including the scope of the arbitrators' jurisdiction), the proceedings are governed by Swiss law.'

But this passage says no more than that (a) the parties can choose which is to be the 'proper law' of their contract; and (b) that they can freely choose where the arbitration shall take place.

It does not support the proposition, nor do the reported cases, that the parties can elect to hold their arbitration in England subject to the procedural law of Switzerland, Kuwait or Jersey. The only proposition the cases support is that, if the arbitration is in fact held in England or Switzerland or Scotland, it will be governed by the law of the place where the arbitration takes place.

There are observations to the contrary in Mustill and Boyd, *Commercial Arbitrations* 1st edition, 1982, page 61, but they do not adequately refute the argument advanced by Dr F. A. Mann in [1969] ICLQ 997.

2.19 The Government Contract GC/Works/1

This is a contract drafted entirely by government officers and as such it must be regarded as exclusively the employer's document and, unlike other contracts in the construction industry, construed *contra proferentem*. There is express authority that the ICE Contract (2nd Edition) should not be so construed (*Tersons* v. *Stevenage District Council* (1963)). and in *Country & District Properties* v. *Jenner* (1974) it was held, with less justification, that the NFBTE/FASS 'Green Form' was not to be construed *contra proferentem* the contractor. It is submitted that this principle is applicable to the other standard forms. They are not, as Lord Pearson said in the *Terson* case, 'drawn up by one party in its own interests and imposed upon the other party'.

That description, however, fits the GC/Works/1 contract exactly and it is submitted further that a contractor who works under it, for the purpose of section 3 of the Unfair Contract Terms Act 1977, is one who deals on 'the other's written standard terms of business'. 'Business' incidentally, by section 25 of that Act 'includes ... the activities of any government department or local or public authority'. The Act does not apply to 'an agreement in writing to submit present or future differences to arbitration': section 13(2), but it does apply to all other terms in the contract.

Condition 61(1) of GC/Works/1 (see Appendix B) requires 'all disputes, differences, or questions between the parties' to be submitted to arbitration. Exempt from these are:

(1) Condition 51 – the fair wages clause
(2) 'as to which the decision or report of the authority or any other person by the contract is expressed to be final and conclusive .'

Those words remove from the possibility of arbitration a large number of matters.

Under condition 3(2), which vests in the employer ownership in all that a contractor brings on site: 'The decision of the Supervising Officer upon any matters arising under this paragraph shall be final and binding.'

Condition 7 deals with the supervising officer's instructions and in 7(3) 'the decision of the Supervising Officer that any such instructions are necessary or expedient shall be final and conclusive'.

Condition 9(3) entitles the quantity surveyor to appraise the value of work covered up without notice from the contractor: 'his decision thereon shall be final and conclusive.'

Condition 11 (4) (c) makes the decision of the employer as 'to the amount of any variation in the Contract Sum' under that fluctuation clause 'final and conclusive'.

Condition 13(3) deals with tests of things intended for incorporation by independent experts and provides: 'The report of the independent experts shall be final and conclusive.'

Condition 28A(6) makes the decision of the supervising officer 'final and conclusive' on all matters dealt with under the whole clause which deals with the consequences of the employer taking partial possession.

Condition 36 authorises the supervising officer to require the contractor to cease to employ and replace his servants and that 'any decision of the Authority or Supervising Officer under this Condition shall be final and conclusive'.

Condition 40(6) deals with non-payment by the contractor of certified sums to a nominated sub-contractor and authorises the authority to make direct payments; condition 39(6) provides that: 'The decision of the Supervising Officer as to whether any such amount has not been paid and of the Authority as to the sum (if any) to be paid to the nominated sub-contractor, or nominated supplier shall be final and conclusive.'

Condition 40 provides in sub-section (3) that the 'amount of any interim advance shall be an approximate estimate only and the decision of the Supervising Officer in regard thereto shall be final and conclusive'.

Condition 44 entitles the employer without giving reason or cause to determine the contractor's employment and it includes the provision under 44(5): 'If upon determination of the Contract under this Condition the Contractor is of the opinion that he has suffered hardship by reason of the operation of this condition he may refer the circumstances to the Authority, who, on being satisfied that such hardship exists, or has existed, shall make such allowance if any, as in his opinion is reasonable and his decision on that matter shall be final and conclusive.'

A similar provision has to be written into every sub-contract with the decision of the contractor substituted for the authority's as 'final and conclusive'.

The authority under clause 45 may also determine the contractor's employment as a result of default or failure by the contractor including in 45(c) where the contractor has failed to comply with condition 56, 'if the Authority (whose decision on this matter shall be final and conclusive) shall decide that such failure is prejudicial to the interest of the State'. Condition 56 refers to access to the site. It also provides in 56(4) that: 'The decision of the Authority as to whether any person is to be admitted to the Site and as to whether the Contractor has furnished the information or taken the steps required of him by this Condition shall be final and conclusive.'

Not every contractual obligation that non-arbitral decisions 'shall be final, binding and conclusive' is necessarily so in law but it would be outside the province of this book to discuss these provisions in detail. Reference should be made to *Burgess & Ano.* v. *Purchase & Sons* (1982) where Mr Justice Nourse explained the earlier cases of *Campbell* v. *Edwards* (1967) and *Baber* v. *Kenwood* (1978).

However, two provisions of GC/Works/1 merit some discussion.

Clause 42 (3) provides that 'Any dispute as to the Contractor's right to a certificate or as to the sums to be certified from time to time, shall be referred to the Authority whose decision shall be final and conclusive' subject to three exceptions. Those words have all the ingredients of an arbitration [1.06], including the vocabulary of one: 'dispute', 'referred', 'final' – except that the employer has appointed himself the arbitrator.

There is an even more extraordinary provision making the authority a judge in its own cause in condition 55 which deals with bribery and corruption. Condition 55 (3) provides that: 'Any dispute or difference of opinion arising in respect of either the interpretation or effect of this condition or the amount recoverable hereunder by the Authority from the Contractor shall be decided by the Authority, whose decision on that matter shall be final and conclusive.'

It is not surprising that the GC/Works/1 contract is not the contractor's favourite contract. All the same, the provisions of GC/Works/1 rarely come before the courts because contractors are well aware that the government has an immense amount of business to place and they set their eyes not on the current contract but on the next one they hope to get.

However, at least three London boroughs have adopted this contract for their work in preference to JCT 80, and it may well be that contractors will feel less inhibited in pursuing actions against them. Also, sub-contractors may seek to challenge the incorporation into their contracts of condition 44(5).

As a result, it may well be argued some day that the provisions of condition 55(3) and condition 44(5) are references to arbitration and that the court under its powers in section 24 of the 1950 Act should revoke the appointment of the arbitrator and appoint an independent one under section 25(2).

It is difficult to decide which way the courts would decide on this. It is not without reason that the *Financial Times* always includes its court reports above the space devoted to its horse racing tipster. The present author is firmly of the opinion that in disputes arising under these clauses, the courts would remove the authority as an arbitrator and appoint an independent one under their powers in section 25(1) of the

1950 Act, as they did in *Veritas Shipping Corporation* v. *Anglo-Canadian Cement* (1966).

Two other matters merit comment: in the absence of express agreement, no reference can take place 'until after the completion, alleged completion or abandonment of the Work or determination of the Contract': Condition 61(2).

Secondly, if the contract is subject to English law, irrespective of where the work is done, 'such reference shall be deemed to be a submission to arbitration under the Arbitration Act 1950'.

2.20 How arbitration agreements are enforced

Contractual obligations are normally enforced in English law by the award of damages for breach or, in rare instances, by an order for specific performance of the contractual provisions or prohibitive or mandatory injunctions. The first is not applicable to agreements to submit disputes to arbitration since the innocent party could rarely prove that he has suffered any damage, and the other remedies, in themselves discretionary, could not be enforced.

Other methods have to be found to enforce the agreement and these vary with the nature of the breach. For example:

(1) *The other party ignores the agreement and issues a writ.*
The remedy here is supplied by statute, namely section 4 of the 1950 Act for domestic arbitrations and section 1 of the 1975 Act for non-domestic ones. In the first class of case, the court has a discretion whether or not to stay the action and the principles on which that discretion is exercised are set out in [2.21].

(2) *The agreement provides for one arbitrator to be appointed by agreement but the other party refuses to agree.*
Here, statute again provides the answer by the power of the court contained in section 10 of the 1950 Act.

Usually the contract provides that in the failure of agreement, a third party, often the president or vice-president of a professional body, should make the appointment. Originally difficulties could arise when such a named person failed to appoint, because it was held that the original section 10 was not wide enough to allow the court to appoint in those circumstances: *National Enterprises* v. *Racal Communications* (1975).

In *Davies Middleton & Davies* v. *Cardiff Corporation* (1964) the Court of Appeal was concerned with the 1939 version of the RIBA form of building contract which, in its printed terms, provided that disputes between the parties should be referred to 'the arbitration and final decision of ... [name to be inserted] and in the event of his unwillingness or inability to act to a person to be appointed by the RIBA'.

The parties did not insert any name in the blank space provided and did not delete the words following the blank space. The president of the RIBA was asked to appoint an arbitrator but he refused to do so, having been advised that he had no power in those circumstances. The plaintiffs applied to the High Court, pursuant to the original section 10, for the appointment of an arbitrator by the court. Master Harwood acceded to their application. The defendants appealed to a judge in chambers who dismissed their appeal and they finally appealed to the Court of Appeal which again dismissed their appeal.

Lord Justice Sellers said that the defendants' grounds of appeal were that the courts had no powers to appoint an arbitrator in these circumstances and that the clause as it stood was meaningless as void for uncertainty. The court accepted neither contention. The parties clearly intended to submit their disputes to arbitration and the courts therefore had power to appoint under section 10.

The section has since been amended by the insertion of the new section 10(2) in the 1950 Act by section 6(4) of the 1979 Act.

If the agreement is silent as to how many arbitrators there should be, the reference is to a single arbitrator as the result of section 6 of the 1950 Act.

(3) *The agreement provides for two arbitrators but one party fails to appoint.*
Section 7(b) of the 1950 Act allows the party who has appointed his arbitrator, after seven days' notice to the other party, to appoint his arbitrator to be the sole one without application to the court.

The terms of the section have to be complied with strictly for the appointment to be a valid one but it is clear that the words 'making default' mean no more than 'fails to appoint' and do not require excessive delay.

Two steps are apparently essential: there must be formal notice to appoint the other arbitrator within seven days and not just to 'name' an arbitrator. Further it would appear that there must be specific reference to both the agreement and the actual dispute or difference that has arisen. In the event of non-compliance there must be a specific appointment of the appointed arbitrator as sole arbitrator. In *Drummond* v. *Hamer* (1942) it was held insufficient to refer in general to 'the disputes and differences now depending between us'; and the words 'I hereby require you within seven days from the service of this notice on you to name an arbitrator to act on your behalf ... failing which the said disputes and differences will be referred to the said R. E. W. alone as sole arbitrator' were held bad, on at least three grounds, for a notice under section 7(b).

A proviso to the section allows the court to set aside an appointment made under this section, so a premature appointment of an arbitrator as the sole one may lead to expensive litigation.

(4) *The other party fails to take steps necessary in the arbitration proceedings*
'The power to dismiss for want of prosecution is not found expressly in the terms of the arbitration agreement nor can it be collected from any provision of the Arbitration Act 1950,' said Mr Justice Bridge, as he then was, in *Crawford* v. *A.E.A. Prowting Ltd* (1973) and this was expressly approved by the House of Lords in *Paal Wilson* v. *Partenreederei* (1982). However, the arbitrator is not without powers to ensure the parties comply with their obligations once he has been appointed.

2.21 Staying an action

Section 4(1) provides:

> 'If any party to an arbitration agreement ... commences any legal proceedings in any court against any other party to the agreement ... in respect of any matter agreed to be referred, any party to those legal proceedings may at any time after appearance, and before delivering any pleadings or taking any other steps in the proceedings, apply to that court to stay the proceedings, and that court or a judge thereof ... may make an order to stay proceedings.'

The approach of the courts to the question of a stay was explained by Mr Justice Donaldson, as he then was, in *Hyams* v. *Docker* (1969). The plaintiff had agreed to purchase the defendant's motor yacht, *The Shemara*, but sought a declaration from the court that he was entitled to cancel the transaction because of material defects in the vessel: the defendant claimed that since there was a binding arbitration clause in the agreement, the action should be stayed and the dispute submitted to arbitration.

'So far as the law on this matter is concerned, I think it is clear that I must approach this application in this way: *prima facie*, the parties have agreed that an arbitrator and not the court shall be the appropriate forum for the determination of disputes arising out of the contract, and therefore there is a bias (a strong bias, I think it has been called) in favour of staying proceedings with a view to the matter going to arbitration.'

In that case, Mr Justice Donaldson held that the court had the power to refuse to stay part of the proceedings, in this case a question about the construction of the agreement, while remitting the rest to arbitration.

The court has to be satisfied 'that the applicant was, at the time when the proceedings were commenced, and still remains, ready and willing to do all things necessary to the proper conduct of the arbitration': section 4(1), Arbitration Act 1950.

This applies *prima facie*, and one would have thought inevitably, to the party that initiates the litigation, and it has been so held: *Weir* v. *Johnson* (1882).

A party is not necessarily unwilling because he has raised the objection that the right to go to arbitration is barred by the terms of the contract: *Bruce* v. *Strong* (1951). But he may be if he raised the objection that any arbitration is out of time because of a statutory provision: *The Escherheim* (1974) and (1976).

However, a party who denies the existence of a valid arbitration agreement is not, when legal proceedings commence, 'ready and willing' to do all that is necessary for the proper conduct of an arbitration: *G. Dew & Co.* v. *Tarmac Construction Ltd* (1978).

Tarmac Construction Ltd, main contractors for a housing estate, employed G. Dew & Co. as sub-contractors for paving and landscape work. The engagement was in the form of letters which, it was alleged, made it clear that the sub-contractors were to be employed in the terms of the NFBTE/FASS 'Green Form' which, in clause 24, contained an arbitration clause. No 'Green Form' was actually signed and in subsequent correspondence Tarmac denied the existence of a contract constituted by the letter and that the 'Green Form' had been the terms of it. G. Dew & Co. issued a writ. Tarmac applied to stay under section 4, but the Court of Appeal held that they were not 'ready and willing' since in the last correspondence before the writ was issued, they had denied the existence of an arbitration agreement.

In its discretion, a court may refuse a stay:

(1) *Where the agreement provides for no immediate arbitration.*

(2) *Where there is delay in applying for a stay.* A stay was refused in *The Elizabeth H* (1962) when 18 months had elapsed from the issue of the writ.

(3) *Where there would be hardship on the plaintiff if the stay were granted.* In *Fakes* v. *Taylor Woodrow Construction* (1973) the plaintiff was a plumber who was a subcontractor under the NFBTE/FASS 'Green Form'. He was insolvent, it was claimed, as the result of breach of contract by the defendants. Legal aid was available for litigation but not for arbitration and this the courts held was a material factor. This decision of the Court of Appeal appears to conflict with the earlier decisions of *Smith* v. *Pearl Assurance* (1939), where it was said that the poverty of the plaintiff was no ground for refusing a stay. In *Ford* v. *Clarksons Holidays* (1971) it was also said that absence of legal aid for arbitration was not material. Attempts are made to reconcile these cases on the basis that (a) *Smith's* case was a *Scott* v. *Avery* clause [2.12] and (b) in *Fakes'* case it said that the plaintiff's poverty was the result of the defendants' breach of contract. They cannot be reconciled and the later case is to be preferred.

Lord Justice Goddard in the Court of Appeal in *Pitchers* v. *Plaza Ltd* (1940) was called upon to express an opinion as to whether the court should stay an action in order that the matter might be dealt with under the arbitration clause of the (then) RIBA contract. He said:

'When an employer reserves the advantage in a building contract of appointing his own architect, who is there to certify and in certifying to protect his interests, and when one finds that the architect and the employer are disputing the certificate, the court should be very slow to take a step which simply means that the building contractor is going to be kept out of his money for a long time as, of course, is the case if it is a proper one to go to arbitration ...'

(4) *Where a stay would result in two sets of proceedings arising out of the same facts, one of which is in the court.* A building owner sued his architect for damages for faulty design and failure to supervise the builders properly. The architect raised the defence that the damages were caused by the builders' breach of covenant; whereupon the owner joined the builders as second defendants in the action. There was an arbitration clause in the contractor's contract with the owner, but not

in his contract with the architect. The contractor was refused a stay: 'Our whole judicial procedure ... would be brought in dispute if ... there was a serious possibility of getting conflicting decisions on questions of fact by two different tribunals': *Taunton-Collins* v *Cromie & Ors* (1964).

But there may be two separate arbitrations arising out of the same facts: one between the owner and the contractor and the other between the contractor and a sub-contractor.

(5) *Where fraud is alleged.* Here section 24(2) of the 1950 Act is applicable.

(6) *Where the sole issue for the arbitrator is one of law*, this is sometimes said to be ground for refusing a stay in spite of the observations of Lord Simon in *Heyman* v. *Darwin* (1942): 'Even if the judge were right in regarding the issue as one in which nothing but a question of law is involved, that circumstance would not necessarily and in all cases make it right to refuse a stay.' Subsequent authorities cannot be reconciled.

Better men than the present author have failed to find a coherent doctrine or consistent principle in the decisions of the courts on this point. The following cases may be consulted: *Hyams* v. *Docker* (1969); *re Phoenix Timber Co.* (1958); *Halifax Overseas Freighters* v. *Rasno Export* (1958); *Eastern Counties Farmers* v. *J. and J. Cunningham* (1962). The so-called 'discretion' seems to depend upon the whims of the court before which the question is raised.

The right to seek a stay is lost if the defendant delivers any pleadings or takes 'any other steps in the proceedings'.

This means, it is said, 'something in the nature of an application to the court ... such as taking out a summons or something like that': *Ives and Barker* v. *Willans* (1894).

This raises problems for a defendant where the plaintiff has issued a writ and then taken out a summons under Order 14 of the High Court Rules. This provides that where a statement of claim (and not just a writ) has been served on the defendant and he has given notice of intention to defend (the post-1979 version of entering an appearance), the plaintiff may apply to the court for judgment on the ground that the defence has 'no defence to a claim included in the court or to a particular part of the claim'. This involves the plaintiff in taking out a summons for summary judgment before a Queen's Bench Master, and swearing the appropriate affidavit to the effect that he verily believes the defendant has no defence.

This summons requires the defendant to send an affidavit of rebuttal to the plaintiffs three days before the date named in the summons.

Pitchers Ltd v. *Plaza (Queensbury) Ltd* (1940) was an action where the plaintiffs sued on an architect's certificate for payment given under the then current JCT form. The defendants filed an affidavit claiming they had a defence to the action and asked for leave to defend. The Court of Appeal, illogically, held they had taken a step in the action, and had lost their right to go to arbitration.

By resisting an Order 14 summons, even on the grounds that there was an arbitration clause in the contract and the matter should be dealt with by arbitration, a defendant can lose his right to go to arbitration. Apparently it is necessary for the defendant to both give notice to the other side and take out a summons under section 4 and then apply for both summonses to be transferred to the same list: *Lane* v. *Hermann* (1939).

Recently the courts seem to have been veering round to a more relaxed approach to the matter. In *Eagle Star Insurance* v. *Yuval Insurance* (1978) the defendants took out a summons to strike out the plaintiff's endorsement on the writ. In *Leigh* v. *English Property* (1976) that had been held to be 'a step in the proceedings'.

The Court of Appeal held that it was not.

Lord Denning said that a step in the proceedings:

'is a step by which the defendant evinces an election to abide by the court proceedings and waives his right to ask for arbitration. Like any election it must be an unequivocal [the published law report says "equivocal" but this is clearly wrong] act done with knowledge of the material circumstances ...

"A step in the proceedings" must be one that impliedly affirms the correctness of the proceedings and the willingness of the defendant to go along with a determination by the courts of law instead of arbitration.'

That, of course, is contrary to all the decided cases, which are collected in para. 3715 of Part 2 of the *White Book*. On analysis, all of them will be found to be cases where the right to go to arbitration has been lost through inadvertence or the defendants' solicitors' ignorance of the rules of the game.

However, without apparently referring to this case, Mr Justice

Graham held in *Roussel-Uclaf* v. *G. D. Searle & Co. Ltd & G. D. Searle & Co. Inc* (1982) that a company which had appeared to resist an application for an injunction and had filed affidavits had taken no step in the proceedings. He based himself on the reasoning of Mr Justice Stirling in *Zalinoff* v. *Hammond* (1898). There it was held that filing affidavits opposing a motion for the appointment of a receiver in a partnership action was not taking 'a step in the proceedings'.

None of these cases appears to be reconcilable with *Pitchers'* case *supra*. But it is apparent that unless great care is taken, a party may end up with an Order 14 judgment against him before his application to stay the proceedings ends.

2.22 No discharge by frustration

An arbitration agreement cannot be frustrated by procrastination on the part of the claimant even if the effect of that delay is to render a satisfactory trial impossible and the circumstances are such that, had it been litigation and not arbitration, the court would have struck the action out for want of prosecution on the principles outlined in *Allen* v. *Sir Alfred McAlpine* (1968).

There are two reasons for this. Firstly, as Lord Diplock said in *Paal Wilson* v. *Partenreederei* (1982):

'It ... is quite impossible to say that the continuance of arbitration proceedings after it has become virtually impossible at the hearing that the arbitrator can be confident that he has been able to ascertain the true facts is a thing radically different from that which was undertaken by the parties when they incorporated the arbitration clause in the main contract.'

The second reason is that the doctrine of frustration only applies where it comes about by some supervening event which makes performance impossible and which is outside the control of either party: *Maritime National Fish* v. *Ocean Trawlers* (1935). In that case Lord Wright said: 'The essence of frustration is that it should not be due to the act or election of the parties.'

Observations in the *Paal Wilson* case in the Court of Appeal, to the effect that arbitration agreements could be discharged by frustration where the claimant procrastinated to such an extent that a fair trial was impossible, were overruled by the House of Lords.

Frustration of the principal contract leaves the arbitration clause standing and effective: *Heyman* v. *Darwins Ltd* (1942); *Government of Gibraltar* v. *Kennay* (1956). The reasons for this were explained by Lord Diplock in the *Paal Wilson* case:

> 'An arbitration clause is collateral to the main contract in which it is incorporated and it gives rise to collateral primary and secondary obligations of its own. Those collateral obligations survive the termination, whether by fundamental breach, breach of condition or frustration, of all the primary obligations assumed by the parties under the other clauses in the main contract.'

2.23 Express or implied agreement to rescind

It is always open to parties to a contract to make a second subsequent agreement whereby they mutually abandon the obligations they have assumed under their original contract. This is possible only when at least one of the primary obligations of the contract remains unperformed and the second contract is known as 'the contract of abandonment'. And, to quote an ancient observation 'as they were bound, so shall they be loosed'.

If a claimant gives notice of arbitration and then goes to sleep on it, so that years pass without the issues being brought to trial, it is possible that a court may hold that the parties have entered into a subsequent agreement to abandon the arbitration agreement.

> 'Where the inference that a reasonable man would draw from the prolonged failure by the claimant in an arbitration procedure is that the claimant is willing to consent to the abandonment of the agreement to submit the dispute to arbitration, and the respondent did in fact draw such inference, and by his own inaction thereafter indicated his own consent to its abandonment in similar fashion to the claimant, and was so understood by the claimant, the court would be right in treating the arbitration agreement as having been terminated by agreement,'

said Lord Diplock in *Paal Wilson* v. *Partenreederei* (1982). He cited the case of *The Splendid Sun* (1981) which he thought had been correctly decided on these grounds (but on these grounds alone).

2.24 Implied terms in arbitration agreements

The 1950 Act writes into all arbitration agreements subject to it various implied terms. These may be summarised:

—*Section 6*: if the agreement is silent as to how many arbitrators there should be, the reference shall be to one arbitrator

—*Section 8* (as amended by Section 6(1) of the 1979 Act): where the reference is to two arbitrators, they may appoint an umpire at any time and shall do so at once if they cannot agree

—*Section 8(2)*: umpire to enter on reference forthwith when arbitrators deliver 'to any party or to the umpire' notice of disagreement

—*Section 12(1)*: parties can be required to give evidence on oath

—*Section 14*: arbitrator's power to make interim award

—*Section 15*: arbitrator's power to order specific performance

—*Section 18*: costs to be in arbitrator's discretion.

These terms are not to be implied if there is contrary intention expressed in the agreement to arbitrate.

According to Lord Diplock in *Bremer Vulkan* (1981), it is also an implied term that 'both parties, respondent as well as claimant ... will join in applying to the arbitrator for appropriate directions to end any delay. This is a mutual obligation so that if both are in breach of it, neither can rely on the other's breach as giving him a right to treat the agreement as at an end.'

There is no implied term that the claimant will use his best endeavours to bring the matter to a speedy conclusion, as was suggested by Mr Justice Donaldson in the High Court in the *Bremer Vulkan* case. Nor is there an implied term, such as was suggested by Lord Justice Roskill in the Court of Appeal in that case, that the claimants will do nothing to frustrate the purpose of the arbitration: *Hannah Blumenthal* (1982).

2.25 Void provisions

The Limitation Act 1980 section 34(2) makes void a provision in an arbitration agreement that the cause of action shall not accrue until an award is made.

For the purposes of this statute (and its predecessor the 1939 Act), a cause of action accrues for breach of contract when the breach takes place whether or not the plaintiff knows of it at that time. In torts, the cause of action accrues not when the wrongful act or omission takes place, but when damage takes place, whether or not the plaintiff knows of it or not. So the House of Lords decided in *Pirelli* v. *Oscar Faber* (1982), overruling a unanimous Court of Appeal in *Sparham-Souter* v.

Town and Country Developments (1976) which was followed in numerous cases and apparently approved by a unanimous House of Lords itself in *Anns* v. *London Borough of Merton* (1976).

As will be seen, it may well be that a building owner's right to go to arbitration may be statute-barred under the Act before he has any right to arbitrate.

Sensible contractual provisions to counter this position are now rendered void by this enactment.

Chapter 3
Arbitrators and their appointment

3.01 Who can be an arbitrator?

Anybody upon whom the parties can agree can be an arbitrator and he is not required to have qualifications, training or even be of full age.

> 'Every person must use his own discretion in the choice of his Judges; and being at liberty to choose whom he likes best, cannot afterwards object the want of honesty or understanding to them, or that they have not done him justice': *Bacon's Abridgement* (1610).

It is not infrequent to find that the parties have agreed that the arbitrator should possess certain qualifications. If the arbitrator does not possess them, his appointment is a nullity, and any award he may purport to make of no effect.

Although formal professional qualifications, e.g. as a chartered quantity surveyor, may be easy to assess, difficulty has arisen where there is provision that the reference shall be to 'a commercial man': see *Rahcassi Shipping* v. *Blue Star* (1967) and *Pando Companio Naviera* v. *Filmo* (1975). The best that can be said apparently is that: 'The use of the words "commercial men" excludes those whose experience is as practising members of the legal profession. Some of them could rightly be described as "commercial lawyers", but while they serve the commercial world, they are not of it.' But apparently a retired solicitor who was a full time maritime arbitrator was 'a commercial man'.

The same principles applicable to the possession of qualifications are equally applicable to express disqualifications, e.g. that the arbitrator 'shall not be a lawyer'. The court has no discretion to allow an award given by a disqualified person to stand.

3.02 Possible disqualifications

There are three other matters which may disqualify an arbitrator, but if he is properly appointed an award by him will be valid unless set aside by the court. They are:

(1) *an interest* in the subject matter of the dispute such as to prevent the arbitrator being capable of being impartial between the parties
(2) *bias* against one party
(3) being *a necessary witness* for one party.

An interest alone will not suffice to disqualify. It is common in the construction industry as under Condition 66 of the ICE Form [2.17) that the engineer shall decide disputes between the contractor and the employer. Those decisions are of course subject to a further tier of arbitration. Formerly, it was the practice in building and civil engineering contracts to provide, as for example in *Stevenson* v. *Watson* (1879), a clause:

'The contractor and the directors will be bound to leave all questions or matters of dispute which may arise during the progress of the works or in the settlement of the account to the architect, whose decisions shall be final and binding upon all parties.'

The clause in *Eckersley & Ors* v. *Mersey Dock* (1894) read:

'All disputes and differences which may arise between the contractor and the Board during the progress, or after the completion, of the works contracted for, in relation to or arising out of any of the plans or drawings, or any of the provisions of the specification or contract, or in relation to any of the works, or the payment to be made for the same, or as to the accounts between the Board and the contractors, shall be and the same are hereby referred to the engineer of the Board, as sole arbitrator, with power to make awards from time to time as he may think proper, and with power to make such orders in any such award as to the costs and charges of and attending any such reference, and of the award, as the said engineer shall in his discretion think proper, and every award of the engineer shall be finally binding and conclusive upon the parties in relation to the disputes and differences as to which such award is made.'

A dispute having arisen between the contractor and the Liverpool Harbour Board, the contractor took out a writ, claiming damages against the engineer's son, who was also a servant of the Board. Opposing an application for a stay and referral to the arbitration of the engineer, counsel for the contractor claimed that the engineer might be biased. Lord Esher MR said:

> 'If you applied the rule which is applied to judges in such a case as this, it is obvious that such a servant, under whose superintendence the work was to be done, never could act as the arbitrator.
>
> Therefore the allegations must be further, and must go, in my opinion, to the extent that it must be shown, I will not say that he would be biased, but that there is a probability that he would be biased. That seems to me to be distinctly the decision in *Jackson* v. *Barry Rail Co* (1893) ... If it is said that the mere fact of the conduct of the engineer himself being likely, or being sure, to come into question is sufficient of itself to satisfy the court that there is a reason why the matter should not be referred to him; all I can say is that it seems to be contrary to other cases and is absolutely contrary to *Jackson* v. *Barry Rail Co*.
>
> It is of the essence of the submission that questions are to be submitted to this engineer, as arbitrator, which must involve matters connected with his competency, with his own case, with his own caution and with the way in which he may have discharged the duties which belonged to him under his contract.
>
> The parties agree that the arbitrator is to adjudicate on matters in which he has an interest. Further than that, I understand it was admitted and was not disputed at the Bar that, if the matter in question here were a matter which involved the professional competency or the professional skill of the engineer himself, he would not be disqualified.
>
> It is therefore not, in my opinion, any objection to the engineer acting in this dispute that his conduct, or the conduct of his son as assistant engineer in directing the other works done in the Canada Dock, would be or might be called in question.
>
> It must have been within the contemplation of the parties that the engineer might have to superintend other works undertaken by the defendants during the progress of the contract works, and it seems to me to be an objection which the contractors waived and deprived themselves of the right to insist on when they agreed that the engineer should be the sole arbitrator as regards themselves.'

Lord Justice Davey added:

'The parties have contracted that the servant of one of them shall be the arbitrator and it appears to me that they have contracted that he shall be the arbitrator in cases which necessarily involve the correctness of his own opinion, the competency of his advice and opinion as an engineer and the regularity of his own proceedings.'

Being an employee of one party is therefore no disqualification. However, a borough surveyor was held disqualified in *Nuttall* v. *Manchester Corporation* (1892) because there was great personal animosity between him and the contractor; and in *Kimberley* v. *Dick* (1871) an architect arbitrator was held to be disqualified because he had made a secret agreement with his employer that the costs of the building would not exceed a certain sum.

A shareholding by the arbitrator in a public company and which is party to a reference should be disclosed to the parties, but shareholdings in a private company which is a party may amount to a disqualification: *Sellar* v. *Highland Railway* (1919).

Section 24(1) of the 1950 Act allows the court to remove an arbitrator on 'the ground that ... [he] is not or may not be impartial'.

Under these powers, the managing director of a company which was a party to a shipping arbitration who had appointed himself as one of two arbitrators was removed: *Veritas Shipping* v. *Anglo-Canadian Cement* (1966). The other party applied to the court for his removal under section 24(1) and Mr Justice McNair said:

'The order they ask for is that the court should remove Dr W. K. Wallersteiner ... on the ground that Dr Wallersteiner has misconducted himself in the arbitration in not only allowing himself to be appointed as arbitrator, but having appointed himself, having as managing director of Anglo-Canadian Cement Ltd signed the letter appointing him to act.

Without making any reflections upon the propriety and skill of Dr Wallersteiner, I am quite satisfied that it would be quite wrong for him to be allowed to continue to act as arbitrator in a dispute of this nature. It is quite true that under the clause, the two arbitrators, according to the customary way in which these matters are dealt with in the City of London, may if they so wish act as advocates. They need not do so but there is nothing wrong in them doing so.

Until that moment arrives, the arbitrators must not only act judicially and show no bias at all but must also appear to be in a position to act judicially and without any bias.

In somewhat similar circumstances in the case of *Burkett Sharp & Co* v. *Eastcheap Dried Fruit Company and Perera* (1962), Lord Justice Pearson, as he then was, expressed the view, with which the other members of the court concurred, that in view of the close association of Mr Perera with the Eastcheap Dried Fruit Company he was manifestly not a suitable arbitrator and their nomination of him as arbitrator was quite unsuitable and, indeed, astonishing.'

Bias is apparent animosity to one party or his witnesses. In *Catalina* v. *Norma* (1938), an arbitrator in an arbitration arising out of the collision of a Portuguese and a Norwegian ship was heard to express an opinion about the credibility of witnesses of Portuguese nationality. He was removed by the court.

3.03 Reference to official referees

Section 11 of the Arbitration Act 1950 provides:

'Where an arbitration agreement provides that the reference shall be to an official referee, any official referee to whom application is made shall, subject to any order of the High Court or a judge thereof as to transfer or otherwise, hear and determine the matters agreed to be referred.'

There are now strictly no official referees since the Courts Act 1971. But there are circuit judges assigned by the Lord Chancellor to official referees' business, and in 1981, when one of these was knighted, the official announcement referred to him as 'The Senior Official Referee'. In practice, the official referees have continued to do what they have always done since they were created in 1854, that is they hear and determine cases referred to them which are too detailed for a High Court judge to entertain. Inevitably, most of the 700 or so cases referred to them each year are construction industry matters.

The obligation of official referees to act as arbitrators appears to have been overlooked by the construction industry. Section 10 of the Arbitration Act 1950 provides that '*any* official referee *to whom application is made* ... shall ... hear and determine the matters agreed to be referred'. It would appear from section 11 that the parties can select which of the circuit judges appointed to deal with official referee's business they wish. The statement (without authority) in *Russell on Arbitration*, 19th Edition, page 115, note 31, to the effect that 'The reference is subject to ordinary rules as to transfer to other referees, arrangement of cause list etc.' is not correct. That is the current practice of the courts but it appears from the terms of the 1950 Act to be wrong. Without separate order from the High Court, it would appear from the words of the statute that the official referee selected by the parties *has* to undertake the arbitration, and that without the fee of £30 currently charged by the court. But only if the arbitration agreement provides for reference to an official referee.

The advantages of nominating an official referee can be considerable. The parties obtain the services of a highly skilled and experienced arbitrator without payment for his services. The hearing, unlike normal official referee business, is in private; the award is not published. Moreover, there is no obligation on either party to engage counsel to represent them; anybody – be he solicitor, quantity surveyor or architect – is, as with all other arbitrations, entitled to appear, whereas only members of the Bar, instructed by solicitors, are entitled to appear before an official referee sitting as such.

Moreover, the parties can agree to exclude any appeal under section 3 of the 1979 Act, which they cannot do with court proceedings before the official referees.

3.04 High Court judges as arbitrators

There is said to be a common law right to appoint any judge, with his consent and that of the parties, to act as an arbitrator to determine matters which are between the same parties but extraneous to those raised in proceedings and which can conveniently be determined at the same time: *Pando Compania Naviera SA* v. *Filmo SAS* (1975).

Also, under section 4 of the Administration of Justice Act 1970 a High Court judge nominated to the Queen's Bench Commercial Court (but none other) can accept appointment as the sole arbitrator or as an umpire. However, there is no obligation on any judge to do so, and there are a number of qualifications. In the first place, he may do so only if 'he thinks fit' and if the dispute appears to him 'to be of a commercial character'. Furthermore, he has to obtain from the Lord Chief Justice confirmation that the state of business in the High Court permits his being made available. If he does sit as arbitrator, his fees have to be paid to the High Court. If he does accept, appellate jurisdiction, which otherwise under the 1979 Act would be exercised by the High Court, becomes exercisable by the Court of Appeal.

County court judges are prohibited from sitting as private arbitrators for a fee to themselves: County Courts Act 1956 section 6(b).

There is, of course, no restriction on a retired judge sitting as an arbitrator and the courts apparently look with favour upon retired judges in appointing arbitrators under section 10 of the principal Act.

3.05 The NHBC panel

The National House-Building Council's panel of arbitrators was originally compiled by the Chartered Institute of Arbitrators and is currently compiled by the Royal Institution of Chartered Surveyors, whose president does the appointing.

3.06 Appointment by the court

Section 10 of the 1950 Act empowers the court, in certain limited circumstances which are set out in the sub-sections, to appoint an arbitrator.

The section has been amended by the 1979 Act, firstly by changing the original 10(c) to read: 'Where the parties or two arbitrators are required or are at liberty to appoint an umpire or third arbitrator and do not appoint him.' This alteration was consequential on the alterations to section 8 which deals with the appointment of an umpire.

Secondly, the 1979 Act adds the additional words now set out as section 10(2). This resulted from a case in which the President of the RIBA refused to appoint and the court held that it had no power under section 10 as it then existed to do so. In an earlier case in similar circumstances, it had done so and this had been approved by the Court of Appeal [2.20].

The procedure under section 10(a) regarding a single arbitrator requires definite and separate steps:

(1) a dispute or difference must have arisen
(2) there must be a formal notice, but there does not first have to be an attempt to agree on an arbitrator
(3) seven clear days, excluding the day of service, must then elapse before application is made to the court: Supreme Court Practice Order 3 rule 2.

UNIVERSITY OF WOLVERHAMPTON
Harrison Learning Centre

ITEMS ISSUED:

Customer ID: 7605300797

Title: Delay and disruption in construction
contracts
ID: 7623722959
Due: 11/03/2009 23:59

Title: Arbitration : principles and practice
ID: 7604541561
Due: 25/03/2009 23:59

Total items: 2
Total fines: £9.20
04/03/2009 10:58
Total Items on Loan: 2
Overdue: 0

Thank you for using Self Service.
Please keep your receipt.

Overdue books are fined at 40p per day for
1 week loans, 10p per day for long loans.

The section is highly unsatisfactory since it does not require that the party giving notice should specify a named arbitrator.

It is also uncertain whether the words 'may … appoint an arbitrator' merely empowers the court to do that or whether they confer a discretion on the court to do so if it sees fit. There are judicial observations in support of both views. Lord Esher and Lord Justice Lopes both thought in *re Eyre and Leicester Corporation* (1892) that the words, which occur first in section 12 of the Common Law Procedure Act 1854, were intended only to confer a power on the court which it had not previously had, and that they should not be read as meaning 'must appoint'. It was said *obiter*, in disregard of those observations in the Court of Appeal, in *Tritonia Shipping* v. *South Nelson* (1966) that the courts have a discretion, and it probably will be held in future that they have an uncontrolled discretion. Certainly in *re Bjornsted & Ouse Shipping* (1924) the Court of Appeal, after an unconvincing attempt to explain away the plain observations in *re Eyre*, held that they were entitled to appoint an arbitrator subject to the applicant, a foreigner, giving security for costs.

Lord Justice Bankes said:

'In this particular case this court has a discretion to refuse to appoint an arbitrator at all under the circumstances of this case, and to refuse because the applicant is a foreigner resident outside the jurisdiction.

If the court has that discretion, it seems to me that it can attach any reasonable condition to the exercise of its discretion in granting the application. One knows that very often in applications under section 4 the fact that an arbitrator has no power to make an order for a commission to examine witnesses abroad is a ground for refusing to stay proceedings. Equally, I think, it would be a ground, or might in this case be a ground, for refusing to exercise one's discretion, that the applicant is a foreigner outside the jurisdiction and, I think, that it is perfectly competent to this court to make an order in this form, that if the applicant within a certain time gives security for the costs of the arbitration, and of this appeal, then the order of Talbot J may stand; but if the security is not given within the time limited then the order is discharged, and in either event that the respondents should have the costs here and below.'

It is however useful to avoid having to go to the president of one of the bodies specified in arbitration agreements, which can involve long delays and may result in the appointment of an unsatisfactory arbitrator. An appointment by the court is preferable and more speedy. Moreover, if there is danger of a claim being statute-barred, it would appear that service of the notice will be sufficient to rank as the 'commencement' of the arbitration. Section 34(3)(a) of the Limitation Act 1980 provides that an arbitration shall be treated as being commenced when one party serves a notice requiring the appointment of an arbitrator. How the notice may be served is set out in section 34(4), but it also provides for other methods being used if specified in the arbitration agreement. It will be noted that the Limitation Act 1980 omits to provide for the situation where the appointment of an arbitrator is to be made by a third party, so that to avoid difficulty if the period of limitation is nearly expired, it may be desirable to adopt this procedure.

3.07 The same arbitrator for two arbitrations

The Court of Appeal has held, however, that it had power under section 10 of the Arbitration Act 1950, where there were two references which were related, to appoint the same arbitrator to both arbitrations.

Liquid gas tanks, erected on Das Island in the Persian Gulf, proved it was alleged to be defective. The employers claimed against the main contractors who in turn claimed against sub-contractors. Both contracts were governed by English law.

Mr Justice Bingham held that there ought to be separate arbitrators for each arbitration because if there were only one, it might be said that an adverse finding in the first arbitration would affect his decision in the second. The Court of Appeal reversed his decision and appointed Sir John Megaw, lately a Lord Justice of Appeal, as arbitrator in both arbitrations, with liberty to the parties or the arbitrator to apply if it were thought that the second arbitration might be prejudiced by findings in the first. Lord Justice Watkin said there was no power in the court to do more than appoint an arbitrator. It had no power to attach conditions to the appointment or direct the arbitrator how he should conduct the arbitration: *Abu Dhabi Gas* v. *Eastern Bechtel Corporation* (1982).

Lord Denning, giving his reasons, said that this course was highly desirable to avoid inconsistent findings.

3.08 Consolidations of separate arbitrations in the United States

In at least eight of the American states, it has been held that under the terms of their enactments, the jurisdiction conferred by statute on the court to enforce arbitration agreements included the power to order that separate arbitrations should be consolidated.

In a case in the State of Maryland, a contractor, alleging delay in receipt of instructions from the architect, demanded arbitration under his contract with the employer. The employer in turn sought arbitration under the contract with the architect. The American Architects' Association wrote to all parties to the effect that 'in the absence of the agreement of all parties or applicable contractual provisions, the Association must administer the cases separately'.

The Court of Appeal in Maryland held that it had inherent jurisdiction under the local statute to order a consolidation of the two arbitration proceedings and it would do so since the issues in the two cases were identical: i.e. if the contractor had been delayed by late receipt of instructions from the architect, the employer would be liable for the loss and expense so caused, but would have a right to an indemnity from the architect for breach of the express and implied terms of his contract. The court also held that the position would be the same under the Federal Arbitration Act.

The English courts do not appear to possess the same power, although the case of *Moody* v. *Ellis* (1982) suggests that it would be useful.

3.09 Immunity of arbitrators

Currently it is generally said that an arbitrator is immune from actions by either party for negligence or for breach of an implied or express term of his acceptance of the appointment that he will exercise due care and skill. But observations made by the law lords in the case of *Arenson* v. *Casson Beckman Rutley & Co.* (1975) suggest that this may not be the position for long.

Lord Kilbrandon said:

'The question which puzzled me ... was: what was the essential difference between the typical valuer, the auditor in the present case, and an arbitrator at common law or under the Arbitration Acts? ... It was conceded that an arbitrator is immune from suit, aside from fraud, but why? I find it impossible to put weight on such considerations as that in the case of an arbitrator:

(a) there is a dispute between parties;
(b) he hears evidence;

(c) he hears submissions from the parties, and that therefore he, unlike the valuer, is acting in a juridical capacity.

As regards (a), I cannot see any juridical distinction between a dispute which has actually arisen and a situation where persons have opposing interests, if in either case an impartial person has had to be called in to make a decision which the interested parties will accept. As regards (b) and (c), these are certainly not *necessarily* activities of an arbiter.

Once the nature and limits of the submission to him have been defined, it could well be that he would go down at his own convenience to a warehouse, inspect a sample of merchandise displayed to him by the foreman, and return his opinion on its quality or value.

I have come to be of opinion that it is a necessary conclusion to be drawn from *Sutcliffe* v. *Thackrah* [3.10] and from the instant decision that an arbitrator at common law or under the Act is indeed a person selected by the parties for his expertise, whether technical or intellectual, that he pledges skill in the exercise thereof, and that if he is negligent in that exercise he will be liable in damages.'

Lord Fraser of Tulleybelton said:

'In *Lingood* v. *Croucher* (1742) Lord Hardwicke LC quoted a *dictum* by Lord King LC that if arbitrators were liable to be sued that "would effectively discourage persons of worth from accepting of being arbitrators".

But the immunity of judges and arbitrators forms an exception to the general rule that a person who professes special skill or knowledge is liable for negligence if he fails to show such knowledge and skill and to take such care and precautions as are reasonably expected of a normally skilled and competent member of the profession or trade in question.'

Lord Salmon said:

'I find it difficult to discern any sensible reason, on grounds of public policy or otherwise, why such an arbitrator with such a limited role, although formally appointed, should enjoy a judicial immunity which so called "quasi-arbitrators" in the position of the respondents certainly do not ...

Such an arbitrator, like any accountant who signs a report in a prospectus, could always protect himself against action for negligence, if he wished to do so, by stipulating that he is willing to act only on condition that he should be under no obligation (which the law would otherwise impose) to use reasonable care.

I do not suppose, however, that insistence on such a condition would be likely to improve his chances of obtaining business; and that no doubt is why such a condition is so rarely imposed.

The question whether there may be circumstances in which a person, even if he is formally appointed as an arbitrator, may not be accorded immunity does not, however, arise for decision in the present case; but it may have to be examined in the future.'

[He then compared the situation of mutual valuers with that of arbitrators.]

Both are giving decisions which will bind parties with conflicting interests. Both have a duty to act impartially between the parties. Both can reach their decision by using their own skill and judgment without hearing evidence, and, unless they have immunity, both are liable to be shot at from opposite sides.

The main difference between them is that the arbitrator, like the judge, has to decide a dispute that has already arisen, and he usually has rival contentions before him, while the mutual valuer is called in before a dispute has arisen, in order to avoid it.

He may be employed by parties who have little or no idea of the value of the property to be valued and who rely entirely on his skill and judgment as an expert. In that respect he differs from some arbitrators.

But many arbitrators are chosen for their expert knowledge of the subject of the arbitration, and many others are chosen from the legal profession for their expert knowledge of the law or perhaps because they are credited with an expertise in holding the balance fairly between parties.

It does not seem possible, therefore, to distinguish between mutual valuers and arbitrators on the ground that the former are experts and the latter are not.

I share the difficulty of my noble and learned friend, Lord Kilbrandon, in seeing why arbitrators as a class should have immunity from suit if mutual valuers do not.'

It appears highly likely therefore that in some future case an arbitrator who has been negligent will be held liable to the parties in negligence.

To err in law or in fact is obviously not negligence, nor is an honest error of judgment, but plainly if the arbitrator so conducts the proceedings that his award is set aside for conduct that no competent arbitrator would have committed, it is likely he will find himself liable for all the costs thrown away.

The position of arbitration costs thrown away where the arbitrator was removed for misconduct and his award set aside was discussed in the High Court, but by no means resolved, in *Fisher & Ors* v. *P. E. Wellfair Ltd* (1981). If the award had been merely set aside, the arbitrator would have continued to be in office and have been empowered to make a fresh award dealing with the costs. As it was, the arbitrator was removed and therefore had no power to award costs. The judge had no power to deal with the costs of the first hearing; nor had the arbitrator subsequently appointed, so that the costs, which would have been the claimant's in any event, were irrecoverable. There seems to be no good reason why the arbitrator whose conduct caused this loss should be protected.

The presumption now is that anybody whose negligence causes reasonably foreseeable loss should compensate the injured, as Lord Wilberforce pointed out in *Anns* v. *London Borough of Merton* (1980).

It would appear from *Jones* v. *Victoria Graving* (1877) that the practice of the court in those days in referring cases to an arbitrator was made subject to the express provision that 'neither the plaintiffs nor the defendants shall bring or prosecute any action of suit at law or in equity against the said arbitrator'. This suggests that under common law at that date arbitrators had no immunity.

In fact arbitrators have been liable under the Supply of Goods and Services Act 1982 as the suppliers of a service who are acting in the course of a business and therefore obliged to use reasonable care and skill. That liability ended under statute on 1 March 1985 as the result of the Supply of Services (Exclusion of Implied Terms) Order 1985 S.I. 1.

3.10 'Quasi-arbitrators': a slight case of genocide

For nearly a century, it was established law that if someone was 'in the position of an arbitrator', in that he was called upon to hold the balance fairly between two parties for the purpose of placing a fair price upon goods or land or to decide any matters upon which the parties had not or could not agree, then he was protected from any action for negligence.

In *Stevenson* v. *Watson* (1879) a contractor sued an architect for negligence in failing to certify sufficient sums in interim payment certificates. The case did not turn, as it well might have done in those early days, on whether or not the architect owed a duty to the contractor; nor even whether financial loss alone was sufficient to support an action for negligence. Those points were apparently conceded.

It turned upon whether the architect, when giving his certificates, was immune from action on the ground that he was performing the role of an arbitrator.

The form of building contract used contained the provision:

'The contractor and the directors will be bound to leave all questions or matters of dispute which may arise during the progress of the works or in the settlement of the account to the architect, whose decisions shall be final and binding upon all parties. The contractor will be paid on the certificate of the architect.'

Lord Coleridge CJ said:

'Where a matter is left by two parties to the judgment of a third who is to determine their rights, and the task is not merely one of arithmetic but involving technical skill and knowledge, that person is in the position of a quasi-arbitrator, and no action will lie against him for negligence in the performance of his duties.

I think this case is within the authority of the cases cited which decide that where the exercise of judgment or opinion on the third person is necessary between two persons, such as a buyer and seller ... an action will not lie against the person put in that position when such a judgment has been given wrongly or improperly, or discretion is ignorantly or negligently exercised.'

Later, the Court of Appeal was called upon to consider the same question in two cases, *Chambers* v. *Goldthorpe* and *Restell v Nye* (1901) in relation to the then Standard Form of Building Contract. In the first case, the architect sued for fees, to be met by a counterclaim for negligent certification. In the second case, the building owner sued the architect directly for negligent certification. The contract provided:

'Clause 21. A certificate of the architect ... showing the final balance due or payable to the contractors, is to be conclusive evidence of the works having been duly completed, and that the contractors are entitled to receive payment of the final balance ...'

The then Master of the Rolls, Lord Smith, said:

'What is the duty of the plaintiff in giving his certificate? The ascertainment of the amount to be paid by the owner to the builder is not a mere matter of arithmetic. The architect's duties are not merely ministerial or clerkly, to use the words of Lord Coleridge CJ, in *Stevenson* v. *Watson* (1879). The matter requires the use of professional knowledge, skill and judgment.

In such circumstances *Stevenson* v. *Watson* appears to show that the position of the architect is that of an arbitrator between the owner and the builder. It was argued that there could be no arbitration because no dispute had arisen between the owner and the builder.

In my opinion there can be an arbitration to settle matters although no dispute has actually arisen with regard to them if it is probable that a dispute will arise unless the arbitration takes place.'
(Author's italics)

Lord Justice Henn Collins said:

'It was contended that there can be no quasi-arbitration unless a dispute is in existence, but I think that there is a fallacy in that argument.

There is a difference between a dispute formulated between the parties, so as to be within clause 22 of the contract as interpreted by the Court of Appeal in *Lloyd Bros* v. *Milward* (1895) and that sort of possible difference which underlies an agreement between two parties, that what one is to pay and the other is to be paid in respect of a certain matter shall be ascertained by a third person. In such an agreement there is involved an underlying assertion of possible difference as to the rights to be so ascertained by the third person, and if he, having notice of the agreement, accepts the responsibility of deciding between the two parties he must ... have duties towards both of them.'

Following these cases, Lord Justice Buckley in the Court of Appeal in *Arenson* v. *Arenson & Ano* (1973) said:

'Where a third party undertakes the role of deciding between two parties a question, the determination of which requires the third party to hold the scales fairly between the opposing interests of the two parties, the third party is immune from an action for negligence in respect of anything done in that role.'

Typical of persons who occupied the position of quasi-arbitrator were: a surveyor appointed to decide the fair open market rent of property under a rent review clause; an architect giving certificates for payment under the JCT Standard Form of Building Contract; an engineer certifying payments under the contract of the ICE conditions; or, as that particular case itself illustrated, an accountant called upon to value shares. Certain other specific professions were recognised as coming within this 'quasi-arbitrator' category, such as average adjusters in insurance contracts.

The fact that an architect was employed and paid by a building owner did not displace the principle that when he gave his final certificate under the JCT contract or earlier building contracts he was 'in the position of an arbitrator'. 'It is established law,' said Lord Radcliffe in *R. B. Burden Ltd* v. *Swansea Corporation* (1957), 'that, in granting a final certificate under a building contract, the architect acts in an arbitral capacity and is not merely in the position of an agent for the building owner'. One judge at least seems to have taken the view that an architect, who was charged with not giving a final certificate within a specified time, was not merely a quasi-arbitrator but a full arbitrator. Lord Justice Slessor in *Neale* v. *Richardson* (1938) said that if an architect neglected or refused to give his final certificate, either party could apply to the court for the appointment of a new arbitrator under Section 10 of the Arbitration Act 1950.

But as Lord Denning said triumphantly, in *Campbell* v. *Edwards* (1975) the House of Lords has since reversed the previous position.

In *Sutcliffe* v. *Thackrah & Ors* (1974) the House was concerned with two interim certificates given under a JCT contract in May and July 1964 for a total of £4457. Shortly afterwards, the contractor's employment was determined and the company became insolvent. Later the interim certificates were discovered to have included defective work not known to the architect but known to the quantity surveyor who was an employee of the same firm.

In the second case, *Arenson* v. *Casson Beckman Rutley & Co.* (1975), a firm of accountants was sued for negligence in placing a valuation on shares under a contractual clause which read:

> '"Fair Value" shall mean in relation to the Shares in A. Arenson Limited, the value thereof as determined by the auditors for the time being of the Company whose valuation, acting as experts and not as arbitrators, shall be final and binding on all parties.'

In the first case, Lord Salmon said the doctrine of *Chambers* v.

Goldthorpe 'clearly is not a doctrine to be lightly overthrown ... But I am convinced that it is contrary alike to principle, sound authority, reason and justice.'

If so, it is somewhat surprising it took nearly a century to discover this.

An architect is only protected from actions for negligence, according to Lord Morris, 'when there is a submission to him either of a specific dispute or present points of difference that might arise in the future and if there was an agreement that his decisions would be binding'.

An architect is now personally liable whenever he gives certificates and he is apparently neither an arbitrator nor a quasi-arbitrator.

3.11 Mutual valuers and arbitrators

Following these decisions, and those of the Court of Appeal in *Campbell* v. *Edwards* (1976) and *Baker* v. *Kenwood* (1978), there arose a neat and tidy division between the award of an arbitrator and the decision of a mutual valuer appointed 'as an expert and not as an arbitrator':

(1) An arbitrator was not liable to actions for negligence or breach of express or implied warranties but his award was subject to challenge in the courts in the manner provided by the common law and/or the 1950 and 1979 Acts.
(2) A mutual valuer's decision was final and binding upon both parties, but he could be sued for negligence and for breach of an express and/or implied warranty that he would use reasonable skill and care.

This appears to have been upset by the decision of Mr Justice Nourse in *Burgess & Ano* v. *Purchase & Son (Farms) Ltd & Ors* (1982) to the effect that if the decision of a mutual valuer is a 'speaking one' (that is, that he gives reasons for his decision), it can be impugned by one of the parties. He said: 'A non-speaking valuation of the right property by the right man in good faith cannot be impugned. It may however be possible in the case of an uncompleted contract for equitable relief to be refused to a party who wishes to sustain the valuation.'

In that he had in mind that equitable decrees, such as those for specific performance, are discretionary and if refused, the party seeking the decree may still 'have a claim at common law for damages,'. He then went on:

'On the other hand, there are at least three decisions to the effect that a speaking valuation which demonstrates that it has been made on a fundamentally erroneous basis can be impugned. In such a case, the completion of the transaction does not necessarily defeat the party who wishes to impugn the transaction. This may be justified on the footing that a valuation made on a fundamentally erroneous basis is in reality no different from one made of the wrong property or by the wrong man, or in bad faith.'

From this it would appear that those who seek finality by making those who have to adjudicate upon disputes, as in the Association of Consultant Architects (ACA) 1982 alternative 1 form, to be 'deemed to be acting as an expert and not as an arbitrator' may well be disappointed.

3.12 The appointment of an arbitrator

No special form is necessary for the appointment of an arbitrator by the parties unless the agreement requires it to be in writing or under seal. Otherwise it does not even have to be in writing. There is nothing to stop it being done by telephone or telex.

There are however three essential elements:

(1) The arbitrator must be told of his appointment.

In *Tradax Export SA* v. *Volkswagenwerk AG* (1970), there was an arbitration agreement between owners and charterers in the standard shipping Centrocon clause:

'Any claim must be made in writing and the claimant's arbitrator appointed within three months of final discharge and where this provision is not complied with the claim shall be deemed to be waived and absolutely barred.'

One party notified the other side on 27 January of the nomination of their arbitrator, but they failed to notify the arbitrator himself until 24 July, when they were out of time. On a motion to hold that there was a valid appointment within the three months allowed by the Centrocon clause Lord Denning said:

'We have to decide: what is necessary to constitute the appointment of an arbitrator? I think the answer is this.

First, it is necessary to tell the other side. That is plain from *Tew* v. *Harris* (1847).

Second, it is necessary to tell the appointee himself. That is obvious because he often has to start acting at once.

Third, it is necessary that he should be willing to act and have intimated his willingness to accept the appointment. In *Russell on Arbitration* (17th edition, 1963 at page 160) it is said: "Acceptance of the office by the arbitrator appears to be necessary to perfect his appointment." There is a passage in *Ringland* v. *Lowndes* (1864) which gives some support to that statement.

[Counsel] by great diligence has discovered the case of *Cox* v. *Johnson* (1914) where it is said:

> "In my view all that is required by the section [a similar section] is nomination by each party to the other of the person whom he has selected to act on his behalf."

I think that statement may have been right in relation to the facts and evidence in that case. But I do not think it is of general application. I think in general it is essential not only that the other side should be told, but also that the arbitrator himself should be told.

I am sure that it was an oversight that Mr Chesterman [the arbitrator] was not told. So much so that if Tradax – as soon as they discovered the omission – had applied to the court to extend the three months, it would certainly have been granted under section 27 of the Arbitration Act 1950, as explained in *Liberian Shipping Corporation 'Pegasus'* v. *A. King & Sons Ltd* (1967). But no such application was made. Instead, Tradax come to the court on the simple point; must the arbitrator be told of his appointment? I think he must. So here the appointment was not made within the three months. And the claim is barred.'

(2) It is also a requirement of a valid appointment that the arbitrator must accept. As it was put in *Fitz. Arbit.*, 1584.

> 'Touching his Ordinance, he is Ordained by these two things, viz., by the Election of the Parties and by his own undertaking of the charge.'

(3) The third requirement is that the other side must be notified of the appointment. 'Neither party can be said to have chosen an arbitrator until he lets the other party know the object of his choice.'

Where there is a clause providing for 'London arbitration,' i.e. each party has to appoint his own arbitrator, and a time clause, it is important that all three requirements are met within the time laid down.

A distinction must now be drawn between the time when any limitation period ceases to run, which by the Limitation Act 1980 section 3(a) is upon 'Notice', and the time when there is a valid appointment. From earlier cases it would appear that the latter is whichever is last in time: acceptance by the arbitrator, or notification to the other side.

3.13 Provision for three arbitrators

Formerly, if the agreement provided for three arbitrators the 1950 Act laid down in section 9(1) that that was to have effect 'as if it provided for the appointment of an umpire'. That section was replaced with a new section 9 in the 1950 Act by the 1979 Act. Now 'unless a contrary mention is expressed in the arbitration agreement ... where there are three arbitrators, the award of any two will be binding'.

3.14 Appointment of an umpire

A third arbitrator sits with the two and takes part in their deliberations and has equal voice with them in the award.

An umpire by contrast is legally without power or function until the two arbitrators fail to agree and have expressed their inability to agree in writing: section 8(1), 1950 Act. There appears to be no objection to an umpire being present at a hearing and even asking questions but he should take no part in the deliberations of the two arbitrators. But it is common practice in many industries for the arbitrators to consult the umpire before he is seized of his function as umpire. At one time the arbitrators were required by section 8(1) of the 1950 Act to appoint an umpire 'immediately after they themselves were appointed'. That provision has now gone as it was largely ignored and the arbitrators now have power to appoint an umpire at any time after they themselves are appointed and 'shall do so forthwith if they cannot agree'.

The court at any time after the appointment of an umpire may, on application by any party, remove the arbitrators and appoint the umpire as sole arbitrator.

3.15 Powers to supply vacancies

Once a party has appointed an arbitrator, he has no power under
section 7(a) of the Arbitration Act 1950 to appoint a new one in his
place unless the one originally appointed conclusively refuses to act at
all.

Section 7 states:

'Where an arbitration agreement provides that the reference shall be
to two arbitrators, one to be appointed by each party, then, unless a
contrary intention is expressed therein ...
(a) If either of the appointed arbitrators refuses to act or is
    incapable of acting, or dies, the party who appointed him may
    appoint a new arbitrator in his place.'

In *Burkett Sharp & Co.* v. *Eastcheap Dried Fruit Co. and Perera*
(1962) Lord Justice Pearson said of this section:

'The refusal required ... is a refusal to act – that is to say, a refusal to
act as arbitrator and not merely a refusal to act in a particular
manner. Secondly, the refusal is in the section associated with the
arbitrator becoming incapable of acting or his death – two events
which would put the arbitrator completely out of action, if I may use
that expression. A refusal should be something equally conclusive. It
should be a definite and final refusal. Thirdly, as in any case of doubt
or difficulty, application can be made under section 1 to revoke the
authority of the arbitrator, there is no need to extend the meaning of
the word "refuse" beyond its natural meaning in its context ...'

3.16 Death of an arbitrator

If a single arbitrator dies before delivering a final award, the
proceedings have to be commenced over again. Since the costs thrown
away can be horrendous and a fresh arbitrator would have no power to
deal with them, the parties have an insurable interest in the life of any
arbitrator who is appointed. Insurance policies are available to cover
such an eventuality and in an arbitration which is expected to last a
long time it is prudent to take out such cover, especially if the arbitrator
appointed is elderly.

It would appear from *obiter* observations by Mr Justice Ackner in
Fisher & Ors v. *P. G. Wellfair Ltd* (1948) that if an arbitrator who has

made an interim award dies before making a final award, the interim award will stand.

The court has power under section 10(b) to appoint a fresh arbitrator if one dies (or otherwise becomes incapable of acting) where the 'arbitration agreement does not show that it was intended that the vacancy should not be supplied and the parties do not supply the vacancy'. The section only has application where there is a single arbitrator.

3.17 Revocation of appointment

It is sometimes thought that revocation of the appointment of an arbitrator is the same thing as the removal of one, but there is a careful distinction drawn in the 1950 Act between the two things.

Normally in arbitrations subject to the 1950 Act – that is, arbitrations where the agreement is in writing (section 32) – the arbitrator, once appointed, cannot have his appointment revoked by either party. Before this provision was first included in the 1889 Act, the appointment of an arbitrator could be revoked at any time and it still can be in the case of arbitrations where the agreement is only oral and not subject to the statute.

Removal under section 1 requires two steps: leave from the court to a party and the actual act of revocation, and it only becomes operative when this has been done. Where each party appoints his own arbitrator, it would seem clear that he can only revoke the authority he has granted to his arbitrator; he cannot revoke the appointment of the other party's arbitrator.

There is little actual authority as to what principles the courts will follow in exercising this power and it seems to be limited to misconduct which is not merely technical: *City Centre* v. *Tersons* (1969). But in spite of *Russell* (19th Edition, 1979, page 165) there is no authority that the appointment of an arbitrator who is disqualified can be revoked by leave.

In the *City Centre* case (also reported as *City Centre* v. *Matthew Hall*) the subject of revocation was discussed at some length. Disputes arose between the building owner, the proposed tenant, and the heating nominated sub-contractor under the Standard Form of Building Contract for the Kensington Palace Hotel.

An arbitrator had been appointed, in accordance with the contract, in a dispute between the site owner and the heating engineers. A Queen's Bench master granted the site owner leave to revoke the appointment on the ground that there was an action pending in the courts in which all three parties were involved. The Court of Appeal reversed that. Lord Justice Harman stressed the difference between section 1 of the 1950 Act, and section 4 that deals with the courts' discretionary powers to stay litigation. He said that section 1 was only to be used sparingly and in unusual cases. Since the issue in the arbitration and those in the action were not the same, it was not right to allow the appointment to be revoked.

3.18 How an arbitrator recovers his fees

The presumption of the common law was that an arbitrator was not entitled to fees; what he was doing was performing the act of a good neighbour and therefore he was not entitled to recover fees even if they had been promised, since the parties did not intend contractual relationships between themselves and the arbitrator [5.05]: *Crampton and Holt* v. *Ridley* (1887).

The residual legacy of this theory is that even to this day the law is uncertain how and for what reason an arbitrator can recover his fees.

The usual procedure is by the arbitrator exercising a lien over the award. He will release it to the parties only when he has been paid. If the arbitrator makes demand for what the parties consider an excessive remuneration and refuses to release the award until this is met, section 19(1) of the 1950 Act provides that on application the High Court may order the arbitrator to deliver the award upon payment into court of the fees the arbitrator has demanded. His fees are then 'taxed' by the Taxing Master.

If the Taxing Master reduces the fees, he may order the arbitrator to pay the costs of the taxation and any excess paid in will be repaid to the applicant.

It would also appear possible for a party to take up the award under protest and then sue the arbitrator for equitable restitution as money 'had and received' to the use of the party.

3.19 Arbitrators' fees for uncompleted arbitration

Difficulties, however, frequently arise when:

   (a) Neither of the parties takes up the award. If it is apparent that the claimant has failed entirely, there is no incentive for either

party to take up the award and pay the arbitrator.
(b) The parties ask an arbitrator to keep certain dates free for an arbitration, with the result that he refuses other work, and he hears no more from them.
(c) The parties settle their dispute (naturally, after briefs have been delivered to counsel which entitles them to the full fee) on the doorstep of the arbitration room. This happens very frequently.
(d) The parties settle after the arbitration has continued for some time and the arbitrator has spent days listening to evidence.
(e) The arbitrator makes an interim award or a final award and then is removed by the court for 'misconduct'.
(f) The reference comes to an end through circumstances other than the misconduct of the arbitrator.
(g) The arbitration ends prematurely through the death or incapacity of the arbitrator.
(h) The appointment of the arbitrator is revoked under section 24 (1) of the 1950 Act; or
(i) The appointment of the arbitrator is revoked under section 24(2) because it appears that the dispute involves the question of whether any party has been guilty of fraud.

It is to be regretted that the cases do not provide a neat and tidy answer to any of these questions and the statutes are completely silent about arbitrators' fees.

In *Burroughes* v. *Clarke* (1831), Mr Justice Taunton said that he remembered a case before he came to the Bar in which Lord Kenyon had ruled that the office of arbitrator was entirely honorary and that an arbitrator could not maintain an action for his fees.

If he was referring to *Virany* v. *Warne* (1801), as seems likely, his recollection was at fault. In that, Lord Kenyon held that an arbitrator could sue on an express promise to pay his fees but there was no promise implied in his appointment and his acceptance that he would be remunerated.

'The appointment of an arbitrator to settle a dispute which had arisen between partners was not of such a nature as to raise a demand for payment and the plaintiff could recover nothing unless he could prove an express promise.'

However, in *In re Coombs* (1851) Baron Parker seems to have thought that an arbitrator could 'maintain an action for work or labour' without an express promise and in *Crampton & Holt* v. *Ridley* (1887), Mr Justice A. L. Smith took the view that in a commercial case there 'is an implied promise by the parties appointing the arbitrator and umpire jointly to pay them for their services'.

It would appear therefore that an arbitrator can recover a *quantum meruit* where the parties have expressly or impliedly agreed with the arbitrator that he shall be paid: *Roberts* v. *Eberhardt* (1857); *re Coombs & Freshfield & Fernley* (1850) but none of the cases explains why that should be.

The most obvious explanation would be that the parties are under a contractual obligation to the arbitrator to remunerate him; and it would appear that this is a *joint* obligation: *Crampton & Holt* v. *Ridley & Co.* (1887). But it is difficult to spell out a contract between the two parties and the arbitrator which does not contain an implied term that he will use reasonable skill and care in deciding the issues between them and the manner in which he conducts the arbitration, and the whole idea that the arbitrator was in a contractual relationship with either party was expressly rejected in *Finnegan* v. *Allen* (1943).

It would also seem that if there is a synallagmatic contractual relationship, the arbitrator is eligible to sue for damages because the issue was settled prematurely before he could give his award. That would not follow if there were two separate unilateral contractual promises.

The other explanation that the arbitrator's right to remuneration arises out of a quasi-contractual obligation does not bear examination. English law knows nothing of an action for benefit conferred, in the absence of an express or implied promise to remunerate. A request that another shall perform a service with an express or implied promise to remuneration is an enforceable obligation as a unilateral contract, if the other person performs what he was asked to do: *United Dominion Trust* v. *Eagle Aviation* (1968). Unjust enrichment and quasi-contractual obligations have clearly no relevance to the position of arbitrators.

The only advice that can be given to an arbitrator in any of the situations given above is that he should sue for his fees without specifying his cause of action.

Only one situation is clear. If an arbitrator is removed under section 13(3) because he has failed to 'use all reasonable dispatch' he is not entitled to any remuneration in respect of his services. In any well drafted legislation it would follow by implication that in all the other circumstances in which the statute provides that an arbitrator may be removed by the court, as for example in section 23(2) for misconduct, the arbitrator is entitled to his fees, especially since there is a separate section 25 which deals with the powers of the court when the arbitrator is removed or his authority removed and this is silent about any power to deprive him of his fees.

3.18 Removal of an arbitrator

The 1950 Act, by two sections, empowers the court to remove an arbitrator.

An arbitrator who fails to use all reasonable despatch can be removed under section 13(3). In those circumstances, the statute provides that he is not entitled to recover any fees whatever work he has done. Apparently this section will apply whether or not the delay is his fault.

Section 23(1) empowers the court to remove an arbitrator who has 'misconducted himself or the proceedings'. The last three words were added to the 1889 Act in 1934 as a sop to arbitrators who disliked being found guilty of 'misconduct' at a time when that was the euphemism used in divorce courts for adultery.

What is misconduct, and the consequences of it, are discussed later [6.10].

Chapter 4
The conduct of an arbitration

4.01 The procedure of arbitration

It is an ironic commentary on the relationship in England between the courts and arbitrators that in the course of one year, 1982, awards made by three Past Presidents of the Chartered Institute of Arbitrators were set aside for disregard of the basic principles on which arbitrators should proceed; and the three arbitrators were removed for 'misconduct'. In one case at least, to which reference will be made subsequently [4.04], the courts, including the Court of Appeal, it is submitted, were gravely at fault.

These cases may serve to emphasise one point. The courts have not laid down any principles as to how arbitrations should be conducted; indeed, it has been said that the courts have no power whatsoever to tell arbitrators how to conduct arbitrations: *Abu Dhabi Gas* v. *Eastern Bechtel Corporation* (1982).

The only guidance that can be derived is from the negative point of view: by consideration of the cases where arbitrators have been held to be guilty of misconduct [6.10] and have either been removed, or had their awards set aside, or had them remitted.

In addition to that, over the years there have been fundamental changes in what the law has accepted as proper procedure for arbitration.

As Mr Justice McNair said in *Henry Bath* v. *Birgby Products* (1962):

'Great care has to be used in reading the decisions of a century or half a century ago as to the powers of arbitrators today. As has been pointed out on many occasions ... the growth of commercial arbitration in the City has been so wide and, as a whole, so beneficial, that the courts show increasing reluctance to interfere with the manner in which these trade bodies carry out their important functions and only interfere in the very rare case where it has been shown that some real impropriety has been committed.'

When the courts first began seriously to interfere with arbitrations at the beginning of the last century, the view generally taken by the judges was that there was an obligation on arbitrators to hold an oral hearing which followed exactly the procedure of the courts.

'Arbitrators, like other judges are bound ... to observe in their proceedings the ordinary rules laid down for the administration of justice ... This court ... is bound to see that those rules have been observed,' said Lord Justice Turner in *Haigh* v. *Haigh* (1861).' 'They must observe the fundamental rules which govern judicial proceedings,' said Mr Justice Mathew in *re Gregson and Armstrong's Arbitration* 1894. 'There are some principles of justice which it is impossible to disregard,' said Lord Halsbury in *Andrews* v. *Mitchell* (1905) of an arbitration hearing.

Some of those principles which are regarded as fundamental can be found in the earlier cases.

'Both sides must be heard and each in the presence of the other,' was the principle laid down by Lord Langdale MR in *Harvey* v. *Shelton* (1844).

Lord Cranworth LC said: 'The person who is prejudiced by the evidence ought to be present to hear it taken, to ... cross-examine and to find evidence ... to meet and answer it; in short, to deal with it as in the ordinary course of legal proceedings.'

Even recent books about arbitration, particularly those concerned with the construction industry, presume that these principles still apply and must be applied, unless the parties expressly agree otherwise.

It is all, however, hopelessly out-of-date. There is no need whatsoever for an arbitration to imitate the court procedure. An arbitrator has an absolute discretion as to what procedure he should adopt. The oral, adversary procedure of the English courts is likely to be the least effective in arriving at a speedy and reasonable decision as most trades recognise by expressly or implicitly providing other systems. In most cases, there is nothing remotely resembling a hearing with both parties present.

In *Wessanen's Koninklijke Fabrieken* v. *Isaac Modiano Brother & Sons Ltd* (1960) only the two arbitrators were present at the hearing and neither of the parties. The arbitration took place under the conditions of the London Cattle Food Trade Association, the arbitration clause of which read:

'Any dispute on this contract to be settled by arbitration in London, in accordance with the rules and regulations of the London Cattle Food Trade Association (Inc), which are indorsed hereon and are deemed to form part of this contract.'

Of those rules, No 1 read:

'Any dispute arising out of a contract embodying these rules shall be referred to arbitration in London, each party appointing one arbitrator, who shall be a member of the association, and not interested in the transaction, and such arbitrators shall have the power, if and when they disagree, to appoint an umpire, who shall be a member of the association, whose decision is to be final.'

Mr Justice Diplock, as he then was, said:

'At the hearing Mr Williams presented the arguments in favour of the buyers. For that purpose he outlined the facts ... and addressed to the umpire his arguments on the effect of the law on those facts. When he had finished, Mr Owen, the arbitrator of the sellers, put forward his conflicting arguments, in the course of which he referred to counsel's opinion which had been obtained by the sellers, a copy of which has been furnished to him.

He read out to the umpire a number of paragraphs of the opinion and, indeed, all the paragraphs of the opinion which dealt with the particular point which he was advocating. It is apparent from his notes that he stressed the importance of the opinion (the author of which he incorrectly described as "a Queen's Counsel"), and suggested to the umpire that the opinion strongly confirmed, and was indeed conclusive in favour of, the contentions which he was advancing.

This was done without protest by the buyers' arbitrator and, at the end of it, the umpire asked the buyers' arbitrator whether he wished to reply – whether he had anything to say in reply or whether he desired to obtain and submit a legal opinion such as the sellers' arbitrator had done. Mr Williams said that he did not. Both parties then handed to the umpire, without any objection from one or the other, their files of documents, which one now knows contained the relevant correspondence in the case of both the arbitrators and, in the case of Mr Owen, contained the copy of counsel's opinion from which he had read and also his own notes from which he had advanced his argument.

In the notice of motion it was contended that the umpire had misconducted himself in three respects.

First, that he had not held a proper judicial investigation of the matter in dispute in the presence of the parties.

Secondly, that he had received as evidence the files of correspondence held by each arbitrator without the other arbitrator seeing the contents of the file.

And thirdly, that he took away counsel's written opinion without seeing the case on which such opinion was obtained.

It is, I think, plain and fully time that the court should take judicial notice of the fact that, in commercial arbitrations of this kind ... where arbitrators are appointed who, on disagreeing, appoint an umpire whose decision is final, the arbitrators, once they have disagreed and having agreed on an umpire, are *functus officio* as arbitrators and act at the hearing before the umpire as advocates for their respective appointors ...

A glance at the cases decided in these courts thirty and forty years ago shows that the practice has been going on since the beginning of this century. And it is clear that the practice, when arbitrators have been appointed in this way, is that the parties themselves are represented at the hearing before the umpire by the arbitrators and by no one else unless they express a desire to be otherwise represented.

It seems to me a necessary implication that a person appointed, as the arbitrators are at this stage of the proceeding, to act as advocate for the parties must have all the necessary powers to agree to the form of the procedure; to admit, for instance, facts, and to agree to the method of proof of fact. It does not seem to me that it can possibly be said to be outside the implied authority of an arbitrator acting in those circumstances to waive or agree to any irregularity in procedure which occurs.'

4.02 'London arbitrations'

The most conspicuous change since the beginning of the century is what is now known as 'London arbitration' or 'arbitration in London in the usual way', which for at least sixty years has been accepted by the English courts.

Each party appoints an arbitrator who is not a lawyer. The parties send their files of papers and observations to the arbitrator they have appointed. The two arbitrators meet and discuss the claims and counterclaims in the absence of the parties. If they agree, they make a joint award. If they disagree they appoint an umpire and each arbitrator then turns himself into an advocate for the party who appointed him before the umpire. Normally no evidence is called, there is no cross-examination and both advocates, when they withdraw, leave their file of papers with the umpire.

This procedure was given the express approval of the Court of Appeal in *The French Government* v. *Owners of SS Tsurushima Maru* (1921). The French Government moved to set aside the award of an umpire on three grounds. Firstly, he had not given notice to the claimants of the date on which he proposed to hold the arbitration. Secondly, he had given no opportunity for the claimants to put forward their contentions; and thirdly, he had made his award without even hearing the parties.

The arbitration agreement did not specifically mention London arbitration but it did provide that each party would appoint a 'commercial man' as their arbitrator and if the two arbitrators failed to agree they were to appoint an umpire.

The Court of Appeal approved this practice, even though as Lord Justice Atkin said, the claimant 'was a Frenchman, who apparently was ignorant as to the nature of the arbitration practice under the contract'.

Further it was said that an agreement providing for arbitration 'by commercial men' carried the implication that the 'rules of evidence as observed in the courts' need not be followed.

Moreover, it would appear that the two arbitrators before appointing an umpire are what has been termed in *Naumann* v. *Edward Nathan* (1930) 'negotiating advocates'; in short, they can act as *amiables compositeurs* even though English law does not recognise such a capacity. It has been suggested that if in that capacity they make an award, it is not an arbitration award. There is no authority whatsoever for such a proposition. If they deliver an award, it is an award, since they are arbitrators. What procedure they take before arriving at their ultimate conclusion is no business of the courts.

4.03 Quality arbitrations

For many years it has been established law that arbitrators in 'quality' arbitrations do not have to hold hearings or receive evidence but are entitled to decide on their own experience or tests. In *Naumann* v. *Nathan* (1930) the arbitration clause provided for arbitrations 'in the usual way'. The buyer of natural cassia oil complained that the oil he had been sold had been adulterated. Each side appointed an arbitrator but these failed to agree, whereupon an umpire was appointed. The buyer's arbitrator called on the umpire by himself, without the seller's arbitrator, and showed him various analyses which indicated adulterants. The umpire was provided with samples and he had them analysed by an independent analyst and in reliance on this report, found in favour of the sellers. The buyers sought to set the award aside on the ground that the umpire had not received evidence.

Lord Justice Scrutton said: 'I daresay if this matter had come before the courts 100 years ago the appellant would have received a very sympathetic hearing... possibly fifty years ago, he would have received a sympathetic hearing ...'

But, he said, 'during the last thirty or forty years business men have formed the view that it is possible to be too accurate in investigating disputes and it is better to have a rough and ready way of getting at the truth than the more accurate, expensive and dilatory methods of the courts.'

Lord Justice Scrutton continued:

'This is particularly the case with the class of disputes which are known as quality disputes. If a buyer rejects goods on the ground that goods do not comply with the contract in many particulars, the question is one which requires someone to understand the trade to decide it properly; and if that quality dispute is to be decided in the courts, the judge, who has the merit of complete impartiality and ignorance of the subject-matter, listens to three or four gentlemen who say it is in accordance with the contract and three or four gentlemen on the other side who say with equal positiveness that it is not. He may, if he is an exceptionally intelligent judge, be able to see through the contradictions of the witnesses; but he may not.

At the end of the proceedings there will be a fairly expensive bill of costs, and commercial men may not be satisfied that the right result had been arrived at.

So in commercial arbitrations many trades have arrived at a system that they think is much better and which probably is very much better than the system of the law courts. They each appoint an arbitrator. That arbitrator is not in the least like a judge. He acts in a way no judge would act. He hears statements from one side without requiring the presence of the other. He uses evidence submitted to him by his client, putting it forward as an advocate and not as an arbitrator.

It is useless to call an arbitrator a judge. He is a negotiating advocate, endeavouring to do the best he can for his client; and the system commercial men have acted on in these quality arbitrations is this.

First of all, they say: "We will appoint our arbitrator who will try to get the best decision he can from the other side" – and no doubt a great many of these commercial arbitrations are settled by give and take between the two arbitrators.

But they may not agree; and when that happens these commercial men appoint an umpire.

It is quite a usual practice in London in simple quality arbitrations that when the umpire is appointed he is told where the goods are, and no further hearing takes place. He sees the goods in the warehouse or gets an agreed sample.

He performs the mystic operations of smelling, tasting, touching and handling, which one sees witnesses do in court; and these tell him the quality of the goods. There is never any further meeting; and there is never any intention of a further meeting; and he makes his award on his own judgment of the stuff submitted to him.

There is one further step. It may be that the nature of the goods is such that you cannot tell by view, or smell, or by taste or by touch, whether the goods are in accordance with contract.

You can on analysis, and it may be that in certain trades a practice has arisen that the umpire may make his own analysis; and in this case the evidence seems to me to be overwhelming that the usual way of settling a quality dispute in respect of this class of goods is that the umpire may make his own analysis and need not have any further meeting, or submit the evidence to either side, unless he has a special request from either party that he shall do so.

"Any dispute arising from this contract to be settled by arbitration in London in the usual way" — it appears to me that the evidence is overwhelming that this arbitration has proceeded in the usual way in this trade – a way which, according to the views of lawyers and the law courts, is quite irregular.

The seller appoints what he calls his arbitrator. These two gentlemen remain in contact with their clients, getting information from them without communicating it to the other side.

The dispute arises as to the quality of the cassia oil. Apparently that dispute may be settled in some cases by mere smell. Evidently in some cases chemical analysis will also be necessary. The arbitrator for the buyer, the negotiating advocate, goes to the umpire who has been appointed and discusses the matter with him without the other side being present.

That, of course, would be hopelessly irregular so far as legal proceedings are concerned, but it is the way business people accept as to the suitable way of investigating disputes like this.

In this particular case, the arbitrator, the negotiating advocate for the buyer, saw the umpire without the other arbitrator being present and saw him before the other arbitrator had been seen, and put his views and two analyses before the umpire.

He admits that the umpire told him that he (the umpire) wanted a sample for analysis and he raised no objection. How, after that, it is possible for the client who appointed the negotiating advocate to object to the umpire taking a sample, I find it impossible to understand.

He has appointed the negotiating advocate. The negotiating advocate has been told that the umpire is going to get a sample for analysis, and a sample is handed to him. When the buyer tells me he did not know what was to be done with the sample, he must think me a very credulous person. What does the umpire want a sample for unless he is going to judge it by his own skill and knowledge, or do what is usual in the trade and get an independent analysis.

The umpire gets an analysis from an independent chemist and he acts on it, and he does not have any further sitting and he does not communicate with the parties asking them to attend before him. The evidence is overwhelming that that is the usual way in which these quality arbitrations – and I am limiting my remarks to them – are conducted in this particular trade; and so far as the question of analysis is concerned, I have not the slightest doubt it is the practice all through London.

The result, therefore, is that there is a clause in the contract "any dispute arising from this contract to be settled by arbitration in London in the usual way". This dispute according to the overwhelming evidence has been settled by arbitration in London in the usual way; and in my view there is nothing that would lead one to say that this procedure in the case of a quality arbitration is contrary to public policy ...

The law of England enforces an agreement between parties as to procedure unless it is so contrary to fundamental principles that it is treated as contrary to public policy.'

It is therefore clear that a commercial man acting as arbitrator is entitled to decide issues without receiving evidence and relying solely on his own knowledge and experience.

In the case of *Mediterranean and Eastern Export Co Ltd* v. *Fortress (Manchester) Ltd* (1948), concerning the rules of the Manchester Chamber of Commerce, Rule 1 stated:

'The object of the tribunal of arbitration shall be the determination and settlement by commercial men of experience and special knowledge of the subject-matter in dispute or difference relating to trade, manufacturers and commerce (including customs of trade) by whomsoever submitted.'

Lord Goddard LCJ said:

'It is obvious, therefore, that parties who submit to the chamber's tribunal intend and expect that they will have benefit of arbitration before a person well acquainted with the class of business in which they are engaged, because he is selected for his knowledge of the trade.

The parties submitted statements to the arbitrator in accordance with the rules. The sellers' document, which was prepared without professional assistance, set out the contract, such letters as were admitted to be material, and certain facts to which I need not refer, and asked for an award of £2,455 2s 6d, the price of the goods plus interest at 5 per cent per annum.

The buyers' statement set out their case and contentions, alleging that they were justified in rejecting the goods. In claiming the price of the goods the sellers, no doubt, fell into an error, often made in such circumstances, of asking for the price on the footing that the property had passed whereas, in fact, as it was a sale of future goods, the property had not passed, and what they were entitled to was not the price, but damages for non-acceptance.

The arbitrator held a meeting at which both parties attended without professional representation, nor did they or either of them seek to call expert evidence.

The reason for this is obvious. They had the advantage of an arbitrator who himself was an expert and he would be in a position as good as or better than expert witnesses to come to a decision on his own knowledge, which was the reason why he had been appointed.'

4.04   Arbitrator relying upon his own knowledge

It is clear from the cases mentioned earlier that an arbitrator is entitled to decide a case on his own knowledge and experience and not on evidence adduced before him.

This was made abundantly clear in *Thomas Borthwick (Glasgow) Ltd* v. *Faure Fairclough Ltd* (1968), where Mr Justice Donaldson said:

> 'A trade arbitral tribunal is fully entitled to use its own knowledge of the trade. Indeed the fact that it has this knowledge is one of the reasons why it exists and performs a most useful purpose.
>
> Experience, however, dictates that this knowledge shall never be used in such a way as to take a party by surprise. If therefore a tribunal considers that both parties have missed the point – this sometimes happens both in litigation and in arbitration – it should invite the parties to deal with this point and, if the point arises for the first time in the course of deliberations after the hearing, should offer the parties a further hearing if either wish to avail themselves of the opportunity.
>
> Equally, if the tribunal has knowledge of facts which do not appear to be known to either party, it is only fair to reveal this knowledge to the parties, giving them an opportunity of putting those facts into different perspective or of persuading the tribunal that they are irrelevant. Such a course is not only fairer to parties; it also enables the tribunal to have additional assistance from the parties in arriving at a just decision.'

In *Mediterranean* v. *Fortress* (1948) it was objected that the award should be set aside because the arbitrator in awarding damages had not relied upon evidence but on his own knowledge of the trade. Lord Goddard CJ said:

> 'The more serious question that was argued was that neither side had tendered evidence with regard to damage and, therefore, the arbitrator had no material before him on which he could fix the amount which the sellers were entitled to receive.
>
> This would be a formidable and, indeed, fatal objection in some arbitrations.
>
> If, for instance, a lawyer was called on to act as arbitrator on a commercial contract he would not be entitled, unless the terms of the

submission clearly gave him power so to do, to come to a conclusion as to the amount of damages that should be paid without having evidence before him as to the rise or fall of the market, as the case may be, or as to other facts enabling him to apply the correct measure of damage; but, in my opinion, the case is different where the parties select an arbitrator, or agree to arbitrate under the rules of a chamber of commerce under which the arbitrator is appointed for them, and the arbitrator is chosen or appointed because of his knowledge and experience of the trade.

There can be no doubt that with regard to questions of quality and matters of that description an arbitrator of this character can always act on his own knowledge. As Lord Esher MR said in *Wright* v. *Howson* (1888), where it was suggested that the umpire ought to have received evidence from experts: "What would this experienced manufacturer care for the opinion of the weaver? He was selected and appointed on account of his own superior experience."

Lopes LJ said: "Such a man is selected for the very purpose of deciding according to his own experience and examination."

No one has doubted – certainly not in modern times – that it is open to an arbitrator skilled in the trade to use his own knowledge and experience on many matters, such as quality, without having witnesses called before him.

One of the reasons why commercial men like to go to arbitration before arbitrators of this description is because it saves the expense of calling witnesses and having the conflicting views of experts thrashed out and decided on.

The parties are content and intend to accept the judgment of a man in their own trade on whose judgment they know they rely.

This indeed, I think, has long been the law. An early illustration is *Eads* v. *Williams* (1854). The arbitrators were there appointed to settle the amount to be paid as the rent of a coal mine and Lord Cranworth LC said:

"I do not agree with the suggestion that it was incumbent upon those parties to examine witnesses; I do not think that is the meaning when a matter is referred to a surveyor, and people of skill to value and settle what the value of the property to be bought or let is ... they are entrusted, from their experience and from their observation, to form a judgment which the parties referring to them agree shall be satisfactory; therefore I do not think that there was anything of importance in their now examining witnesses, provided *bona fide* they meant to say, "We know sufficiently of the subject to decide properly without examining witnesses."

There are other decisions to a like effect and I would only mention *Jordeson & Co* v. *Stora, etc Aktiebolag* (1931). Branson J in giving judgment, said:

"Now, I think that the fact that this umpire was an expert in the timber trade and was appointed because he was such an expert must not be lost sight of. I think the parties must be taken to have assented to his using the knowledge which they chose him for possessing; I do not mean to say knowledge of special facts relating to a special or particular case, but that general knowledge of the timber trade which a man in his position would be bound to acquire."

I can see no reason why this principle should not be applied to a question of damages just as much as to a question of quality.'

This view of the law does not appear to have been appreciated by some arbitrators concerned with the construction industry. One arbitrator appointed by the Chartered Institute of Arbitrators under the NHBC scheme arrived to hold a 'hearing' at a house which, because it had been built upon an inadequately filled pond, was tilting at an angle of 15 degrees from the vertical. He refused to proceed unless there was expert evidence to confirm what he could see with his own eyes, taking the entirely erroneous view that his duty as an arbitrator required him to act on evidence and nothing but evidence. Nor is it always followed by the courts.

In *Fisher & Ors* v. *P. G. Wellfair Ltd* (1981) the arbitrator, a qualified architect, surveyor and barrister, was concerned with two arbitrations arising from the National House-Building Council's contract, HB5. In the first, twenty-eight purchasers of long leases of flats in a block built by the respondents were the claimants and the arbitration related to alleged defects in the 'common parts' of the building. In the second, the claimants were the owners of one of the flats and it related to alleged defects in their flat. By the time the hearing took place, more than four years after the appointment of the arbitrator, the respondents had gone into liquidation and were no longer represented. This, however, did not concern the plaintiffs since any award would be honoured by the National House-Building Council under the statutory approved scheme.

The hearings therefore took place *ex parte* and in the absence of the respondents or any to represent them. Nevertheless, the one about common parts lasted eight days initially and there were subsequent hearings at the request of the arbitrator and also further written submissions. The claim was for £93,000, the cost of repairing defects, and a further £37,000 for the strengthening of part of the roof for use as a roof garden. In spite of being an undefended case, six witnesses in all were heard, four of them experts. Eighteen months later the arbitrator gave an interim award disallowing the claim in respect of the £37,000 roof strengthening. Another four months later he made a non-speaking award granting the claimants £12,471 instead of the £93,000 they had claimed. Even then the award was not final, since he had reserved to himself the taxation of his own costs.

The claimants brought a motion in the High Court, under section 23 of the 1950 Act, that 'the arbitrator be removed on the grounds that he misconducted himself and for an order that some fit and proper person may be appointed; alternatively, that the award be set aside.'

The trial judge, Mr Justice Ackner, removed the architect under section 23(1) for misconduct and set aside the award under section 23(2). He said:

'Of course, an arbitrator when dealing with the facts need not accept *in toto* the evidence of either side. Moreover, where he is chosen for his own expertise (which is not this case) he may of course rely upon that. He was sitting as a legal arbitrator and not as a lay expert.'

He found that the proceedings were not conducted in accordance with the principles of natural justice:

'the applicants being in effect condemned unheard to lose a greater part of their claim.

The officious bystander who had had the resilience to listen attentively at all stages of these arbitrations, who had heard the very careful and detailed manner in which every aspect of the claims had been supported both by arguments and by evidence, would have been justifiably provoked, on reading the awards, into saying to the applicants "Well, you've been badly treated by the arbitrator".

Translated into forensic language, the arbitrator failed to provide the applicants with a fair hearing in that he failed to give them any opportunity to deal with the very serious deficiencies which he must ultimately have found in the presentation and/or proof of their claim.

There must have been major matters of criticism to have resulted in the dismissal of so large a part of the claim. An arbitrator is not, in my judgment, entitled ... to hide behind his hitherto immunity from giving a reasoned decision and thus enable it to be claimed that, since it cannot be established that the deficiency he found was one of fact or law or both, the aggrieved party has no remedy.

If the result of my judgment is that arbitrators in general are obliged to give to the parties an opportunity to deal with any major points, be they matters of fact or law which the arbitrator alone is finding difficulty in accepting, then it is not a result which should cause any anxiety at all.

It is of the very essence of a fair hearing that the parties should have an adequate opportunity of dealing with any substantial criticism of their claim or defence, whether the source of that criticism comes from the opposing party or the tribunal who makes the decision.'

The decision of the Court of Appeal affirming the judgment was based on different grounds. The arbitrator was treated as having been an expert with a special knowledge of the particular subject matter and to have relied upon that in rejecting a substantial part of the claim. Lord Denning said:

'There are some arbitrations in which the arbitrator is expected to act on his own knowledge and form his own opinion without recourse to evidence such as an arbitrator deciding whether goods are up to sample.

In others the arbitrator is expected to receive evidence and the submissions of advocates and be guided by them in reaching his conclusions.

In such a case the arbitrator is often chosen for his knowledge of the trade so he can follow the evidence and submissions but he must act judicially.'

It was not right, in his view, that the arbitrator should do for the builders what they could and should have done for themselves. (Lord Denning did not appear to be aware that the builders were insolvent and in compulsory liquidation and that their insurers, the NHBC, had no right to be heard.) The arbitrator, he continued:

'should use his special knowledge so as to understand the evidence that was given but not to provide evidence on behalf of the defendants which they had not chosen to provide for themselves, as he would then be discarding the role of an impartial arbitrator and assuming the role of an advocate for the other side.

At any rate, he should not use his knowledge to derogate from the evidence of the plaintiff's experts without putting his knowledge to them and giving them a chance of answering it and showing that his own view was wrong.

The arbitrator fell into error because he felt it was his duty to protect the interests of the unrepresented party ... There was no such duty. If the defendants elected not to appear and protect themselves, it was no part of an arbitrator's duty to do it for them.'

Lord Justice Dunn said that, where the arbitrator relied upon general expert knowledge, there was no need to disclose it.

'Where he relies on knowledge of special facts relevant to the particular case, he should disclose the details. He should not in effect give evidence to himself or act on his own private opinion without signalling his intention to the parties.'

Leave to appeal to the House of Lords was refused, as was an application for leave to the House itself. But, it is understood, Lord Denning has since expressed the opinion extra-judicially that the Court of Appeal in its decision was wrong.

There are a number of comments that could be made about this case. The first is to express some concern about an arbitrator who could extend an undefended case to such a hearing and over such a prolonged period of time.

But the decision of the courts also seems open to criticism. To start with, it is always the duty of the claimant or plaintiff to prove his case. A judge in an undefended case is not obliged to accept all the evidence tendered on behalf of a plaintiff; nor is he obligated before judgment to indicate to the counsel for the plaintiff what he accepts and what he does not accept. That would be an unacceptable and intolerable burden. It is sufficient if in his judgment he says 'the plaintiff has failed to satisfy me that he is entitled to these damages'. Why then should an arbitrator (a) be regarded as guilty of misconduct and (b) have his award set aside, if he follows the same course of conduct that would be followed by a High Court judge?

The judgment of the Court of Appeal was even more surprising since the court held that the arbitrator was sitting as an expert. If he rejected the damages put forward on behalf of the claimants on the basis of his expert knowledge of the industry, the court had no excuse for interfering.

4.05 Steps following appointment

The arbitrator's first step, following his acceptance of appointment, is to call for the agreement and satisfy himself that his appointment is a valid one, that he is properly qualified if qualifications are called for and that he is not disqualified [3.02].

He should also satisfy himself that the dispute referred to him is within the scope of the agreement. If issues outside the terms of the original agreement are raised, he should obtain written confirmation from both parties that he has jurisdiction to deal with them.

His next task is to decide what law is applicable. And that may not always be as easy as it seems, unless, of course, the dispute arises out of construction work done under an English contract in England with the arbitration being held in England.

4.06 What law?

Earlier in England, as has been observed [1.04] all arbitrators were entitled to decide disputes not according to law but in accordance with whatever they thought was right. Only since the last century has English law not allowed them to do so even where the terms of their appointment expressly authorise them: see *Knox* v. *Symmonds* (1791). The arbitration agreement in *Orion Compania Espanola* v. *Belford Maatschappij* (1962) provided that the arbitrators were to be relieved from all 'judicial formalities' and might abstain from following the strict rules of the law. 'They shall settle any dispute under this agreement according to equitable, rather than strictly legal, interpretation of its terms.' It was held that arbitrators had to apply a fixed and recognisable system of law.

The arbitrator therefore in English law must decide according to law, but what law?

Four things must be distinguished:

(1) the 'proper' law of the contract, which is usually the law to be applied by the arbitrator
(2) the law of the place where the contract is to be performed, as for

example, building regulations applicable in cases of construction work

(3) the law which the parties have expressly agreed should be applied in the arbitration

(4) the law of the place where the arbitration is to be held.

The difficulties which can arise from the conflict of these laws is well illustrated by the case of *James Miller and Partners Ltd* v. *Whitworth Street Estates (Manchester) Ltd* (1970).

A Scottish company made an agreement on the standard JCT contract form with an English company for building work to be done at the English company's Scottish factory. There was at the time no separate JCT form for Scotland, although there was a separate Scottish Standard Form. Differences having arisen, the President of the RIBA appointed a Scottish architect as arbiter and the arbitration was held in Scotland in the Scottish form [1.15]. The English company asked for a case stated on a point of law under the Arbitration Act 1950 at a time when there was no procedure for special cases in Scotland.

On an application to a master of the English High Court, he ordered the arbiter to state his award in the form of a special case. A judge reversed this and rescinded the order. The Court of Appeal reversed the judgment and reinstated the order. The House of Lords allowed the appeal and again rescinded the order. A majority (Lords Hodson, Guest, Dilhorne) held that the 'proper' law of the contract was English, notwithstanding that the work took place in Scotland, because the use of the JCT printed form showed that to be the intention of the parties. Lords Reid and Wilberforce dissented and thought the proper law of the contract was Scottish.

The whole court was agreed, however, that the conduct of the parties after the appointment of the arbiter showed that they intended the curial law (i.e., that of the tribunal) to be Scottish law and under that there could be no case stated.

Lord Reid said that in the case of courts, the *lex fori*, the law of the country in whose courts application was being made, applied:

'I see no reason why this principle should not be applied to arbitration proceedings. It appears from *Norske Atlas Insurance Co. Ltd* v. *London General Insurance Co. Ltd* (1927) that Mackinnon J was of this opinion.

An opinion to the same effect is to be found in Dicey and Morris,

Conflict of Laws (8th Edition, 1967), where the editors submit, at page 1048:

> "Where the parties have failed to choose the law governing the arbitration proceedings, those proceedings must be considered, at any rate *prima facie*, as being governed by the law of the country in which the arbitration is held, on the ground that it is the country most closely connected with the proceedings."

I agree with this submission.'

Lord Guest said that the question must be: 'What procedural law did the conduct of the parties evince their intention to adopt?' He found the answer:

'At this stage of the appointment of an arbiter, I am satisfied that neither party applied his mind to what procedural law should be adopted. But as soon as the arbiter was in the saddle, matters took a more definite turn.

The arbiter appointed a Scottish solicitor as his clerk. He made it clear to the parties that he was adopting Scots procedure. The respondents instructed Scots solicitors and Scots counsel, as did the appellants. The pleadings took Scottish form and the respondents tabled pleas to the relevancy in Scots form and used Scots terminology for the remedies which they sought on the counter-claim, namely "decree arbitral". The form of order by the arbiter was a Scots interlocuter. The seat of the arbitration continued to be in Scotland. With all these proceedings the respondents acquiesced and took not a single objection.'

Lord Wilberforce held that the proper law of the contract was Scottish law but he said:

'It is a matter of experience that numerous arbitrations are conducted by English arbitrators in England on matters governed by contracts whose proper law is or may be that of another country, and I should be surprised if it had ever been held that such arbitrations were not governed by the English Arbitration Act in procedural matters, including the right to apply for a case to be stated ... The principle must surely be the same as that which applies to court proceedings brought in one country concerning a contract governed by the law of another, and that such proceedings as regards all matters which the law regards as procedural are governed by the *lex fori* has been accepted at least since Lord Brougham's judgment in *Don* v. *Lippmann* (1837). In my opinion, the law is correctly stated by Professor Kahn-Freund and Dr Morris in *Dicey and Morris* op. cit., page 1048, where they say:

> "It cannot however be doubted that the courts would give effect to the choice of a law other than the proper law of the contract. Thus, if parties agreed on an arbitration clause expressed to be governed by English law but providing for arbitration in Switzerland, it may be held that, whereas English law governs the validity, interpretation and effect of the arbitration clause as such (including the scope of the arbitrators' jurisdiction), the proceedings are governed by Swiss law." [Then follows the passage already quoted by Lord Reid above.]

The first part of this is well supported by *Hamlyn & Co.* v. *Talisker Distillery* (1894) *per* Lord Herschell LC and Lord Watson, and also by *N. V. Kwik Hoo Tong Handel Maatschappij* v. *James Finlay & Co. Ltd* (1927) and both parts rest solidly on common-sense.'

It is submitted that the current position is:

(1) The parties may expressly select for themselves what law is to be applied by the arbitrator, even though it is not the 'proper law' of the contract.

(2) If they do not do so expressly, an implication as to what law the arbitrator is to apply *may*, but does not inevitably, arise from their choice of the place of arbitration: i.e. 'London arbitration' may mean arbitration in London according to English law: *Tzortzis & Sykias* v. *Monark Line* (1968); *Compagnie d'Armement Maritime SA* v. *Compagnie Tunisienne* (1971). 'An arbitration clause is as capable as any other clause of providing *by implication* for the law which is to be applied.'

(3) In all matters up to the moment of the commencement of the hearing, the law applicable to the contract applies to the arbitration proceedings: *International Tank* v. *Kuwait Aviation Fuelling* (1975). A contract between the parties, both Kuwait companies, for construction work in Kuwait was in the standard FIDIC form, but amended and with an additional clause 75:

'Construction of contract: This contract shall in all respects be construed and operated in conformity with the laws of England and the respective rights and liabilities of the parties shall be in accordance with the laws for the time being.'

It was held by the Court of Appeal that as a result of this, section 27 of the Arbitration Act 1950 could be invoked to extend time for giving notice of arbitration – even though it was known that the arbitration would not take place in England.

(4) Once the hearing has begun in any jurisdiction, from that moment the hearing is to be subject to the *lex fori*, the law of the country in which the arbitrator holds the proceedings.

The Rules of the International Chamber of Commerce, Article 16, provide that arbitration should be under:

'the law of procedure chosen by the parties or, failing such choice, those of the law of the country in which the arbitrator holds the proceedings.'

It is submitted that the parties cannot by contract in fact elect to make the arbitration hearing subject to any law other than that of the *lex fori*.

A misconception about this has influenced the Joint Contracts Tribunal to write an extraordinary provision into Article 5 of JCT 80:

'Article 5.5 Whatever the nationality, residence or domicile of the Employer, the Contractor, any sub-contractor or supplier or the Arbitrator and wherever the works or any part thereof are situated the law of England shall be the proper law of the contract.'

So far the clause is unobjectionable. But it continues:

'and in particular (but not so as to derogate from the generality of the foregoing, the provisions of the Arbitration Acts 1950 (notwithstanding anything in s.34 thereof) to 1979 shall apply to any arbitration under the Contract *wherever* the same, or any part of it, shall be conducted.'

Section 34 of the Arbitration Act 1950 (as amended by the Arbitration Act 1975) provides:

'Extent of Part I

Save as aforesaid none of the provisions of this Part of this Act shall extend to Scotland or Northern Ireland.'

The idea that the parties can by contract apply the Arbitration Acts 1950, 1975 and 1979 to Scotland, Northern Ireland, Switzerland or anywhere else in the world, can only be on a misreading of the judgments set out above. Once a hearing starts, it must be subject to the law of the place where the arbitration is held. As Lord Wilberforce said *supra*, the principle must be the same for the courts and for arbitration. 'Such proceedings as regards all matters which the law regards as procedural are governed by the *lex fori*.' They can no more contract to alter this, it is submitted, than there can be a contract that the English High Court shall follow the procedure of Pakistan.

The provision of Article 5.5 of JCT 80, it may be suspected, is aimed at arbitrators who have chosen to hold construction industry arbitrations in the Channel Islands because there is no power of the courts to interfere with an award and they are in fact final and binding and not subject to appeal to any court, but registrable in the English High Court as a judgment.

Parties to JCT 80 who do not seek litigation up to the House of Lords should ensure that the latter part of Article 5.5 is deleted before they sign.

Just to make the situation thoroughly confusing, an arbitrator is not entitled to decide the case on a point of law which has not been argued before him by either party: *Société Franco-Tunisienne d'Armement-Tunis* v. *Government of Ceylon* (1959). Not even, apparently, if he applies the law correctly.

The position regarding illegal contracts is even more obscure although it frequently occurred during the last war that disputes arose out of unlicensed building work. Was it fair that a building owner who had procured a contractor to do unlicensed work for him, and had been enriched thereby, could evade paying the proper, or any sum, for it on the grounds that it was illegal and the courts cannot enforce illegal contracts? *Halsbury* and *Russell* both contend that there can be no valid arbitration arising out of an illegal contract. The references they make to the cases of *Prodexport* v. *Man* (1972), *Taylor* v. *Barnett* (1953) and *Birtley District Co-op* v. *Windy Nook* (1960) do not support this proposition and while a judge, as the servant of the Crown, may be obliged to raise the issue of illegality, even if neither party has pleaded it, an arbitrator has no such obligation.

But he is in a difficult position if the respondent claims that the contract which included the arbitration clause was void *ab initio* for illegality. The only guidance he can find is in the case of *Dalmia Dairy Industries* v. *National Bank of Pakistan* (1978) which deals with the law of India.

4.07 Arbitrators and limitation periods

An arbitrator has to apply the law and this includes the law relating to limitation of actions now contained in the Limitation Act 1980, so far as England is concerned, and the Prescription and Limitation (Scotland) Act 1973.

There is however a fundamental distinction between the two statutes. In Scotland, as in most Roman law countries, the plaintiff's right to action is extinguished by negative prescription after the elapse of time specified in the Act. Moreover, time begins to run from the date when he 'first became or could with reasonable diligence have become so aware.' By contrast in England the plaintiff's rights are not extinguished but still subsist — it is just that he cannot enforce them by an action. Therefore unless the defendant raises in his pleading the issue that the plaintiff's claim is statute-barred, the court will not take the point and the action will proceed. The observation in Mustill and Boyd *Commercial Arbitration*, 1st edition, 1982, page 161 that 'Since the arbitrator is obliged to give effect to legal grounds of defence, he must dismiss any claim which has become time-barred by the expiry of a statutory period of limitation' is therefore very misleading. An arbitrator is not entitled to dismiss a claim on the ground that the claim is statute-barred unless the respondent has specifically raised this in his pleadings. The arbitrator is not entitled to take the point on his own initiative.

Until the Limitation Act 1980 came into force there were no statutory provisions regarding arbitrations and limitation periods, although the courts held, incorrectly and without good reason, it is submitted, that they were statute-barred in exactly the same way as an action although none of the Limitation Acts has ever so suggested. Consequently difficulty arises as to when an arbitration commenced for the purpose of the Limitation Act. However, the point at which an arbitration commences has now been clarified to some extent by section 34(1) of the Limitation Act 1980, which also expressly provides that: 'This Act and any other limitation enactment shall apply to arbitrations as they apply to actions in the High Court.'

Another statute which includes a limitation period is the Defective Premises Act 1972, section 5.

The Limitation Act 1980 provides that in the case of contracts under seal an action shall not be brought after twelve years from the date on which 'the cause of action accrued': section 8(1). In the case of other contracts the period is the expiration of six years from the date on which 'the cause of action accrued': section 5. Where the action is founded on tort the period is six years from the time when 'the cause of action accrued'.

Difficulties arise as to the interpretation of these words. The 'cause of action accrues' in contract at the date of the breach of contract, which is normally an easily ascertainable time. In the case of defective construction work it will normally be the time when the work is done. This applies whether the innocent party knows of the breach or not, so that it could happen that his cause of action is statute-barred before he knows of the breach. But this is subject to section 32 that, where the action is based on the fraud of the defendant or any fact relevant to the plaintiff's right of action is deliberately concealed from him by the defendant, time shall not begin 'until the plaintiff has discovered the fraud ... or could with reasonable diligence have discovered it'. 'Fraud' does not in this context mean moral fraud: *Beaman* v. *A.R.T.S. Ltd* (1949). It merely means that it would be unconscionable to allow the defendant to rely upon his rights under the statute: *Kitchen* v. *R.A.F. Association* (1958). It has repeatedly been applied to building contracts: *Clark* v. *Woor* (1965); and *Applegate* v. *Moss* (1971). If a contractor does bad work and covers it up that is 'fraud' for the purpose of this section and its predecessor, section 26 of the Limitation Act 1939.

When the cause of action accrues in tort is a much more difficult question. All that can safely be said is that it is never the same time as for breach of contract. Since it is current practice to plead everything these days as both breach of contract and tort in the form of negligence, nuisance or breach of statutory duty etc., it may often be of utmost importance.

In any tort, three elements can be discerned: (a) the wrongful act or omission or negligent statement, (b) the time when the plaintiff suffers damage in the sense of incurs loss or expense or suffers physical damage, and (c) the time when he knows he has suffered loss or expense or experienced personal injury. In some torts, such as battery, the three incidents can be contemporaneous. In others, as in *Davie* v. *New Merton Board Mills Ltd* (1959), the negligent act of the defendants in manufacturing a tool with a latent defect occurred years before the other two incidents, when the tool a fitter was using broke off and went into his eye. In other cases, the three incidents may be long separated, as with the negligent omission to provide filter apparatus which would prevent workmen inhaling noxious dust which gave them pneumonoconiosis which they only discovered years later, as were the facts in *Cartledge* v. *Jopling* (1963).

The House of Lords, in that case, held that the plaintiff's action was statute-barred six years from the time when he suffered the damage of pneumonoconiosis although that was years before he knew or could have known that he now suffered it. Lord Reid, who was a party to the decision, admitted in a subsequent case that it 'was an absurd result that a man's claim may be time-barred before it is possible for him to know that he has suffered any damage', and Parliament immediately set to work the same year to correct this by the Limitation Act 1963, which provided that in the case of personal injuries time should only begin to run when the plaintiff knows of his injury.

So far as buildings were concerned, a strong Court of Appeal consisting of Lord Denning MR, Lord Roskill, as he now is, and Lord Lane, the present Lord Chief Justice, decided that in the case of defects in buildings 'time does not begin to run, until such time as the plaintiff discovers it has done damage or ought, with reasonable diligence, to have discovered it.'

Lord Roskill said:

'Principle requires me to hold that the earliest moment at which a plaintiff in the position of a first or subsequent purchaser can be said to suffer damage is when, by agreeing to buy the premises ... he acquires his interest in that property ... but it seems more consistent with principle and logic to hold that he suffers the damage which is the second prerequisite of his cause of action in tort when, but only when, the defective state of the property first appears.'

Lord Lane said:

'The cause of action accrues when the damage caused by the negligent act is suffered by the plaintiff and that cannot be before that damage is first detected or could by the exercise of reasonable skill or diligence have been detected.

Whatever the disadvantages may be to local authorities ... that is the law and we in this court are not entitled to alter it ...

Two results flow from this view of the law. First the period of limitation may be postponed indefinitely ... This I regard as less obnoxious than the alternative, which is that a house owner may be deprived of his remedy against a negligent defendant by the arbitrary imposition of a limitation period which started to run before the damage caused by the defendant could even be detected.'

However, six years later, the House of Lords overruled that decision and held that, so far as buildings were concerned, time begins to run when physical damage is suffered by the building (not loss or expense to the plaintiff) whether the plaintiff knew of it or not: *Pirelli* v. *Oscar Faber* (1982). Lord Scarman, who agreed with this, described the decision as 'harsh and absurd'.

Lord Fraser, in giving his reasons, added: 'There may perhaps be cases where the defect is so gross that the building is doomed from the start and where the owner's cause of action will accrue as soon as it is built.'

In other words: the worse the architect's work, the sooner he will be protected from negligence actions. He continued:

'Except perhaps where the advice of an architect or consulting engineer leads to the erection of a building which is so defective as to be doomed from the start, the cause of action accrues when physical damage occurs to the building ... The true view is that the duty of the builder and of the local authority is owed to owners of the property as a class, and that if time runs against one owner, it also runs against all his successors in title ... No owner in the chain can have a better claim than his predecessor in title.'

With this the four law lords agreed, although it is hard to understand how this can be reconciled with *Anns* v. *London Borough of Merton* (1977), in which Lord Wilberforce said:

'The Court of Appeal was right when in *Sparham-Souter* it abjured that the cause of action arose immediately upon delivery i.e. conveyance of the defective house. It can only arise when the state of the building is such that there is present or imminent danger to the health or safety of persons occupying it.'

4.08 Deciding the procedure

If Lord Justice Watkin was right when he said in *Abu Dhabi Gas* v. *Eastern Bechtel Corporation* (1982) that the courts had no power to direct any arbitrator how he should conduct an arbitration, it would appear that neither have the parties. Even if the parties have expressly or impliedly agreed what procedure an arbitrator should follow, how can he be bound by it? He is not a party to that contract and in all probability he is under no contractual obligation to either party as to how he will conduct the arbitration. Suggestions which have been made that an arbitrator is bound by the procedural terms of an arbitration agreement to which he is not a party are notably unsupported by authority, or by any explanation as to why he should be: see Mustill & Boyd, *Commercial Arbitration*, page 243. The 'failure to comply with the agreement is misconduct,' say these authors, without quoting any authority. Indeed, there is authority that it is misconduct if the agreed or customary procedure violates some principle of law, as where it was the established practice for an umpire to retire with the board of appeal which was considering an appeal against his award: *London Export Corporation Ltd* v. *Jubilee Coffee Roasting Co. Ltd* (1958)

It may, of course, be a quite different matter when the parties have agreed to be bound by the rules of a particular trade association and an arbitral board is appointed from its members and subject to its rules. In that case there may be a separate contractual relationship between parties and arbitrators similar to that which exists between members of a club; in short, an agreement, by reason of membership, to be bound by the rules.

But this cannot apply, for example, in a construction industry case where the contract merely provides that the President of the RIBA, or the RICS or the Chartered Institute of Arbitrators shall appoint in default of agreement. On the other hand, it may apply to the provisions of the FIDIC contract [2.18] where the parties submit to resolution of disputes in accordance with the Rules of the Chamber of Commerce in Paris and the Chamber appoints the arbitrator or arbitrators and determines their fees.

There is a widespread belief in the construction industry that where it is clear that the parties themselves want a formal hearing, then the arbitrator is under an obligation to follow the procedure of the High Court. That is, there have to be formal written pleadings by particulars of claim, further and better particulars of the claim, defence, further and better particulars of defence, reply, further and better particulars of reply, rejoinders and rebuttals and all the other ingenious methods lawyers have invented to extend time and increase their fees. There has to be discovery of documents, which often means listing every bit of paper that has ever passed between the parties over the three, four or more years that the construction work has been in progress. (In one case, the Court of Appeal complained that 1285 agreed documents had been filed but only 14 had been referred to.) There are interlocutory hearings and orders before, years later, a hearing is fixed.

Then the arbitrator has to listen to a Queen's Counsel opening the case for the claimant at length extending over days or weeks and to him or his junior reading all the agreed correspondence and documents — in spite of the fact that the arbitrator, if he is any good, has read them already.

Witnesses are called, examined at length, cross-examined, re-examined. Counsel for the respondent then opens his case, calls witnesses. Both end by making exhausting speeches which traverse every aspect of the matter again.

It is no wonder that the simple issue as to whether the contractor for the Peterborough Hospital had been unduly dilatory in performing the contract lasted 200 days and made the *Guinness Book of Records* as the longest lasting English arbitration (since beaten by another construction industry case).

It is very much to be regretted that many arbitrators are all too willing to follow the procedures of the courts. English lawyers are firmly convinced that the English legal system is faultless. As a once well-known young lady said to a judge, 'They would, wouldn't they?'.

The reality however is that the civil and criminal procedures of the English courts can not only conceal the truth, but also deny justice. The following should be noted:

(a) The English 'adversary' system may result in both sides suppressing facts which are, perhaps for different reasons, inconvenient.

(b) The judge is not allowed to call evidence, even if he knows it exists, which could be decisive of the issues if the parties themselves do not call it.

(c) The complex procedure of the courts prevents any lay person from conducting his own litigation as effectively as keeping secret the *dies fasti* on which cases could be heard did in ancient Rome. It increases enormously the costs. It is full of illogical inconsistencies, such as the rule that if something is not denied in the defence it shall be taken to have been admitted. In view of the fact that it is said that it is always for the plaintiff to prove his claim, this is a barbaric and unjustified denial of justice.

(d) The written 'pleadings' must contain only allegations of fact, and must not plead the law applicable. There is no provision in English law, as there is in American and European systems, for 'briefs' or 'submissions' in writing to be made to the judge as to what the law is. The result is that at an oral hearing the judge is entirely dependent upon the legal arguments which are advanced to him and is deprived of any opportunity of prior consideration or research into what the law really is.

As a result of this, and the haphazard system of leaving law reporting to private enterprise, many erroneous decisions are arrived at each year which, if reported, become the basis of subsequent erroneous decisions. The only consistency in the common law is that introduced by textbook writers, and then only by ignoring the decisions hostile to their views.

(e) To limit evidence to that which is admissible in a court of law is to exclude, very often, the most relevant. English law of evidence is a hotch-potch of inconsistencies.

(f) There are other major defects in the English system but the most fatal flaw is the concept that there must be an oral hearing to which the judge or judges come with their minds like a clean slate, so that until counsel for the plaintiff addresses them they have no knowledge of the facts or law, and are entirely dependent upon what is adduced before them. This, to start with, is a spurious assumption.

However, it may be debated whether this is what any arbitrator is called upon to do.

The 1950 Act, by section 12(1), provides that 'the parties to the reference ... shall ... submit *to be examined by* the arbitrator, on oath or affirmation in relation to the matters in dispute' (author's italics). The critical word of the statute is *'by'*. It is not *'before'*. These words are derived from the Arbitration Act 1889 and originate in section 40 of the Civil Procedure Act 1833. It is instructive to go back to that statute. By section 40 of that 1833 Act, the court or any judge thereof was empowered to 'command the attendance *and examination of any person* to be named' *by* an arbitrator. That is, not only the parties but 'any person'.

What the statutes from 1833 onwards clearly contemplated in arbitration proceedings is not an adversary procedure but an inquisitorial procedure whereby the arbitrator was empowered, through the courts, to compel the attendance of any witness whom he regarded as having relevant evidence to attend and *be examined* on oath.

Parliament clearly intended that, unlike the courts, arbitrators should have inquisitorial powers similar to those of a *juge d'instruction* in France, and the right to require not only that the parties should appear before him and give evidence on oath, but that any person the arbitrator thought had information relevant to the issues before him should be required to do the same.

Regrettably, the courts have not adopted this view of the statutory requirements. In 1969, for example, Mr Justice Donaldson, as he then was, insisted in *The Myron (Owners)* v. *Tradax Export SA* that if a hearing was called for, it had to follow the full-blown procedure of the courts. However, with respect, that is not what any of the statutes have said. In fact they have all said quite the opposite: that witnesses were to be examined *by* the arbitrator – i.e. that the procedure was to be inquisitorial and not adversary.

4.09 No power to call witnesses

The courts have held that, in spite of the statute, an arbitrator should not call witnesses of his own accord and against the will of the parties. In the case of *In re Enoch and Zaretsky, Bock & Co* (1910), an umpire insisted that a partner in one of the parties to the arbitration, 'a gentleman who was not personally acquainted with the matter', should attend and give evidence. The arbitrator then called a witness of his own, who produced documents in the form of copies of an award 'which were said to show that certain parcels of rice had been purchased in Rangoon from certain people at certain prices and of certain qualities'. Lord Justice Fletcher Moulton said it was clear 'that there is an idea that an umpire, a person in a judicial position, has the power to call witnesses in a civil dispute which the parties do not either of them choose to call. In my opinion there is no such power.' The idea, he thought, was based on an observation made by Lord Esher MR in *Coulson* v. *Disborough* (1894) and of this he said:

'There is no basis for that dictum ... it is not based upon any course of reasoning and no authority is cited for it. It would be destructive of fundamental principles of our law of procedure ... The dictum does not justify ... and it is certainly not the law, that a judge or any person such as an arbitrator in a judicial position, has any power to call witnesses to fact himself against the will of either of the parties.'

Lord Justice Farwell said:

'If an umpire knows of a witness who can give evidence, he should inform both parties and invite them to call him ... the conduct of the umpire in calling this witness and examining him and admitting the copy award as evidence is legal misconduct.'

Much the same sort of thing happened in *Royal Sugar Supply Commission* v. *Kwik-Hoo-Tong* (1938), where the arbitrators called their own expert witness in the absence of the parties and their award was held to be bad.

It is difficult to reconcile that law with the provisions of Article 27 of the UNCITRAL Arbitration Rules. That reads:

'1. The arbitral tribunal may appoint one or more experts to report to it, in writing, on specific issues to be determined by the tribunal. A copy of the expert's terms of reference, established by the arbitrators, shall be communicated to the parties.

2. The parties shall give the expert any relevant information or produce for his inspection any relevant documents or goods that he may require of them. Any dispute between a party and such expert as to the relevance of the required information or production shall be referred to the arbitral tribunal for decision.

3. Upon receipt of the expert's report, the arbitral tribunal shall communicate a copy of the report to the parties who shall be given the opportunity to express, in writing, their opinion on the report. A party shall be entitled to examine any document on which the expert has relied in his report.

4. At the request of either party the expert, after delivery of the report, may be heard at a hearing where the parties shall have the opportunity to be present and to interrogate the expert. At this hearing either party may present expert witnesses in order to testify on the points at issue. The provisions of article 25 shall be applicable to such proceedings.'

The result is that, by adopting these rules, the parties have in effect given *carte blanche* to the arbitrator to call expert witnesses himself. Possibly this will be effective, since the decision in *Enoch and Zaretsky* (1910) was limited to cases where the arbitrator called a witness of fact and without the consent of either party. But it seems open to the same objections as were given in that case. As Lord Justice Farwell then said:

> 'It puts the party against whom the witness gives evidence in a very difficult position when the umpire has made him his own witness by calling him and examining him. How can he effectively object to the umpire's questions? How can he ask him to reject a document which the witness produced on which the umpire relies? ... It is not open to counsel on either side to comment on the evidence given and to say he is either the plaintiffs' witness or the defendants' witness.'

The insistence of the English courts that an arbitration must be of an adversary nature creates difficulty in this country, for under the UNCITRAL Rules an inquisitorial role is clearly implied.

4.10 Must the parties give evidence?

Section 12(1) provides that 'unless a contrary agreement is expressed therein every arbitration shall contain an implied term that *the parties to the reference* ... shall submit to be examined by the arbitrator ... on *oath or affirmation*' (author's italics). That means what it says. It is not just authority for the arbitrator or umpire to administer the oath: that is contained in section 12(3).

The only meaning that can be attached to section 12(1) is that it is a statutory obligation upon the parties to submit themselves to being examined by the arbitrator or umpire.

The words are derived from clause (f) of the Schedule to the 1889 Act which dealt in detail with procedure, including a requirement that the arbitrators publish their award within three months and an umpire within one month. The original wording in clause (f) was even more emphatic:

> 'The parties to the reference ... shall, subject to any legal objection, submit to be examined by the arbitrators and umpire on oath or affirmation in relation to the matters in dispute ...'

The words 'subject to any legal objection' make it clear that giving evidence on oath was intended to be a statutory obligation subject only to the provisions of the law, such as those against self-incrimination in criminal matters.

If these interpretations be correct, and it is submitted that they must be, the statute makes it plain that in no way was the procedure of the courts intended to be followed. It is much to be regretted that none of this was raised in *In re Enoch and Zaretsky, Bock & Co.* (1910).

Of course, in 1889 the likelihood that both parties to an arbitration would be individuals was much greater than now, and how the provisions of the statute on this point can be applied to corporations is far from clear.

4.11 Admission of inadmissible evidence

'One of the reasons for going to arbitration is to get rid of the technical rules of evidence and so forth,' said Lord Denning in *GKN* v. *Matbro* (1976). Arbitrators, therefore, are not guilty of misconduct if they accept evidence not in accordance with the strict rules of the court or do not require a document to be proved with the strictness required by the law. In *Henry Bath & Sons Ltd* v. *Birgby Products* (1962) the particulars of claim were delivered only on the morning of the arbitration and then contained the allegation, as the most important point, that one Lane as agent for the respondents' buyers had inspected material as it left a warehouse and had found it was according to contract and had actually seen it loaded on to the lorries. The buyers therefore got in touch with Mr Lane and in the course of the arbitration produced a telegram which read: 'Strongly repudiate any suggestion that at any time I saw and supervised any loading of material at Birgby warehouse. [signed] R. W. Lane.' Application was made to set aside the award, *inter alia*, on the ground that the arbitrators should not have admitted the document in evidence. In the judgment it was said:

> 'It is clear that parties can, by express or implied agreement, give their arbitrators power to act on any evidence they like: just as parties in the Commercial Court can give the judge power to act upon inadmissible evidence even if it is documentary evidence not strictly proved ...
>
> The whole basis of these documentary arbitrations (which result in the disposal of countless cases in the City of London) is that a certain amount of informality both as to evidence and as to other matters will be indulged in without any right of protest by anybody.

The practice of allowing each party to submit his evidence and arguments to the arbitrators separately only works on the assumption that neither party will be taken by surprise by either the evidence or the arguments advanced by the other party.

Normally both parties are fully aware of the issues, the arguments and the evidence available for consideration, and no problem arises. If, however, the arbitrators have the slightest grounds for wondering whether one of the parties has fully appreciated what is being put against him, or whether he might reasonably wish to supplement his evidence or argument in the light of what has been submitted by the other party, it is their duty to take appropriate steps to resolve these doubts. This would normally be done by one of the arbitrators writing to the party concerned summarising the case made against him and inquiring whether in the light of the summary he wished to add anything by way of evidence or argument.

I am not for one moment suggesting, and I do not think that Mr Justice Megaw has ever suggested [i.e. in *Montrose Canned Food* v. *Eric Wells (Merchants) Ltd* (1965)] that the evidence and argument submitted by one party must be copied and submitted by the other with a right to reply thereto. That would lead to an indefinite exchange of correspondence.

If either party wishes to see the whole of the other party's evidence and to be informed in detail of his arguments, he should require a formal hearing. Any such request must be granted and at the hearing the usual court procedure will be followed.

The usual court procedure includes the granting of an adjournment on appropriate terms if the justice of the case so requires. What I am saying is that each party to an arbitration conducted on informal lines is entitled to rely upon both the arbitrators to safeguard his interests by ensuring that he is fully informed of any issue of fact or law which is raised by the other party and which he may not have anticipated.'

The application was therefore rejected.

The courts appear to adopt a different position regarding this in cases where there is a single arbitrator and cases where there are two arbitrators, one appointed by each party, who are expected to become advocates before an umpire if they disagree. In the latter circumstances, there is apparently nothing irregular in the party appointing the arbitrator making communications to him without any necessity for him to communicate it to the other party: *Ritchie* v. *Jacks* (1922). As long as each party knows in general terms the case against him and has the opportunity of refuting it, in the case of informal arbitrations with two arbitrators, this it would appear is sufficient: *Franz Haniel* v. *Sabre Shipping* (1962).

4.12 Evidence may be admitted *de bene esse*

The case of *F. G. Whitley & Sons* v. *Clwyd County Council* (1982) was concerned with the ICE contract and as to whether certain infilling of embankments ordered by the engineer was within the work specified or not. It was claimed that the contract was ambiguous on this point, but that other contracts between the same parties would make the position clear that similar infilling had been regarded by both parties as something for which the contractor was entitled to extra money.

In the Court of Appeal, Lord Justice Donaldson said:

'It must not be forgotten that ambiguity in a contract may be latent, and if this is alleged the evidence must be admitted before deciding whether or not the contract is ambiguous. That may not always be the case, but in general it is more satisfactory in terms of simplicity, speed and economy to admit any evidence which the party wishes to adduce, while reserving all questions of whether any facts so established are permissible aids to the construction of the contract.'

He rejected the suggestion that although a judge could safely be trusted to admit evidence *de bene esse*, for possible future use, and then later reject it, an arbitrator could not.

His Lordship said that it was 'a wholly unjustified aspersion on the profession of arbitrator' to believe that they could not like judges disregard evidence which was not a permissible aid to the construction of the contract.

4.13 Communications from the parties

If a single arbitrator receives a communication from one party, he should immediately disclose the fact to the other and communicate to him the full text of it. That would seem such an elementary and obvious aspect of judicial impartiality, that it need not be stated. As Mr Justice Megaw said in *Government of Ceylon* v. *Chandris* (1963):

'It is, I apprehend, a basic principle, in arbitrations as much as in litigation in the courts (other of course, than *ex parte* proceedings) that no one with judicial responsibility may receive evidence, documentary or otherwise, from one party without the other party knowing that the evidence is being tendered and being offered an opportunity to consider it, object to it, or make submissions on it. No custom or practice may override that basic principle.'

In *Ireland & Co.* v. *Bowring* (1920) this was described by Mr Justice Bailhache as 'a sacred principle'. There are at least a dozen cases where this has been accepted as axiomatic, even for informal arbitrations.

In *C.M.A. Martin Engineering Ltd* v. *J. Donne Holdings* (1980) J. Donne Holdings ordered vehicle chassis from C.M.A. Martin Engineering to fulfil an order from the Algerian government for mobile communication vehicles. A dispute having arisen, an arbitrator (who was an engineer as well as a barrister) was appointed to resolve the issues. At the preliminary meeting, it was accepted that the arbitration should be conducted informally without legal representation.

A document was sent to the arbitrator by C.M.A. Martin Engineering which was extremely damaging to the reputation of the other party. At a hearing, J. Donne Holdings learned of this document and demanded a copy. The arbitrator refused to provide it or order that they should be supplied with a copy.

At the time the representative of J. Donne Holdings made no formal protest, in the belief that the arbitrator was acting within his powers.

But subsequently, after two interim awards had been made, the High Court was moved to set them aside. Mr Justice Bingham held that a party who agrees to dispense with a formal hearing does not thereby agree to dispense with the rules of natural justice. The failure to order that a copy be provided was a breach of the fundamental rules underlying the administration of justice. In the circumstances the party had not waived his rights.

Much the same thing happened in *Woolridge Timber Ltd* v. *Branntorps Travaru* (1982) where Mr Justice Parker held that if an award was, or might have been based on points which were not put to the other side, the interests of justice required that the award be set aside or remitted.

However, there are numerous cases where information has been received by two arbitrators in the absence of either party and the position about this was explained by Mr Justice Donaldson in *The Myron* v. *Tradax Export* (1969):

' ... the practice of allowing each party to submit their evidence and arguments to the arbitrators separately only works on the assumption that neither party will be taken by surprise by either the evidence or the arguments advanced by the other party. Normally both parties are fully aware of the issues, the arguments and the evidence available for consideration, and no problem arises. If, however, the arbitrators have the slightest grounds for wondering whether one of the parties has fully appreciated what is being put against him, or whether he might reasonably wish to supplement his evidence or argument in the light of what has been submitted by the other party, it is their duty to take appropriate steps to resolve these doubts. This would normally be done by one of the arbitrators writing to the party concerned summarising the case made against him and inquiring whether in the light of the summary he wished to add anything by way of evidence or argument.'

4.14 Consulting lawyers

An arbitration is a private hearing and members of the press and public have no right to be present. A party can be represented by anybody he chooses, whether legally qualified or not; barristers have no exclusive right of audience before an arbitrator as they have before the higher courts.

If one party proposes to employ a barrister, however, it is his duty to advise the other side, so that they may have the opportunity of instructing one if they see fit. In an old case where one party appeared with counsel and the other asked for an adjournment so that he could instruct one and was refused by the arbitrator, the award was set aside for misconduct.

The extent to which an arbitrator is entitled to obtain assistance in the form of advice from a solicitor or barrister is uncertain. He is essentially the sole judge of both fact and law and it is his duty to make up his own mind on both after listening to the evidence and arguments presented to him.

It was said in a Privy Council case that an arbitrator may, without the consent of the parties, take the advice of counsel about the general principles applicable to the type of case in question but not on the specific questions of law that arise. But this does not seem to be the view taken by the court in *Giacomo Costa fu Andrea*. v. *British Italian Trading Co. Ltd* (1961) where, after the hearing had concluded, the arbitrator took the advice of a firm of solicitors on the interpretation of a clause in the contract and the Court of Appeal held there was nothing irregular about that. It appears to be accepted practice in the construction industry for an arbitrator to take counsel's opinion if he is in doubt about the law after the hearing, and that without notifying the parties.

With the consent of the parties he can always take the opinion of counsel, in which case he should show it to both sides. But the opinion of one counsel is no more likely to be right on a difficult point than the arbitrator's own opinion and it is a fallacy to think there is such a thing as *the* law which counsel is bound to know.

It is not contrary to public policy to insert in an arbitration agreement that neither counsel nor solicitor shall be instructed for either party or for the arbitrator in such circumstances to refuse leave for the parties to be legally represented: *Henry Bath & Son Ltd* v. *Birgby Products* (1962).

4.15 Further evidence

Further evidence should not be admitted after closing the hearing. In *Eastcheap Dried Fruit Co.* v. *N. V. Gebroeders Catz* (1962) it was said:

'Having regard, however, to the authorities, and in particular to that of *Royal Commission on Sugar Supply* v. *Trading Society Swik Hoo Tong* (1922), it appears that, when fresh evidence comes before the arbitrators after the conclusion of a hearing, then that is in law misconduct, vitiating the award unless, perhaps, it is affirmatively shown that it could not have affected that award. It is not as a rule for the court to embark upon conjecture as to whether their minds were affected or not.'

4.16 Viewing property

If an arbitrator indicates to the parties that he intends to have a view of the property in dispute, he is guilty of misconduct if he does not do so. In *Micklewright* v. *Mulluck* (1974), an arbitration between a house owner and the builder who carried out alterations for him included two points:

(1) what was the reasonable price for work carried out and
(2) what allowance ought to be made for work alleged to be badly done by the builder.

On a motion to set aside the award made in the builder's favour by the arbitrator, the court held that:

> 'An arbitrator who states that he intends to inspect the property in dispute and thereby induces a party to the arbitration to conduct his case on the basis that the arbitrator would do so, should not depart from his intention, or, if he did, should not do so without giving both parties notice of his intention to do so and an opportunity to call such further evidence as might be necessary in the changed circumstances.'

4.17 Oaths and affirmations

The form of oath commonly in use in the courts is: 'I swear by Almighty God that the evidence I shall give shall be the truth, the whole truth and nothing but the truth.'

By The Oaths Act 1909 sections 2 and 3:

> 'The person taking the oath shall hold the New Testament or, in the case of a Jew, the Old Testament, in his uplifted hand and shall say or repeat after the officer administering the oath the words "I swear by Almighty God that ..." followed by the words of the oath.'

It will be observed from the statute (contrary to popular impression) that: (a) the book can be held in either hand; and (b) the words 'so help me God' (a relic of the pagan Roman *sic me adjuvet Deus*) form no part of the oath.

At common law, persons of other religious faiths must be sworn in a manner binding on their conscience: on the *Koran*, the *Granth*, the *Vedas, Zend Avesta* or whatever particular holy book they believe the Deity inspired. Chinese witnesses kneel and break a saucer, and the only valid oath for the Nagas of Assam is to hold a live animal with another person and chop it in half with a single blow of a dao – a procedure the arbitrator may prefer to take place in an abattoir rather than the room where the hearing is taking place.

Until The Oaths Act 1888, no other form of giving evidence was permissible but as the result of that and subsequent legislation, currently The Oaths Act 1978, a witness may be allowed to affirm:

(a) if he has no religious belief
(b) if his religious belief precludes him from swearing an oath (as with the Quakers and the Moravians)

(c) if the oath binding on his conscience is not capable of being administered, eg because one of the only two copies of the *Granth* in Great Britain is not available.

The prescribed words of the affirmation are:

'I, A.B., do solemnly, sincerely and truly declare and affirm that the evidence I shall give shall be the truth, the whole truth and nothing but the truth.'

4.18 Limiting evidence

An arbitrator may, it would seem, for good reason limit the evidence which the parties wish to adduce.

Carlisle Place Investments engaged Wimpey Construction (UK) to build two office blocks. Defects were alleged in relation to the work on eighty-three separate roofs of the two blocks and in due course the dispute came to the arbitration of an experienced architect.

Since there was a possibility that this arbitration might be somewhat prolonged, Wimpey's applied to the arbitrator for an order that the issue of liability be determined by a maximum of twenty-five roofs. He made the order and gave the parties liberty to apply, expressing the opinion subsequently that his order in no way inhibited either party from raising issues about the other roofs if there were any additional defects requiring his attention.

He suspended his order, so that Carlisle Investments might apply to the courts for an order requiring him to state a special case as to whether he had such powers. They did so, seeking that the High Court should make an order under section 21(1) (c) of the 1950 Act (since repealed) that, a question of law arising in the course of the reference, the arbitrator should state a special case [6.05] for the decision of the High Court, as to whether he had power to limit the reception of otherwise admissible evidence.

Mr Justice Goff rejected the application. There was, he held, no requirement that an arbitrator must allow each party to call all the evidence which he wishes to call: *Carlisle Place Investments Ltd* v. *Wimpey Construction (UK) Ltd* (1980).

4.19 Powers to speed up proceedings

The 1979 Act includes a curious and highly ambiguous section 5 which is headed 'Interlocutory Orders'.

Before that Act, the standard method of enforcing interlocutory orders made by an arbitrator was for him to serve formal notice on the party in default that if the order was not complied with within *x* days, the arbitrator would proceed with the hearing *ex parte* or with the exclusion part excluded: *Congimex SARL* v. *Continental Grain* (1979). See also [1.14].

In addition, by section 12(6) of the 1950 Act, the High Court have power to make orders in respect of the large number of matters which include discovery of documents and interrogatories.

Section 5 of the 1979 Act seems to confuse matters. Where one party has failed to comply with an order by the arbitrator, the arbitrator or any party can apply to the High Court for an order. But an order for what?

Section 5(1) speaks of an order 'extending the powers of the arbitrator ...' Section 5(2) then professes to give him the power 'to continue with the reference in default of appearance or of any other act by one of the parties in like manner as a judge of the High Court might continue with proceedings in that court where a party fails to comply with an order of that court.'

What does it mean?

It is thought that it was intended to allow the arbitrator to deliver a 'default' judgment e.g. by striking out a defence filed by a respondent and making an award without holding a formal hearing or being satisfied by the claimant. At least, that is what the law lords in *Bremer Vulkan* (1981) seem to think it means.

But that is not what it says. It uses the word 'proceed with the reference' which means in real English that the arbitrator is empowered to continue it. And clearly he does not need the authority of the court to do that. Nor does it mean he can dismiss a party's case unheard.

Moreover 'in default of appearance' meant, in 1979, sending in to the court a piece of paper, 'an appearance', in response to a writ, which was a technical and necessary step before filing a defence and allowed the court 'in default of appearance' to grant summary judgment to the plaintiffs. The rest of section 5(2) is hardly more intelligible.

The only merit of section 5 will be that the arbitrator can write to a party in default and tell him that 'unless you comply with my orders within seven days I shall apply to the court for an order under section 5 of the Arbitration Act 1979 and ask for my costs on a solicitor and own client basis against you'. That will be equivalent to a fine of about £5000.

The other virtue of the section is that the court could possibly make an order that the arbitrator should 'proceed with the reference' by holding a hearing *ex parte*. Although an arbitrator clearly has that power at the moment, most are fearful of exercising it for fear of being accused of misconduct. That can hardly happen if they have the court's blessing.

In short, the section can be a valuable piece of bluff and a prudent arbitrator will make full use of it to speed up the proceedings.

4.20 Construction industry procedures

As has been seen, all the major construction industry contracts have an arbitration clause and most provide that for most disputes no arbitration shall take place until after practical completion. They all imply that arbitration should be a full formal hearing.

Although it is always open to the contracting parties to agree that the terms of their contract shall be varied by, for example, holding an arbitration before practical completion, this is rarely done. The result is that arbitrations take place years, if not decades, after the dispute has arisen, when most of the relevant witnesses have dispersed to the ends of the earth, and the arbitration becomes outrageously expensive.

All this means that arbitration does not work well for the construction industry. Disputes neglected fester. Goodwill vanishes. Site relationships deteriorate. The contractor's zeal to get the job done well evaporates.

In all other industries, provision is made for settlement of disputes as and when they arise and while the parties continue to trade amicably with one another. As Mr Justice Donaldson, as he then was, observed in *Pando* v. *Filmo* (1975) the shipping and commodity trades of the world regard arbitration as a normal incident of commercial life.

The construction industry cannot apparently be induced to provide its own arbitration procedure through a central body. But it would save itself an enormous amount of money, if it could be persuaded to have a rapid, streamlined procedure to be put in force as soon as disputes between employer and contractor or contractor and sub-contractor arise.

A streamlined arbitration procedure could consist in the following:

(1) *All lawyers are banned*. 'Parties shall not be represented by or have present at the hearing ... counsel or solicitors' runs the rule of one important federation. There is good reason for this. Any marriage where either party consults a solicitor is doomed. The expertise of lawyers consists of formulating issues, and drawing battle lines to the exclusive advantage of their clients.

'Experience teaches us every day,' Lord Denning once said, 'that judges and courts can disagree on the intepretation of words right up to the House of Lords, so that one can end up with three judges one way and six the other and no one can say one side is more right than the other.' On commercial contracts, he admitted 'the only certain guide is to be found in applying sound ideas of business, convenience and sense.'

(2) *Each party appoints his own arbitrator*, who should be experienced and qualified in the particular problem at issue. For example, quantity surveyors are often better qualified to settle disputes about site conditions, the effect of architects' instructions, pricing, clashes between different sub-contractors, and even the meaning of the JCT contracts than many an architect would be.

(3) *The two arbitrators should meet on site within a fixed time of their appointment and give their award within a fixed period of days*, or, of course, register their inability to agree.

(4) *No formal hearing should be held and no oral evidence be given unless requested by the arbitrators.* As Lord Justice Scrutton said in *Naumann* v. *Nathan* (1930): 'Businessmen have formed the view that it is possible to be too accurate in investigating disputes and that it is better on the whole for business to have a rough and ready way of getting at the truth than the more accurate, expensive and dilatory method of the courts.'

5. *If the arbitrators disagree, then they appoint an umpire.*

6. *Once an umpire is appointed, the former arbitrators are at liberty to become advocates* before him for the party who appointed them.

7. *The parties should agree an exclusion clause* under section 3 of the 1979 Act [6.17].

4.21 Formal hearing for construction disputes

Even where the parties wish to have a formal hearing of a construction dispute there is no reason whatsoever why it should be conducted like a court hearing – and probably good statutory reasons why it should not be [4.08].

A more effective procedure would be if the arbitrator required the parties to file with him within a specified reasonably short period of, say, four weeks:

(1) *An agreed statement in writing of the issues in the dispute*

The Romans in the halcyon days of the republic had a wonderful system whereby an arbitrator, agreed upon by the parties from a list of senators, was charged to decide the issues between them by, in essence, answering 'yes' or 'no' to a formula.

In fact most disputes can be reduced to a single sentence issue. To illustrate this it is possible to take construction cases which have been fought over years through the courts at vast expense right up to the House of Lords and where the costs in any case cannot have been less than £150,000.

In *Bilton* v. *GLC* (1982) the issue was simply: 'Does the architect have powers under clause 23(f) of the JCT 63 contract to extend time for completion because of delay in renomination of a sub-contractor?'

In *Sindall* v. *North West Thames Regional Health Authority* (1977) the issue was simply: 'Does a bonus recommended by the National Council rank as a fluctuation under the JCT 63 contract?'

In either case, the issue could have been settled by a competent arbitrator in half an hour.

(2) *A statement in writing of agreed facts*

A vast amount of time is wasted in court proving facts which are not seriously in dispute.

(3) *An agreed statement in writing of facts which are in dispute, with the contentions on either side*

(4) *A brief from each side setting out in writing what the law is on each issue, with reference to all the authorities upon which they rely*

(5) *An agreement excluding appeal under section 3 of the 1979 Act*

In the vast majority of construction industry cases the arbitrator could, after studying these documents, indicate to the parties (to adopt part of the Scottish procedure) what his preliminary conclusions were – within days rather than weeks – and invite them, if they so wished, to make oral submissions to him, after which he would make an interim award declaratory of the issues at stake, leaving the parties to work out for themselves the implications in money terms.

Most construction industry disputes fall into one of two categories:

(a) claims by the contractor for extra money other than that provided for by the contract, for various reasons such as variations or fluctuations, or by way of loss and/or expense claims

(b) actions by the building owner for defects in the structure.

The latter are invariably the subject of litigation, since the owner will wish to sue not only the contractor but also his architect, the structural engineer, the contractor and sub-contractors, and possibly the local authority with responsibility for building inspectors. In turn, various defendants may wish to bring in as third parties those with whom they had contractual relationships or from whom they can claim a contribution under the Civil Proceedings (Contribution) Act 1977. Even though there are arbitration clauses in his contract with the contractor and the architect, the owner will wish to proceed by litigation rather than arbitration since his claim will be against many defendants and the current philosophy is to sue everybody in sight and leave them to apportion liability amongst themselves. No court is likely to stay any such action [2.21].

This leaves for arbitration procedure only the most simple of issues between contractor and owner or contractor and sub-contractor, and the procedure suggested should be capable of settling these with expedition and at trifling cost.

If there is a serious dispute as to the facts, the parties can be invited to submit evidence on this and before making any award the arbitrator can send to each party his 'findings of fact'. This is not an interim award, and having found the facts the parties can, if they wish, address argument in writing and orally to the arbitrator upon the effect. Usually they will be agreed upon the effects of these findings of fact.

At all costs, the imitation of a court hearing should be avoided.

Chapter 5
The award

5.01 Essentials of a valid award

For an award to be valid it must do the following:

(1) *Settle all matters submitted in the arbitration* – and no more. There are two qualifications to this principle:

  (a) An award will be presumed to have done that unless the contrary is proved otherwise. In *Falkingham* v. *Victoria Railways Commissioner* (1900), the arbitrators awarded a lump sum. The Privy Council held that if it could be shown that they had included in that lump sum matters which they had no jurisdiction to consider, the award was bad; but although there was some evidence that the arbitrators had listened to matters not within the terms of reference, it must be presumed to have been a valid award.

  (b) 'All matters within the arbitrator's jurisdiction' means all matters that have in fact been raised before him; that is, upon which either party relied. Points which have not specifically been raised by either party or argued will not invalidate an award: *Tatem Steam Navigation* v. *Anglo-Canadian* (1935).

(2) *The award must be certain.* This means that the party that is to perform what the arbitrator directs must be made clear; so also the party that is to benefit. They must both be correctly named: *The Azuero* (1957). If money is to be paid, the amount must be specified with accuracy and which party is to pay and which to receive. If any act other than payment of money is ordered, *the time* within which it is to be done must be specified.

An arbitral award ordered that three contracts for sale should be set off against three contracts for purchase and that the respondents should pay the difference. But the contracts were not for specified quantities of goods, being 'about' figures (x per cent more or less). It was held that the award could not be enforced: *Margulies Bros Ltd* v. *Dafnis Thomaides* (1958).

In this case there were six contracts of sale between the parties, three for the purchase of cocoa by one party and three for the purchase of cocoa by the other. The contracts were not for specified quantities but were for '3 per cent more or less'. Disputes having arisen, the Board of Appeal of the Cocoa Association of London made an arbitration award:

> 'that contracts nos 2101, 2168, 2174 shall be applied against contracts nos 2184, 2297, 2265 respectively and the resultant differences plus interest at eight per cent per annum from 14 December 1957 to date of payments shall be paid by (the applicants) to (the respondents) within seven days and we further award that the fees and expenses of the original arbitration shall be paid by (the respondents).'

Mr Justice Diplock (as he then was) said:

> 'This award on its face is uncertain and comes within the first category described in *Montgomery, Jones and Co.* v. *Liebenthal & Co.* (1898) in which awards can be remitted to the arbitrator ... It is, in my view, an implied term of an arbitration agreement made since 1889 (when the provision for enforcing an award in the same manner as a judgment was first introduced) that an award for the payment of money – as contrasted with a mere declaratory award – shall be in a form which is capable of being enforced in the same manner as a judgment.'

But if the amount can be accurately calculated by some formula, 'that is certain which can be made certain'. Therefore an order just for 'costs' will be valid, since a taxing master can assess these, but an order for 'expenses' to be paid will not be unless, of course, these are quantified. In one case where the arbitrator decided the value per acre of land and directed the number of acres to be determined by measurement it was said that this was a valid award, since all that was necessary was a 'ministerial act'.

(3) *The award must be consistent.* In a claim for damages based solely

on fraudulent misrepresentation, the arbitrator acquitted the respondent of all fraud but nevertheless ordered him to make a payment to the claimant. 'The conclusion this arbitrator has come to ... is quite absurd. He says, I think he is innocent and then awards against him': Park J in *Ames* v. *Milward* (1818).

(4) *The award must be in conformity with the submission.* If the arbitration agreement contains specific instructions as to how the award is to be made or when it is to be made, it is not a valid award unless it conforms. Therefore, if the arbitration agreement specifies that each item of claim shall be assessed separately by the arbitrator, it is not permissible to make a lump sum award.

(5) *The award must be final.* An interim award may be made at any time by the arbitrator, provided it expressly professes to be one. Such an award may be in respect of part of the sum claimed or in respect of some of the issues: section 14, 1950 Act.

But if it is not an interim award it must be final in the sense that, after it is given, nothing remains to be done.

If the issue of a certificate by the architect is a condition precedent to payment, no certificate has been issued and the dispute in arbitration arose out of that refusal, the arbitrator is entitled to order payment to be made directly to the builder on the principle of *Neale* v. *Richardson* (1938).

The award is still final even if it does not deal with the costs of the reference.

Nothing in the Arbitration Acts or at common law requires the award to be in writing, but it is normal practice for such awards to be in writing and signed by the arbitrator and for his signature to be witnessed.

Three copies are usually made, one signed by the arbitrator which is the award itself and handed to the party taking up the award. Another copy is for the other party and the arbitrator retains the third.

The award is said to be 'published' as soon as it is signed by the arbitrator. The Rules of the Supreme Court provide for six weeks in which an application to set aside the award can be made; thus, this period does not begin to run until 'the award has been made and published to the parties'. This has never been closely defined by the courts but would appear to begin when the parties have been notified that the award is ready to be taken up and when one party has actually taken it up.

In practice, it is common to divide the award into two parts: *the recitals* and *the award*. There is no necessity to include a recital. A mistake in the recitals is not grounds for setting the award aside but it is an incitement to litigation and there are on the records numerous cases where a party has sought, unsuccessfully, to have the award set aside because of errors in the recitals. The briefer the recitals, therefore, the better.

All that they should contain is a brief reference to the agreement for arbitration and the appointment of the arbitrator.

5.02 Speaking or non-speaking awards?

Because of interference [6.01] by the courts in arbitration awards, it became the universal practice in England to give non-speaking awards, i.e. ones that merely required one party to pay a fixed sum to the other without explaining the arbitrator's reasons.

The Lord Chancellor, Lord Mansfield (1705-93), once wrote: 'Consider what you think justice requires and decide accordingly. But never give your reasons: for your judgment will probably be right but your reasons will certainly be wrong.'

English arbitrators on the whole have tended to agree with him. They have preferred to give what are called 'non-speaking' awards – that is, no reasons are given.

Before the 1979 Act explanation for this was admirably summarised by Mr Justice Mocatta in *The Tres Flores* (1972).

'England unlike, I think, most other countries including Scotland, has a rule that if an error of law appears on the face of an award, even though that award be not stated in the form of a special case for the decision of the court, the award can be set aside. Accordingly, rather than allow that to happen in cases where no special case has been requested, most arbitrators adopt the policy of making and publishing non-speaking awards.

If the parties to such award wish to be appraised of the arbitrator's reasoning, then very often the arbitrators are prepared to state their reasons, but in a document separate from the award itself and forming no part of it and on the basis that their reasons shall not be used by either party to set aside the award.'

The courts were not entitled to look at a contract unless the award specifically referred to it. Lord Denning more than once said that he had no regrets on that score. When parties go to lay arbitrators the matter ought to be left to them and not queried later on points of law: *D. S. Blaiber & Co.* v. *Newborne* (1953).

Similarly, although there are observations to the contrary, the better view was that the pleadings formed no part of the award and could not be looked at by a court unless the award specifically referred to them or they were 'accompanying and forming part of the award' or 'a document forming part of an award': *Belsfield Court Construction Co. Ltd* v. *Pywell* (1969).

The practice of giving non-speaking awards does not appear to have been challenged in any English court and was apparently approved by Mr Justice Mocatta in *The Tres Flores supra*. In Australia in *Madafferi Construction Co.* v. *Morling* (1973) in a building dispute, the arbitrator made his award and at the same time delivered to both parties a document headed 'Arbitrator's Notes on Award: without prejudice: these notes do not form part of the award and may not be used in any action without my permission'.

Lord Chief Justice Foster said:

'It was contended for the builder that the notes should be read as forming part of the award, notwithstanding the express declaration to the contrary because, it was said, the document itself coupled with its contemporaneous delivery indicated an intent to make it, in truth, part of the award. I am unable to agree. It seems to me the arbitrator has made his meaning clear, not only by his express statement that the notes do not form part of the award, but also by the somewhat inept phrase "without prejudice" and by directing that the notes may not be used in any action. To add the words "without my permission" does not depart from the intention thus expressed."

There may be some statutory arbitrations in which it is obligatory for an arbitrator to state his reasons. But in ordinary private arbitration, there is no such obligation: *Norman Hughes & Co.* v. *Ruthen Borough Council* (1972).

However, the practice of not giving reasons in English arbitration awards has raised difficulties with the enforcement of such awards in several civil law countries. There were instances where it was held that this amounted to a violation of a constitutional principle that a party condemned should be provided with the reasons for his condemnation and therefore the English award was unenforceable in that country.

5.03 The 1979 Act and non-speaking awards

It appears to be widely thought that the 1979 Act has changed the arbitrator's obligations about giving reasons.

That is not so. Nothing in the Act requires him to give reasons on any occasion.

Section 1(5) does, however, empower the High Court to order an arbitrator to 'state the reasons for his award in sufficient detail to enable the court should an appeal be brought under this section to consider any question of law arising out of the award.'

That power is, however, circumscribed by sections 1(5) and 1(6). It can only be exercised *after* the award is made and not before. It can only be exercised on application to the High Court by one of the parties, and then only with the consent of all the other parties to the reference or by special leave.

Moreover, even in those circumstances, the court shall *not* make an order unless it is satisfied:

(a) that *before* the award was made one of the parties had given notice to the arbitrator that a reasoned award would be required, or

(b) there was some special reason why such a notice was not given: section 1(6) (b).

The 1979 Act is studded with the ambiguous phrase 'special reason'. In *Hayn Roman & Co. SA* v. *Cominter (UK)* (1982) Mr Justice Robert Goff held that it was a 'special reason' under this section that the party applying had thought that in a 'London arbitration' [4.02] a reasoned award would be published. This appears to contrast with the lack of sympathy shown by the Court of Appeal to one of the parties in *The French Government* v. *SS Tsurushima Maru* (1921), where the claimant was 'a Frenchman who was apparently ignorant as to the nature of the arbitration practice under the contract.'

It will be observed that the 1979 Act does not go as far as the Commercial Court Committee would clearly have liked, but it did anticipate what would happen. 'Armed with reasons for an award, the unsuccessful party could apply to the court for leave to appeal,' observed the Committee. They have indeed.

The prudent arbitrator in the light of this, and in the real interests of the parties, will continue to give non-speaking awards, particularly in construction cases.

There has already been litigation as to what constitutes 'some special reason' and much more may be expected.

The fact that *one* of the parties has given notice that a reasoned award would be required does not mean that the arbitrator *has* to give a reasoned award. Mustill & Boyd (*Commercial Arbitration*, page 332) without authority say: 'If he receives such notice the arbitrator should incorporate his reasons into the award.' Why?

5.04 Giving a reasoned award

In an address to the Chartered Institute of Arbitrators, Lord Justice Donaldson said:

> 'I know that some arbitrators feel that giving reasons is a difficult and technical exercise. This is quite wrong. Nothing technical and above all nothing legalistic is required.
>
> The reasons might be as simple as "I award the plaintiff £500 and costs. I did not believe a word of the evidence called for the respondent. He never delivered the goods. I believe the claimant when he says that he had to buy other goods and that it cost him £500 more than the contract price."
>
> Or, "The issue is whether the goods were fair average quality beans. I have been in the trade for 30 years. I looked at a sample of the goods and they were not fair average quality. In fact, most of the sample was not even beans."'

However, in a judgment he went into more detail.

In *Westzucker GmbH* v. *Bunge GmbH* (1982) and another case, heard at the same time (neither of which cases was under the Arbitration Act 1979), Lord Justice Donaldson as he then was, discussed what reasons an arbitrator should give for his award. The passage must of necessity be *obiter*, since it did not in any way relate to the cases before him, but can be taken as a piece of judicial advice.

> 'It is of the greatest importance that trade arbitrators working under the 1979 Act should realise that their whole approach should be different. At the end of a hearing, they will be in a position to give a decision and the reasons for that decision. They should do so at the earliest moment.
>
> The parties will have made their submissions as to what had actually happened and what was the result in terms of their

respective rights and liabilities. All that will be fresh in the arbitrators' minds and there will be no need for further written submissions by the parties.

No particular form of award is required. Certainly, no one wants a formal special case.

All that is necessary is that the arbitrators set out what, in their view of the evidence, did or did not happen. They should explain succinctly why, in the light of what happened, they reached their decision and what the decision was. That is all that is meant by a "reasoned award".

For example, it may be convenient to begin by explaining how the arbitration came about.

The award can briefly tell the factual story as the arbitrators see it. Much will be common ground and will need no elaboration. On controversial matters it will be helpful if arbitrators not only give their view of what occurred but also make it clear that they have considered any alternative version and rejected it.

The arbitrators should end with their conclusions as to the resulting rights and liabilities of the parties.

It is sometimes said that the new approach means arbitrators are delivering judgments and that is something which requires legal skills. That is something of a half truth. Much of the art of giving a judgment lies in telling a story, logically, coherently and accurately. That is something that requires skill, but it is not a legal skill and it is not necessarily advanced by legal training. It is certainly a judicial skill, but arbitrators for the purpose are judges and will have no difficulty in acquiring it.

Where a 1979 Act award differs from a judgment is in the fact that arbitrators will not be expert to analyse the law and the authorities. It will be quite sufficient that they explain how they reached their conclusions. *It can be left to others to argue that that is wrong in law and to a professional judge, if leave is given, to analyse the authorities* [present author's emphasis].

That is not to say that where arbitrators are content to set out their reasoning on questions of law in the same way as judges, that will be unwelcome to the courts. Far from it.

The point I want to make is that a "reasoned award" in accordance with the 1979 Act is wholly different from an award in the form of a special case. It is not technical, it is not difficult to draw, and above all, it is something which can and should be produced promptly at the conclusion of the hearing.'

If this speech is analysed it will be seen that in fact arbitrators are now expected to deliver what is in effect a judgment. The arbitrator is to set out five things:

(1) a narrative of events that led up to the hearing, including his appointment
(2) the contentions raised on either side as to the facts
(3) the arbitrator's findings of fact
(4) the contention raised on either side as to the legal effect of those facts
(5) the arbitrator's conclusions as a result.

In construction cases this will necessitate reference to the specific contract and relevant clauses of it and to all the pleadings.

5.05 Interim awards

It is always open to the arbitrator to make an interim award and frequently it is in the interests of the parties that he should do so. In almost any dispute there is a conflict about liability, which not infrequently turns upon the interpretation to be placed upon the contract; and there is conflict about the consequences resulting from liability. It is usually therefore convenient to decide issues of liability initially and to make an interim award thereon before going on to decide the quantification of that decision. Once issues of liability are decided, the parties can often agree questions of *quantum*.

Section 4 of the 1950 Act specifically provides that it shall be an implied term of every arbitration agreement, unless there is a term to the contrary, that the arbitrator or umpire may make an interim award.

In arbitrations subject to the 1979 Act, an interim award can be appealed to the High Court under section 1(2). This requires the consent of all parties but not that of the arbitrator, or otherwise leave of the court. The position where only one of the parties wishes to appeal an interim award and obtain the leave of the court is unclear. It is submitted that there is no analogy with the previous procedure of case stated, so that the arbitrator is not obliged to await a decision on this application before proceeding. In fact, he should refuse to adjourn or prolong the arbitration while this application is made, in view of the professed intention of the 1979 Act to restrict the courts' interference with arbitrations. Of course, if both parties agree on an appeal on this section, it would be prudent for the arbitrator not to proceed further, although there is no statutory obligation on him not to do so.

There is an awkward over-lap between those provisions for appeal and section 2 of the 1979 Act. In that case, the High Court has no power to grant leave for a determination of a point of law unless the arbitrator has given his consent or all parties have agreed.

There is also a fundamental difference between the two procedures. If an appeal is made under section 1(2) the decision of the court (and any appeal court) about an interim award is *res judicator*; it cannot subsequently be appealed or disputed. Whereas the advice, given under section 2 is mere advice, so that even if an arbitrator follows it, it could still be reversed on appeal, as happened in *British Westinghouse* v. *Underground Electric Railways* (1912) where the arbitrator, having had a consultative case stated, followed the directions of the High Court as to the law and then had the mortification of seeing his award set aside by the House of Lords on the grounds that an error of law appeared on the fact of the award.

5.06 Successful litigant entitled to costs

'There is a settle practice of the courts that in absence of special circumstances a successful litigant should receive his costs, and that it is necessary to show some grounds for exercising the discretion of refusing an order which would give them to him, and the discretion must be judicially exercised. Those words "judicially exercised" are always somewhat difficult to apply, but they mean that the arbitrator must not act capriciously and must, if he is going to exercise his discretion, show a reason connected with the case and one which the court can see is a proper reason': Lord Goddard LCJ in *Lewis* v. *Haverfordwest RDC* (1953).

There are various types of costs and the High Court Order 62 which deals with costs which can be awarded by the court reminded the head of the Chancery Division, Sir Robert Megarry VC, of Oliver Cromwell's phrase, 'an ungodly jumble'.

He said there were five main bases of taxation of costs used in the courts:

— *Party and party*: 'all such costs as are necessary or proper for the attainment of justice ...'

— *The common fund basis*: (earlier known as solicitor and client basis): 'a more generous basis than party and party.'
— *The trustee basis*: 'where no costs will be disallowed unless they fall within certain exceptions.'
— *The solicitor and own client basis*: 'costs allowed except in so far as they are of an unreasonable amount or unreasonably incurred.'
— *The indemnity basis*: 'For years the courts have been making such orders, particularly against contemnors, and taxing masters have had to do their best to tax costs under such orders.'

He held in *EMI Records Ltd* v. *Jan Cameron Wallace* that the court was not restricted under section 50(1) of the Judicature Act 1925 to making orders only on a 'party and party basis' or a 'common fund' basis. The court had power to order the payment of costs on an indemnity basis. The result of an indemnity order was that all costs incurred were to be allowed, except those unreasonably incurred or of an unreasonable amount, and the receiving party should be given the benefit of any doubt.

The arbitrator should confine himself to making orders which deal with the normal 'party and party' basis. In exceptional cases where the unsuccessful party has shown a wanton disregard of the rights of the successful party, he might consider an application on the 'common fund basis'. The exact subtle distinctions between other forms of costs are best left to the Taxing Masters of the Queen's Bench since they alone, if anyone, might understand them.

If the word 'costs' alone is used it will mean 'party and party' costs. Section 18 of the 1950 Act provides:

'If no provision is made by an award in respect of costs of the reference, any party to the reference may, within fourteen days of the publication of the award, or such further time as the High Court or a judge thereof may direct, apply to the arbitrator for an order directing by and to whom these costs shall be paid, and thereupon the arbitrator shall, after hearing any party who may desire to be heard, amend his award by adding thereto such directions as he may think proper with respect to the payments of costs of the reference': section 18(4)

5.07 Principles on which costs are awarded

Costs are usually divided between costs of the reference and costs of the award.

The costs of the reference are those which are incurred by the parties in the course of the whole procedure from the moment when an agreement to submit to arbitration was first signed to the final award.

The costs of the award are the arbitrator's fees and expenses. In respect of both, unless the arbitration agreement specifies otherwise, the arbitrator has a discretion to award them or not; and this is an implied term of the arbitration agreement.

Section 18 of the 1950 Act confers these powers on the arbitrator:

  (i) to exercise his discretion to award costs
 (ii) to settle the amount of such costs himself
(iii) to award costs not merely on the usual party and party basis but on a solicitor and client basis (now called the common fund basis) or indeed on any basis on which a court could award costs.

If in an agreement made before the dispute has arisen it purports to order that each party shall pay his own costs, this clause is void by reason of section 18(3). It follows that in these circumstances the arbitrator should exercise his own discretion in accordance with usual principles.

An arbitrator ought not without special reasons deprive a successful party of his costs, still less award costs to a completely unsuccessful one.

In *Pepys* v.*London Transport Executive* (1975) a claim for compensation for injurious affection caused by the construction of the Victoria Line extension of the underground was referred to the Lands Tribunal which has power to receive 'sealed offers' under its statutory rules. A sealed offer was made but the claimant was awarded nothing; nevertheless the tribunal gave her costs up to the date of the sealed offer.

Lord Denning said:

'The practice of the courts, as also of tribunals and arbitrators, is that if a plaintiff or claimant fails altogether, no order is made whereby the successful party is to pay the costs of the plaintiff or claimant, except for very special reasons.

If that rule is departed from, the tribunal or arbitrator or whoever it might be ought to set out the reasons, particularly where there is an appeal on costs to a higher court or tribunal which will want to see whether they are proper reasons'.

In *Matheson & Co Ltd* v. *A. Tabah & Sons* (1963) Mr Justice Megaw
(as he then was) said:

'The principles on which the arbitrator has got to act are indentical
with the principles on which a judge in a court has got to act in
awarding costs.

Where a party is successful, by which I understand to be meant
that he obtains judgment for a sum of money, in the ordinary way, he
is entitled to recover the costs which he has incurred in the
proceedings which have been necessary for him to obtain an order
for the payment of that sum to which he is entitled. But that is subject
of course to exceptions and provisos in relation to particular cases.

If, for example, the claim has been grossly exaggerated and the
award is for a much smaller sum than the award claimed, that is a
factor which the court is entitled to take into consideration in
depriving a successful claimant of his costs or of part of them.

There are all kinds of other matters which may also properly be
considered in the exercise of the court's discretion. They would
include the conduct of the parties in the course of the hearing.

They would include questions whether one particular facet of the
claim failed on which a large amount of time had been spent and so
forth. The principles which an arbitrator is, by his legal duty, obliged
to apply are the same but there is a difference in practice that
whereas if a judge in court makes what I may call an unusual order
for costs, such as depriving a successful claimant of his costs or a
large part of them, the judge would normally be expected to indicate
his reasons for following that course and his decision would of
course be available to a higher court, and if that court took the view
that he had applied the wrong principle having regard to the matters
which he had stated as being his grounds for decision, or if it were
apparent from the proceedings in the court that he had applied a
wrong principle or had failed to act on a proper principle, then his
award as to costs could and would be upset.

But it had been held by authority by which I am undoubtedly
bound that, where there is an order as to costs in an arbitration and
that order is challenged in the court, the court is not entitled to
require the arbitrator to state the reasons why he made that order.'

5.08 How the discretion is to be exercised

In spite of the wording of the section, an arbitrator has not *carte blanche* to make any order concerning costs that tickles his fancy. His duty is to exercise that power judicially and that means in the same way as the courts do.

The basic rule of the courts is that *'costs follow the event'*. That means unless there are substantial reasons why they should not be given to the successful party, he is entitled to receive the costs of the reference and the award from the loser. At one time it was said that an arbitrator's failure to make an award of costs in favour of the successful party without giving any reasons was no ground for the court setting aside the award; but that has been strongly criticised and it is submitted that it is the arbitrator's duty, if he decides to depart from the invariable rule that a successful party is entitled to his costs, to give his reasons. Lord Goddard LCJ, in *Lewis* v. *Haverfordwest RDC* (1953) said:

'It is a curious circumstance – and one experiences it time and time again – that lay arbitrators always seem to think that parties should pay their own costs. ... In the absence of special circumstances a successful litigant should receive his costs, and ... it is necessary to show some grounds of exercising the discretion of refusing an order which would give them to him, and the discretion must be judicially exercised.'

However, the law is less than clear about that and two subsequent cases seem to suggest that at least the court is not entitled to require the arbitrator to state the reasons why he made the order he did – even where a successful claimant was deprived of costs; though, in *Messers Ltd* v. *Heidner (No 1)* (1960) the court remitted an award to the arbitrator to explain why he had divided the costs two-thirds to one party and one third to the other.

There is, however, some guidance on decided cases about what are *not* sufficient grounds for depriving a successful party of his costs. These include:

(i) Because no serious attempt had been made to settle the matter before arbitration: *Lewis* v. *Haverfordwest RDC* (1953).
(ii) Because a 'without prejudice' offer had been made before the proceedings which was more than the arbitrator found was due

from the respondent: *Stotesbury* v. *Turner* (1943).

(iii) Because in a building arbitration the respondent builder had alleged in his defence that he had always been willing to put right the defects: *Dineen* v. *Walpole* (1969).

It is no ground for depriving a successful claimant of his costs in a building dispute that the builder was given no opportunity of putting right the defects.

In *Dineen* v. *Walpole* (1969) the award of the arbitrator read:

'I award the Claimant D. M. Dineen against the Respondents the sum of Forty Pounds ... to put right the items under clause 3 of the Points of Claim under (a), (b) and (c). I award that the costs of the arbitration be paid by the Claimant'.

But it may be grounds for depriving a successful party of part of his costs that he has called more evidence than is necessary, that his claim was exaggerated, that he has failed on important issues or has otherwise by his conduct prolonged the proceedings.

In *Tharros Shipping Co. Ltd* v. *Mitsubishi Corp of Manila* (1981) Mr Justice Mocatta held that notwithstanding the principal sum had been paid and accepted before an award, an arbitrator still had power to make an award of costs.

5.09 'Sealed' offers

Under the rules applicable to claims for compensation in cases of compulsory purchase before the Lands Tribunal, provision is made for the acquiring authority to make an unconditional offer of compensation in a sealed envelope. If the award exceeds the sum offered, the claimant receives the costs of the proceedings; if the award is the same or less than the offer, the claimant is deprived of his costs, since if he had in fact accepted the offer the proceedings would then have been unnecessary.

In the High Court and county court it is always open for a defendant to make a payment into court with or without a denial of liability. If the plaintiff accepts that sum he may discontinue the action by taking the sum out of court, in which event he will be entitled to his costs up to that date at a rate appropriate to the sum recovered. If he does not accept the sum paid in, he will continue the action. If he loses the action entirely, the plaintiff will in most circumstances have to pay the defendant's costs. If the plaintiff recovers more than the sum paid in, he will normally recover his costs against the defendant. If on the other hand, he recovers *less* than the sum paid in he will not be allowed to recover his costs after the date of the payment in.

As a result of these two practices, some arbitrators have allowed the respondent to make an offer in a sealed envelope and have deprived the claimant of his costs if the award does not exceed it.

This is a practice which should not be followed. There are considerable differences between the Lands Tribunal, the High Court and the ordinary arbitration:

(1) In the case of the Lands Tribunal, there is statutory authority for the practice of allowing a sealed offer; in the High Court, payments in are authorised by SCR Order 22. There is no statutory authority for the practice in arbitration.

(2) In the court, the judge is not allowed to know that a payment into court has been made; nor is the Lands Tribunal allowed to know of a sealed offer. An arbitrator is bound to know that a sealed offer has been made since it can only have been handed to him.

(3) In the case of court practice, money is actually paid into court and in the Lands Tribunal the offerors are always local authorities who can be relied upon to make a payment. In many arbitrations even an accepted offer will not necessarily result in the money being actually paid.

These views, expressed by the present author in his book *The Law and Practice of Arbitrations*, published in 1974, have now been confirmed by comments in the Commercial Court Committee Report on Arbitration of 1978 (Cmnd 7284):

'*Offers to settle and payment into Court*:
62. In an action, the defendant can pay into Court a sum which he considers to be sufficient to meet the amount which the plaintiff will eventually be awarded. Within a limited period the plaintiff can, if he wishes, take this sum out of Court in full satisfaction of his claims and will thereupon be entitled to the costs of the action. Alternatively he can go on with the action in the hope that he will recover more than the sum in Court. If his hopes are realized, he will *prima facie* be entitled to the costs up to the date of payment into Court, but will have to pay the defendant's costs incurred after that

date. It is a very strict rule of Court that the judge cannot be told that money has been paid into Court and, still more, how much has been paid in until he has given judgment. He is then told and makes the appropriate order as to costs.

63. There is difficulty in adapting this procedure to arbitrations since the award usually deals with liability, damages, interest and costs all in the same document and the parties have no opportunity of making submissions about costs after the other issues have been determined. A somewhat imperfect solution has been adopted whereby the respondent in the arbitration makes a "sealed offer" of settlement. The claimant can accept it or reject it. If he rejects it, the offer is placed in a sealed envelope and handed to the arbitrator on terms that it shall not be opened until after he has decided upon all issues other than costs. The system is open to the objection that the arbitrator, unlike a judge, will know that some offer of settlement has been made, although he will not know how much. There is a further objection that the arbitrator must be subject to a great temptation to open the envelope before deciding how much to award.

64. The Committee recommends that an arbitrator should make his award on all issues including costs without being told that any offer of settlement has been made, but that he should be empowered to re-open so much of the award as relates to costs upon subsequent proof that an offer of settlement was made before or during the hearing of the arbitration.

65. There is a further objection to the system in that it is one thing to make an offer in settlement but quite another to produce the necessary money to back that offer. Under the Court system, the offer is of no effect unless accompanied by the money. Under the arbitration system, there is no guarantee that the party making the offer has the money to back it if the offer is accepted. The Committee recommends that the respondents in arbitration proceedings who wish to make an offer or settlement which may affect the arbitrator's decision as to costs should be obliged to pay the amount offered into Court.'

No action has been taken on this recommendation.

This practice in ordinary arbitrations was considered in *Stotesbury* v. *Turner* (1943). The respondent made an offer, without prejudice, of £550 in full settlement of the claim and costs. The arbitrator knew of this and, having found for the respondent for a lesser sum, made an order to the effect that the claimant should pay all the costs of the proceedings. The court set aside the award as to costs on the ground that there were no grounds on which he could properly exercise his discretion to deprive a successful claimant of his costs. See also *Demolition and Construction* v. *Kent River Board* (1963).

The principle will not be altered by an alteration in procedure, such as giving the conclusions of the arbitrator in the form of an interim award and then listening to arguments about costs before making a final award. An arbitrator should not deprive a successful claimant part of his costs just because an earlier offer might have given him the same as he has won.

5.10 'Open' and 'without prejudice' offers

An offer to settle may be made in the form of an 'open' letter to the other side. That is, one that can be put before the arbitrator in the course of the proceedings.

Or it can be made in the form of a 'without prejudice' offer, which cannot, without the consent of the party making it, be put before an arbitrator.

The practice of making 'open offers' was considered in *Tramountana Armadora SA* v. *Atlantic Shipping Co* (1978). There in spite of the fact that the claimants had won in the sense that an award of $2710 was made in their favour and the contract had been rectified in their favour, the arbitrator had awarded the whole of the costs both of reference and the award to the respondents.

One of the reasons he gave in a subsequent affidavit was:

'My apportionment of costs is made in the exercise of my discretion, and in consideration of the fact that the respondents offered to pay the claimants a much larger sum than has now been awarded and that the claimants refused to accept the said offer.'

In fact, he was totally wrong in that the offer made in an 'open letter' was $6000 exclusive of costs to that date (after two days of hearing) and interest and was in reality less than the sum ultimately awarded.

The award as to costs was remitted to the arbitrator since it was manifestly wrong in law, but little guidance can be deduced from the judgment of Mr Justice Donaldson (as he then was).

But it was said in *Demolition and Construction Co. Ltd* v. *Kent*

River Board (1963) and *Dineen* v. *Walpole* (1969) that a written offer from the respondent of the maximum figure for which he is prepared to settle made in an *open* letter in the course of the arbitration might be grounds on which a successful party could be deprived of his costs, if he recovered only that sum or less than that sum, but in neither case was that part of the *ratio decidendi*, and although it appears to be the practice in commercial arbitration it has yet to be fully considered by the courts. From *Martin French* v. *Kingswood Hill Ltd* (1960) it would appear that it is only where the offer is open (that is, *not* made 'without prejudice') and before the arbitrator as such, that it should be allowed to affect costs.

The most satisfactory procedure, if it is desired to settle a claim or counterclaim, is that a 'without prejudice' offer be made and that the other party should require that the money be deposited with a banker in the joint names of the parties or their solicitors, and that the parties should agree that the arbitrator be asked to give an interim award as to the substantive sum due, if any, and hear argument as to costs thereafter.

In those circumstances, and only in those circumstances it is submitted, would an arbitrator be entitled to ask himself the question, 'Has the claimant achieved more by rejecting the offer and going on with the arbitration than he would have achieved if he had accepted the offer?'

In those circumstances alone, it would be possible for the arbitrator to apply the reasoning of Mr Justice Donaldson in the *Tramountana* case:

'If the claimant in the end has achieved no more than he would have achieved by accepting the offer, the continuance of the arbitration after that date has been a waste of time and money. *Prima facie*, the claimant should recover his costs up to the date of offer and should be ordered to pay the respondent's costs after that date.'

5.11 Costs in 'string contracts'

Where there are 'string contracts' of sale and the arbitration relates to whether the goods are of contract quality, each party is entitled to receive the costs he has to pay out to the previous party and not merely his costs against his supplier.

In *L. E. Cattan Ltd* v. *A. Michaelides & Co. (a firm) (third party, Turkie; fourth party, George, trading as Yarns & Fibres Co)* (1958) an action commenced by specially endorsed High Court writ was remitted by consent of all parties to the tribunal of arbitration of the Manchester Chamber of Commerce.

The arbitrator made an award which contained the words:

'viii: that the defendants shall pay the plaintiffs' costs of and incidental to this reference and to the said action but not including the amount paid by the plaintiffs to the third party under paragraph (vi) hereof. By that paragraph (vi) the plaintiffs were condemned to pay the costs of the third party.'

Lord Diplock said:

'I think that I should make these observations about the way in which costs should be dealt with where third, fourth, fifth and sixth parties have been brought in in these string contract cases, which are very common.

In doing so, I want to make it clear that I am not seeking to substitute my discretion for that of the arbitrator, or to suggest that there may not be reasons in some circumstances for making a different award.

In the ordinary way, however, where damages are claimed for breach of contract on one contract in a string of contracts, and the seller brings in his immediate seller as a third party, and the third party brings in his immediate seller as a fourth party, then, provided that the contracts are the same or substantially the same so that the issue whether the goods comply with a description is the same, the defendant (in this case it was the plaintiffs because it was a counterclaim), if successful, should recover against the plaintiffs not only his costs but any costs of the third party which he has been ordered to pay; the third party in like manner should recover from the defendant his own costs and any costs of the fourth party which he has been compelled to pay, and so on down the string.

That is the normal way in which costs should be dealt with in this kind of action where there is a string of contracts in substantially the same terms. In saying that, I am not excluding the possibility that there may be special reasons for departing from normal practice.

Whether it was reasonable for the defendant to bring in a third party at all is always a question to be considered, and that is a matter on which a lot of facts may be relevant.'

5.12 Duty to award interest

'In a commercial transaction, if the plaintiff has been out of his money for a period, the usual order is that the defendant should pay interest for the time for which the sum has been outstanding. No exception should be made except for good reason': *Panchaud* v. *Pagnan* (1974).

Indeed, it has been said that an arbitrator is under a duty to award interest from the date when the cause of action accrued up to the date of his award, in the absence of special circumstances: *Wildhandel NV* v. *Jacker & Ors* (1976).

In *The Myron* (1970) Mr Justice Donaldson, as he then was, said that matters of costs in the arbitration and interest upon any money found due were for the arbitrator or umpire.

'However, it may assist if I express my views upon the principles which are applicable. It is of paramount importance to the speedy settlement of disputes that a respondent who is found to be under a liability to a claimant should gain no advantage and that the claimant should suffer no corresponding detriment as a result of delay in reaching a decision. Accordingly, awards should in general include an order that the respondent pay interest on the sum due *from the date when the money should have been paid.* [author's emphasis]

The rate of interest is entirely in the discretion of the arbitrators, but I personally take the view that in an era of high and fluctuating interest rates the principle which I have expressed is best implemented by an award of interest at a rate one per cent in excess of the Bank of England discount rate for the time being in force.

When interest is awarded arbitrators commonly award it for a period ending with the date of the award.'

Care should be taken however that a claimant does not recover interest twice. If damages for the repair of defective structures are given as at the date of the award, where for good reason the repairs have not been carried out it is inappropriate to award interest from the date when the cause of action arose since the effects of inflation have been taken into account already. That is a trap the courts fell into by giving damages for personal injuries as at the date of judgment.

5.13 Interest before award

Interesting though these observations of judges are, and in spite of the fact that they had been implemented by them, arbitrators had in fact no power in law to award interest, for the simple reason that the power of the courts to award interest was entirely statutory and was confined to 'courts of record', i.e. the High Court. However, the Administration of Justice Act 1982 amended the Arbitration Act 1950 and allows an arbitrator to award interest, at such a rate as he thinks fit, on monies due.

Three things should be distinguished: interest from the date when a cause of action arises; interest from the date of institution of proceedings in court or the initiation of an arbitration; and interest subsequent to a judgment or award.

In 1826, Chief Justice Best said: 'However a debt is contracted, if it has been wrongfully withheld by the defendant after the plaintiff has endeavoured to obtain payment of it, the jury may give interest in the shape of damages for unjust detention of the money.': *Arnott* v. *Redfern* (1826).

Three years later, *all* the judges of the King's Bench Court held that was wrong: *Page* v. *Newman* (1829). No damages could be given at common law for the non-payment of money due. The decision in *Page* v. *Newman* (1829) stood unchallenged throughout the nineteenth century and was reaffirmed by an authoritative judgment of the House of Lords in *The London, Chatham and Dover Railway Co.* v. *South Eastern Railway* (1893), and has since been confirmed by the House of Lords in *The President of India* v. *La Pintada* (1984).

Because the common law courts had no inherent powers to award interest, Parliament had to intervene to alter the common law rule in order to empower the courts to give interest on judgments. This was done by the Judgments Act 1838.

Parliament did not give power to the common law courts to award interest on sums due, as from the date when they were due, until the Common Law Procedure Act 1852.

This became in due course the Law Reform (Miscellaneous Provisions) Act 1934.

Section 3 of that Act read:

'(1) In any proceeding *tried* in any *court of record* for the recovery of any debt or damage, the court may, if it thinks fit, order that there shall be included *in the sum for which judgment is given* interest at such rate as it thinks fit on the whole or part of the debt or damages for the whole or any part of the period between the date *when the cause of action arose* and the date of the judgment.' (author's emphasis)

That section did not apply to county courts since they are not 'courts of record', and judges in those courts had no power to award interest before judgment, until the Administration of Justice Act 1982 became law.

Since the 1934 Act applied only to 'courts of record', excluding thereby county courts, it clearly had no application to arbitrations and the Queen's Bench Divisional Court, Lord Goddard presiding, correctly so held in *Podar Trading Co.* v. *Tagher* (1949). However, in *Chandris* v. *Isbrandtsen-Moller Co.* (1951) Lord Denning and his colleagues in the Court of Appeal held that an arbitrator *has* such power. In that case, Lord Denning said:

'I cannot see why any distinction should be drawn between the duty of an arbitrator to give effect to such statutes as the Statute of Limitations and his jurisdiction in his discretion to award interest. An award of interest is only a part of the *damages recoverable.*' (author's emphasis)

It will be observed that his reasoning was exactly contrary to the judgment of the House of Lords in the *London, Chatham and Dover Railway* case *supra,* by which his lordship was bound.

However, that judgment has ever since stood enshrined as law on the basis that the parties impliedly give the arbitrators the same powers as a High Court judge, including those powers which are conferred on him by the 1934 Act.

It was disputed in *Tehno Impex* v. *Gebr van Weelde Scheepvaart-kantoor* (1981). But this time the arbitrator was dealing with a dispute, it was said, which by virtue of section 1 of the Administration of Justice Act 1956 would, if tried by a court, have come within the jurisdiction of the Admiralty Court.

For that reason it was held that the arbitrator was entitled to award interest since the Admiralty Court has always awarded interest. It has always awarded interest, not only simple interest but compound interest; so presumably can an arbitrator dealing with matters which would otherwise have been within the jurisdiction of that court.

It would appear, however, that in statutory arbitrations interest can only be awarded by the arbitrator if the statute expressly authorises it: *Monmouthshire County Council* v. *Newport Borough Council* (1947).

In *Tharros Shipping Co Ltd* v. *Mitsubishi Corporation of Manila* (1981) Mr Justice Mocatta held that an arbitrator had no power to award interest when the principal sum due had been paid and accepted before an award. In that he followed *Tehno-Impex* v. *Gebr Van Weelde Scheepvaartkantoor* and *The Medina Princess* (1962).

The position so far as the courts are concerned (including the county court) has been altered by the Administration of Justice Act 1982.

5.14 Interest on the award

Interest after the award is dealt with in section 20 of the 1950 Act:

> 'A sum directed to be paid by an award shall, unless the award otherwise directs, carry interest as from the date of the award and at the same rate as a judgment debt.'

The House of Lords, however, decided that an arbitrator under that section has power only to order that no interest shall be paid on his award and not to vary the rate fixed by statutory instruments for judgment debts.

The arbitrator who wishes to incorporate interest after his award as part of his award should be careful to ascertain what is the correct current rate of interest: all the counsel and the judges in the *Chandris* case were unaware that it had been increased.

5.15 Summary of the present position regarding interest

The present position can therefore be summarised as follows:

(1) Although the common law courts had no power to award interest on monies due, that power was conferred on the High Court and other courts of record by statute in 1854 (but not on the county courts until 1982).

(2) Since the case of *Chandris and Isbrandtsen-Moller* (1951), the courts have held that an arbitrator has implied authority to award interest.

(3) He should normally do so in commercial cases of debt and no

exception should be made except for good reason: *Wildhandel NV* v. *Tucker and Cross* (1976).

(4) Arbitrators in statutory arbitrations, however, have no power to award interest unless the statute specifically authorises it: *Monmouthshire County Council* v. *Newport Borough Council* (1947).

(5) The amount of interest is at the discretion of the arbitrator but should normally be a commercial rate such as will provide the party with adequate compensation for being kept out of his money.

(6) The period for which the arbitrator is entitled to award interest is from the date when the money is due up to the date of the award.

(7) Interest should be simple interest: the arbitrator has no power to award compound interest except in such circumstances as the Admiralty court would.

(8) In cases where the arbitrator awards damages, e.g. for the cost of rectification of a defective building, rather than debt, the damages should be assessed as at the date of the award: *Dodd* v. *Canterbury City Council* (1980). In those circumstances the damages should not carry interest. Otherwise the claimant will be getting paid twice over.

(9) The award will bear interest at the statutory rate for judgments unless the arbitrator orders that it shall bear no interest: section 20, 1950 Act, as construed in *Timber Shipping Co. SA* v. *London and Overseas Freighters Ltd* (1972).

(10) The Administration of Justice Act 1982:
   (a) authorised county courts to award interest
   (b) allowed the High Court to award interest after the writ on debt (but not on damages) paid before judgment, thereby reversing the law laid down in *The Medina Princess* (1962). The Act makes no mention of arbitration, but if the *Chandris* case is to be followed, by analogy interest can be awarded on sums paid before award. But as indicated earlier, the present author regards *Chandris* as bad law. Statutory powers conferred expressly only on 'courts of record', and therefore not on county courts, cannot possibly confer powers on arbitrators.

5.16 Suing on the award

If the losing party does not pay in accordance with the arbitration award, there are two methods available whereby it can be enforced:

(i) the successful party can use the award as a cause of action and take out a writ to sue on it; or, more conveniently, he can

(ii) register the award as a judgment of the High Court in accordance with section 26.

If he elects or has to sue on the award it will be as a breach of a contractual agreement to abide by the terms of the award. He will therefore have to prove:

(a) the original agreement for arbitration under which the reference took place

(b) a dispute arose within the terms of it

(c) the arbitrator was validly appointed

(d) the award was properly made

(e) the sum named in the award has not been paid – or something ordered under it has not yet been performed.

The defendant can dispute any of these points and it will also be a good defence if he can show that:

(i) the arbitrator's authority was validly revoked before the award was made

(ii) the award had ceased to be binding for any good reason

(iii) the arbitrator had no power to make the award he did because it was outside his jurisdiction

(iv) the arbitrator was disqualified and the proceedings were a nullity

(v) there had been a subsequent agreement between the parties, good in law, that the award should not be enforced.

The defendant however will not be allowed to plead as his defence that there was misconduct on the part of the arbitrator or that the proceedings in some other way were irregular. The proper procedure if he wishes to adopt this is to move the court to set aside the award.

Contrary to statements in *Russell on Arbitration*, 20th edition, page 350, and Mustill and Boyd's *Commercial Arbitration*, 1982 edition, page 369, an overseas arbitration award based on a contract made within the English jurisdiction can be enforced by an Admiralty action *in rem*: *Bremer Oeltransport* v. *Drewry* (1933); *The Saint Anna* (1983).

5.17 Enforcement of an award as a judgment of the court

Section 26 of the Arbitration Act 1950 provides for enforcement as a judgment of the court of the award.

At one time there was a substantial body of law, including at least seven decisions of the Court of Appeal, which held that an award was not entitled to be enforced as a judgment of the court unless it was reasonably clear. In *Re Boks and Peters Rushton & Co* (1919) where the issue was raised that the contract might have been illegal because a necessary licence had not been obtained, Lord Justice Scrutton said: 'This summary method of enforcing awards is only to be used in reasonably clear cases', and he refused to make an order under section 26.

But the Court of Appeal in *Middlemiss and Gould* v. *Hartlepool Corporation* (1973) decided that Lord Justice Scrutton had gone too far. Earlier cases must now be regarded with suspicion, for the Court of Appeal in this case laid down the rule that once an award has been made and the time limit for challenging it has expired, the award becomes irrevocably final and binding; it can therefore be entered as a judgment and enforced accordingly. The earlier decision of the same court, *Smith* v. *Martin* (1925), must therefore be regarded as no longer good law. There the arbitration clause in a building contract contained the words 'the reference shall not be opened until after the completion of the work'. The court decided that arbitration had begun before the completion of the work and refused to allow the award to be registered as a judgment, leaving the successful party to sue on it, when, presumably, the unsuccessful one might raise the issue whether the arbitrator has any jurisdiction. In view of the latest decision of the Court of Appeal, there can apparently be little scope to raise such issues on application for leave to register as a judgment.

An award is to be enforced as a judgment unless there was real ground for doubting its validity, Lord Denning held in the *Middlemiss and Gould* case. The mere fact that there was a point of law which one side or the other thought had been wrongly decided did not make the award invalid.

Chapter 6
Arbitration and the courts

6.01 Interference by the courts

'It is well known that English law is nearly unique in the degree of interference it permits the courts in the conduct of arbitrations and the settlement of disputes thereby,' said Mr Justice Mocatta in *Prodexport* v. *E.D. & F. Man Ltd* (1972). The word 'interference' was his lordship's word. It is very apt and will be used here. One of the reasons advanced for the Arbitration Act 1979 by its supporters was that interference by the courts over arbitrations held in England was so great that parties to disputes avoided holding arbitrations in England and thereby the country was losing a valuable invisible export (i.e. lawyers' fees) which had somehow been quantified at £500 million a year, according to the Commercial Court Committee.

The 1979 enactment has done nothing to commend arbitration in England to overseas parties and, as the present author and many others prophesied at that time, has actually increased the interference of the courts. The history of the first case to be heard under the provisions of the Act, *The Nema* (1981), is eloquent proof of that, as is the vast flood of applications to the courts for leave to appeal under the Act.

'Litigation and arbitration are but two branches of the same industry, one public the other private,' said Mr Justice Donaldson, as he then was, in the *Bremer Vulkan* case (1981). One is tempted to ask 'what industry can that be?' unless it be the industry of creating work for lawyers. Certainly the 1979 Act has done that whatever other arguments may have been advanced in support of it.

6.02 Had the courts inherent jurisdiction to set aside awards?
The Arbitration Act 1698 conferred power on any court of law or equity to set aside 'any arbitration or umpirage procured by corruption

or undue means' which should, as a result, be 'judged and esteemed void and of none effect'.

The power of the High Court to set aside an award is conferred by section 23(2) and is limited to situations where:

(a) The arbitrator has misconducted himself.
(b) The arbitrator has misconducted the proceedings. These words were added by the 1934 Act to the 1889 Act as a sop to arbitrators who complained that 'misconduct of an arbitrator' suggested moral delinquency. There is no reason to believe that they changed the law in any way whatsoever.
(c) The arbitration has been improperly procured (whatever that may mean).
(d) The award has been improperly procured.

There are a number of early cases in which one party deliberately deceived an arbitrator: *South Sea* v. *Bumstead* (1734); *Mitchell* v. *Harris* (1793); *Medcalfe* v. *Ives* (1737); *Gartside* v. *Gartside* (1796).

Where an award is set aside, the court has power to order that any money payable on the award shall be brought into court pending the determination of the application: section 23 (3) of the 1950 Act.

In recent times, it has been claimed that the courts have always had an inherent jurisdiction to set aside awards for any 'misconduct' of the arbitrator: see Lord Justice Parker in *Meyer* v. *Leanse* (1958). No authorities were quoted in support of that proposition, or by *Russell on Arbitration*, 19th edition, 1979 for the statement on page 128: 'At common law there was an inherent jurisdiction to set aside.' The proposition is not supported by earlier textbooks. Had it existed, there would have been no need for the 1698 Act, which was strictly limited to cases of dishonesty on the part of the arbitrator.

There appears to be no case before 1802 when a court set aside an award for anything other than corruption or fraud, pursuant to the Act of 1698.

6.03 'Errors of fact or law' on the face of the award

Section 1(1) of the 1979 Act provides that:

'the High Court shall not have jurisdiction to set aside or remit an award on an arbitration agreement on the ground of errors of fact or law on the face of the award.'

The curious may wonder when the High Court ever acquired such a jurisdiction, since such power is not contained in any statute. The history can be traced back to the case of *Kent* v. *Elstob* (1802) in which the court held that it had jurisdiction to set aside a *speaking* award for error of law on the face of it.

A host of spurious reasons have been advanced to justify that invasion of the authority of arbitrators. Since it is now ancient history, it is not proposed to rehearse them.

But as Lord Denning explained in an ingenious argument, what the judges currently think is the law, and always has been the law, may conflict with binding authority to the contrary.

'When the House of Lords held in 1976 that judgment could be given for a debt in a foreign currency, it held that that was the law of the land and always had been the law of the land, but the judges had never appreciated it before.

From 1854, when attachment of debt was introduced, a sum owing in foreign currency by a person within the jurisdiction here was "a debt" which could be attached, although no one had ever thought so before, and the courts had previously held to the contrary': *Choice Investments Ltd* v. *Jeromimnon* (1980).

Mr Justice Mocatta in *Prodexport* v. *E. D. & F. Man Ltd* (1972), said that power to set aside arbitrators' awards for errors of law or fact was a development which has 'often been regretted and which led to highly technical and unsatisfactory refinements'. It is also the reason why the practice of giving non-speaking awards became established in England, and why there was a strong disincentive for parties to an international contract to agree to have an arbitration in England.

By 1857, Mr Justice Williams could say:

'The law has for many years been settled and remains so to this day, that where a cause or matters of difference are referred to an arbitrator ... he is constituted the sole and final judge of all questions, both of law and of fact.

Many cases have fully established that position ... the court has invariably met these applications by saying "you have constituted your own tribunal. You are bound by its decision."

The only exceptions to that rule are cases where the award is the result of corruption or fraud and one other, which, although it is to be regretted, is now I think firmly established, *viz*: where a question of law necessarily arises on the face of the award or upon some paper accompanying and forming part of the award.

Though the propriety of this latter may very well be doubted, I think it may be considered as established': *Hodgkinson* v. *Fernie* (1857).

No statute has ever expressly authorised judges to remit or set aside awards for 'error of fact or law on the face of the award'. It is a power the judges took to themselves without the authority of the common law or the legislature. On this point the 1979 Act is therefore merely declaratory of what the common law was formerly. The difficulties which arose because of it were therefore entirely of the judges' own making and arose from an assumption of authority not conferred by statute or the common law.

6.04 Power to remit to an arbitrator

It was formerly generally accepted, however, that the power of the High Court to remit a case to an arbitrator for reconsideration is entirely statutory and did not exist as common law: *Simpson* v. *IRC* (1914).

It first appeared in section 8 of the Common Law Procedure Act 1854 and is now contained in section 22 of the 1950 Act.

The High Court or a judge thereof may remit 'the matters referred or any of them, to the reconsideration of the arbitrator or umpire.' The Rules of the High Court provide that that application shall be by way of motion before a single judge, except where the arbitrator or umpire is a High Court judge, in which case application has to be made to the Court of Appeal.

Of the original enactment, it was said:

'It was not intended ... to alter the general law as to the principles upon which the courts had been in the habit of acting in determining whether they would or would not set aside awards but merely to give the court power to remit the matter to the arbitrator for reconsideration ... where it turned out that there was a fatal defect in the award, but of such a nature as not to render it expedient to set aside the award and thus render nugatory all the expense that had been incurred': Cockburn CJ in *Hodgkinson* v. *Fernie* (1857).

The grounds on which a case may be remitted to an arbitrator for reconsideration were classified by Lord Justice Chitty in *Montgomery*

Jones v. *Liebenthal & Co* in 1898 as:

(i) want of any of the requirements of a valid award
(ii) *misconduct* on the part of the arbitrator
(iii) *additional evidence* discovered after the award
(iv) *mistake* admitted by the arbitrator.

However, it is said that a case can be remitted where it is expedient to ensure that no injustice has been done: *Compagnie Financière* v. *Oy Vehna A B* (1963).

In the case of *European Grain and Shipping Ltd* v. *Cremer* (1982) Mr Justice Bingham remitted a clear and unambiguous finding by the Grain and Feed Trade Association Board of Appeal so that the Board might 'elucidate the basis of its decision. The parties are entitled to as just an answer as the court can give,' he said.

Since 1954, in fact, the courts have claimed a power to remit any award even if there is no misconduct by the arbitrator, and quite apart from the provisions of the statute. This started with the case of *Peter Cassidy Seed* v. *Osuustukkukauppaa* (1954) and continued in *Franz Haniel* v. *Sabre* (1962), *Compagnie Financière* v. *Oy Vehna* (1963), *Aktiebolaget* v. *Berg* (1964), *Exormis Shipping* v. *Oonsoo* (1975), *GKN* v. *Matbro* (1976), *The Aros* (1978).

The better view, however, is that cases should only be remitted if there is such inconsistency or ambiguity in the operative parts of the award that it cannot be enforced as a judgment of the court: Mr Justice McNair in *Oleificio Lucchi SPA* v. *Northern Sales Ltd* (1965), expressly approved by Sir John Donaldson MR in *Moran* v. *Lloyd's* (1983) where he said: 'Neither section 22 nor section 23 is available as a backdoor method of circumventing the restrictions upon the courts' power to intervene in arbitral proceedings which have been created by the 1975 Act.'

County court judges, whose jurisdiction is entirely statutory, had been given no power to remit awards but apparently had power to set them aside: *Meyer* v. *Leanse* (1958). This power is not affected by the 1979 Act which is expressly limited to the High Court.

6.05 The former case stated procedure

The 'case stated' procedure originated with the medieval criminal courts of Quarter Sessions: it came to be applied to arbitration by the Common Law Procedure Act 1854 and ended up as section 21 of the 1950 Act. A case could be stated for the opinion of the High Court:

(a) at any time in the course of the reference, or

(b) in the form of an interim award: or

(c) in the form of the final award with alternatives.

Those in the course of the reference were termed 'consultative case'.

Section 21(1) of the 1950 Act, since repealed, entitled an arbitrator to state such a case and required him to do so if so ordered by the court.

The Commercial Court Committee in its *Report on Arbitration* explained why they recommended the repeal of section 21(1). It started by pointing out that a case stated was a 'somewhat formalised document', for which arbitrators often felt the need for legal advice. But it continued:

'A much more serious objection is that the procedure is capable of being used by undeserving parties for the sole purpose of postponing the day when they have to meet their commitments. Applications to the court and possible appeals created enormous delays. As a result of the existence of the entrenched right of judicial review which exists in England, these arbitrations are held elsewhere ... Whilst it is impossible to compute the resulting loss to the national economy, it is not inconsiderable and has indeed been put as high as £500 million a year.'

That being so, it is surprising that although section 21 of the 1950 Act has been repealed, judicial review has been retained and the consultative case stated has been brought back under another name by section 2 of the 1979 Act.

6.06 Case stated could not be excluded

In a most unfortunate decision, it was held by the Court of Appeal in *Czarnikow & Co.* v. *Roth Schmidt & Co.* (1932) that if the parties contracted not to seek the opinion of the courts on a case stated, this was void as contrary to public policy, as ousting the jurisdiction of the courts. Members of the Refined Sugar Association entered into contracts which included the term:

'It is expressly agreed that the obtaining of an award from the tribunal shall be a condition precedent to the right of either party to sue the other in respect of any claim arising out of any such contract. Neither buyer, seller, trustee in bankruptcy, nor any other person as aforesaid, shall require, nor shall they apply to the court to require any arbitrators to state in the form of a special case for the opinion of the court any question of law arising in the reference, but such question of law shall be determined in the arbitration in manner herein directed.'

Lord Justice Barker said:

'As an agreement it ousts the jurisdiction of courts of law and is consequently against public policy and void. The importance of maintaining in its integrity the rule of law in reference to public policy is, in my opinion, a matter of considerable importance at the present time. Powerful trade organisations are encouraging, if not compelling, their members and persons who enter into contracts with their members to agree, as far as they lawfully can do so, to abstain from submitting their disputes to the decision of a court of law.'

Lord Justice Scrutton added:

'In my view, to allow English citizens to agree to exclude this safeguard for the administration of the law is contrary to public policy. There must be no Alsatia in England where the King's writ does not run.' (Alsatia: the name of the precinct of White Friars in London at one time a sanctuary for debtors and criminals.)

All of the judges dilated upon the evils that would follow if the parties were able to exclude review by the courts on a case stated. None seemed to have noticed that originally arbitrators in England were entitled to exercise their powers in accordance with their own sense of justice and not in accordance with the law [1.04]. Nor did they observe that in Scotland at that time, there was no reference to the courts by way of case stated, without any of the evils they all confidently predicted. If there could be no Alsatia in England, the whole of Scotland could be one.

The Court of Appeal was patently smarting under the recent reversal of its judgment in *Atlantic Shipping* v. *Louis Dreyfus & Co.* (1922) by reason of 'the House of Lords putting an entirely different construction upon the agreement between the parties from that which was put upon it in this court'.

Moreover, one of its strong objections to the arbitration scheme of the Refined Sugar Association was that it excluded lawyers from appearing at the hearing. As Lord Justice Scrutton said: 'When they are persons untrained in law and when, as in this case, they decline to

allow persons trained in law to address them on legal points, there is
every probability of their going wrong.'

The court chose to ignore the fact that it is always possible for parties
to an agreement to exclude the jurisdiction of the courts. In *Rose &
Frank* v. *Crompton Bros* (1925) the parties entered into an agreement
which provided (no doubt to avoid USA law about monopoly
agreements) 'this is not entered into as a formal and legal agreement
and shall not be subject to legal jurisdiction in the law courts either of
the United States or England'. Similarly the jurisdiction of the courts is
ousted by all football pool forms which provide that 'it shall not be
attended by or give rise to any legal relationship, rights, duties or
consequences whatsoever or be legally enforceable or the subject of
litigation': *Appleson* v. *Littlewood* (1939). In that case Lord Justice
Scott said: 'The rule of public policy, which takes precedence of all
others in a case like this, is that people must be bound by the
arrangement they have made.'

It was a principle which was disregarded by Court of Appeal in the
Roth Schmidt case.

6.07 Preliminary points of law

Consultative case stated has been abolished. But it has been re-
introduced under another name by section 2 of the 1979 Act.

As Lord Justice Donaldson said in *Babanaft International Co. SA* v.
Avant Petroleum Inc (1982) section 2 is the 'successor in title to the old
consultative case which aptly describes its nature. Put colloquially, the
arbitrator or the parties nip down the road to pick the brains of one of
Her Majesty's judges, and thus enlightened, resumes the arbitration.'

The willingness and alacrity with which Her Majesty's judges will
answer questions is perhaps overestimated by his lordship. Lord
Devlin as a High Court judge refused to deal with one case stated,
saying: 'The court is not at the beck and call of an arbitrator to answer
whatever questions an arbitrator may want to put to it.' The question
he had been asked to decide in the case was the then highly relevant and
difficult one of the finality of an architect's final certificate under the
JCT contract (the RIBA contract, as it was called in those days). In
Windsor RDC v. *Otterway and Try Ltd* (1954) the employers alleged
that the builder had been overpaid, and the arbitrator needed to know
whether the architects' final certificate was conclusive as to the amount
due or whether he had power under the arbitration clause to reopen it.

Section 2 of the 1979 Act allows reference at any time in the course of a hearing by any of the parties for the High Court to determine 'any question of law arising in the course of the reference'. There is, as a condition precedent, a requirement that either:

(a) the arbitrator has to give his consent: or
(b) *all* the parties have consented

It is too early to say whether the courts will find some way of reviewing whether an arbitrator should give his consent or not. Under the old law not only could he be ordered to state a case for the opinion of the High Court but if he refused to do so, he was guilty of misconduct if he did not adjourn the proceedings while application was made to the court for an order that he should do so: *re Palmer & Co. and Hosken & Co* (1898).

Section 21 may have been repealed but some ingenious way may well be found of re-introducing it by the back door.

In any case, parties to an arbitration may find it less than fruitful to 'pick the brains' of Her Majesty's judges. In *British Westinghouse* v. *Underground Electric Railway* (1912), turbines supplied to the railway proved defective and, without prejudice to the right to claim damages for breach of contract, they were used for a time and then replaced by others. In an arbitration to assess damages, a case was stated for the High Court as to whether the cost of the replacement turbines was recoverable as damages. The High Court directed that it was and the arbitrator made his award, as he was bound to, accordingly. The party who had lost then moved the High Court to set aside the award on the ground that an error of law appeared on the face of the award. After an expensive trip from the High Court to the Court of Appeal and thence to the House of Lords, that tribunal held that the award should be set aside on the grounds that an error in law appeared on the face of the award.

From a determination under section 2 of the 1979 Act, an appeal would be to the Court of Appeal and thence to the House of Lords, with all the potentiality for delay involved.

However, the Supreme Court Act 1981 section 148(3) and Schedule 5 of that Act altered the 1979 Act by adding a new section 2A, that no appeal would lie from such a decision unless the High Court gives leave to appeal and certifies that the decision is 'either one of general public importance or one which for some other special reason should be considered by the Court of Appeal'; but the Court of Appeal itself, if such leave was refused, has power to grant leave.

It is surely a poor statute that requires amendment less than two years after it has been enacted; particularly as the amendment still permits a multiplicity of hearings.

6.08 Appeals under the 1979 Act

Having abolished appeals by way of case stated and removed the jurisdiction of the High Court, if it ever had any, to set aside an award on the ground of errors of fact or law appearing on the face of the award, the 1979 Act re-introduces the same thing in a slightly different form in section 2.

An appeal now lies to the High Court on 'any question of law arising out of an award'. What is a question of law will be discussed shortly [6.10]. To ensure that one can be found, arbitrators can be required now to give reasons [5.04] subject to the conditions set out in section 1(6) and 1(6A) added by the Supreme Court Act 1981.

The appeal may be brought with the leave of all other parties to the reference. The consent of the arbitrator is not required.

If all the parties do not agree on an appeal the court can give leave, subject to the proviso that it shall only do so 'if the determination of the question of law could substantially affect the rights of one or more of the parties'.

Not content with an appeal on a point of law alone, the House of Lords in *The Nema* (1981) appears to have widened the powers of the courts to interfere with awards by writing into the Act the principles it laid down for subordinate tribunals in an income tax case *Edwards* v. *Bairstow* (1956).

The General Commissioner of Income Tax had found as a fact that certain transactions in which a taxpayer had entered were not an 'adventure ... in the nature of trade'. Lord Simonds said that: 'though it is a pure finding of fact, it may be set aside ... if it appears that the Commissioners have acted ... upon a view of the facts which could not reasonably be entertained ...'

Lord Radcliffe said: 'If the case contains anything which *ex facie* is bad law ... it is obviously erroneous in point of law. But without any misconception appearing *ex facie*, it may be that the facts found are such that no person acting judicially and properly instructed as to the relevant law could have come to the determination under appeal. In those circumstances, too, the court must intervene ...'

In *The Nema*, without reference to the words of the 1979 statute, Lord Diplock said expressly that in appeals under section 1 of that Act, the court should proceed on the principles laid down in what he referred to as 'the classic passage' in the speech of Lord Radcliffe in the *Edwards'* case. He then added that he approved of Lord Denning's observation in the present case that the court should interfere with an award not only where the arbitrator misdirected himself in law but also where *'the decision was such that no reasonable arbitrator could reach'*. (author's italics)

The effect of this decision appears to be that the courts have greater powers under the 1979 Act, as thus interpreted by the House of Lords, than they did under the old case stated procedure and the former 'error of law' on the face of the award.

However, leave to appeal to the High Court should only be given by 'commercial judges' as defined by the Rules of the Supreme Court.

In the case of *F. G. Whitley & Sons Co. Ltd* v. *Clwyd County Council* (1982) Clwyd County Council entered into a contract with F. G. Whitley & Sons Ltd on the ICE Conditions (5th Edition June 1973 version) modified in important respects. A dispute arose as to whether the cost of infill materials to form embankments to a road was covered by the contract or amounted to a variation, for which an additional £340,000 was claimed by the contractor. An arbitrator was appointed by the President of the ICE.

Leave was given by Mr Justice Mais, who is not a 'commercial judge', for the Council to appeal, under section 1(2) of the Arbitration Act 1979 from an interim award of the arbitrator. From his decision, he gave leave to appeal to the Court of Appeal.

There, Lord Justice Donaldson said:

'Under the terms of Order 73 rule 6 of the Rules of the Supreme Court all applications for leave to appeal to the High Court against an award of an arbitrator "shall be heard by a commercial judge, unless any such judge otherwise directs".

This rule has the effect of channelling all applications under rules 2 and 3 in the first instance to the commercial court. This rule recognises that in practice the subject of arbitration is substantially a commercial matter and should be dealt with by a commercial judge ... and also to enable uniformity of practice and procedure.'

He said Mr Justice Mais was wrong to grant leave to appeal from the award.

'This is a one-off contract and the construction of it depends upon familiarity with the terminology and practices of the construction industry. It is clearly a case in which leave to appeal should not have been given.'

And in *Babanaft International Co. SA* v. *Avant Petroleum Inc.* (1982) it was decided that leave to appeal to the Court of Appeal from a High Court judge under section 1(2) of the Arbitration Act 1979 will be restricted in future to cases where the point of law is definitive enough to settle the entire dispute between the parties and, so far as 'one-off' clauses are concerned, where it is apparent on the reading of the judgment without the benefit of argument that the decision is patently wrong.

Thus the courts have sought by their own legislation to limit the unhappy consequences of the 1979 Act.

6.09 What is a question of law?

The difficulties of deciding what is a question of law are well illustrated by the question which Lord Denning raised, but did not answer, in *Prota Nacional* v. *Skibsaktieselkapet* (1981). 'Is a question of war or no war a question of fact or a question of law?' A charterparty had a clause which provided for revocation in the event of war involving England or France. Both countries were then engaged in the Suez misadventure.

The following have been accepted as questions of law:

— 'Whether on the facts found, the claimants are entitled to the relief claimed or any part thereof': *Woodhouse AC Israel Cocoa Ltd* v. *Nigerian Produce* (1972).
— 'Whether there was any evidence to support' a particular finding of fact: *Nello Simoni* v. *A/S etc. Straun* (1949).
— 'Whether or not a contract has been frustrated by some supervening event which prevents one or other party from performing what he has undertaken': *The Angelica* (1972).
— 'Whether there are implied terms in a contract.'
— 'Whether a term of a contract is a condition or a warranty': *Oppenheim* v. *Fraser* (1876).
— 'Whether there has been a subsequent variation of the terms of a contract': *Woodhouse AC* v. *Nigerian Produce* (1972).
— 'Whether a contract has been repudiated': *Charles Weis* v. *Peters, Rushton* (1922).

Even the period of delay which has to elapse before a contract is frustrated is now held to be a question of law and not of fact.

The interpretation of the meaning of the words in contracts and documents, the 'construction' as lawyers term it, is always a question of law, even though what the parties meant is best known to themselves and an arbitrator from their particular industry. A valiant attempt by Lord Denning to bind a court to the meaning of a term which had been found by a trade arbitrator failed in *The Hadjitsakos* (1975).

The first case to come to court under the 1979 Act, *Pioneer Shipping Ltd & Ano* v. *BTF (The Nema)* (1981), was concerned with whether or not a voyage charterparty was frustrated by a prolonged strike at the loading port. An experienced and widely respected shipping arbitrator held that it was. After eight court hearings, three in the House of Lords, it was decided that he was right.

A strong reasoned dissent by one of the arbitrators is no reason for giving leave to appeal: *Halcoussis & Co.* v. *Stinnes Interact GmbH* (1982).

6.10 What is misconduct?

Section 23 of the 1950 Act [6.02] empowers the courts to set aside 'where an arbitrator or umpire has misconducted himself or the proceedings'.

'The settlement of disputes by arbitration is a consensual process, and what is usually meant by misconduct is a departure by the arbitrators from the procedure which has the express or implied agreement of the parties, although considerations of public policy can be involved,' said Mr Justice Diplock, as he then was, in *London Export Corporation Ltd* v. *Jubilee Coffee Roasting Co.* (1958).

> 'In deciding whether or not there has been such a departure, the courts now recognise that the parties may well intend to confer upon the tribunal of their choice a wide discretion as to the procedure to be adopted and are properly reluctant to intervene.
>
> However, in the absence of express agreement to the contrary, the courts assume that the parties, as reasonable people, intended that the procedure should be such as would not only tend, but appear to tend, to the achievement of a just result.'

The following have been held to be misconduct by the courts:

(a) receiving documents from one party without showing them to the other: *Woodridge Timber Ltd* v. *Branntorps Travaru* (1982)
(b) where one party appeared represented by counsel, refusing to

adjourn to allow the other party to instruct counsel: *Tatem Steam* v. *Anglo–Canadian (1935)*

(c) receiving evidence after the close of an oral hearing: *Eastcheap Dried Fruit* v. *N. V. Gebroeders (1962)*

(d) indicating to the parties that the arbitrator intended to view the property in dispute and failing to do so: *Micklewright* v. *Mullock* (1974)

(e) accepting documents, without translation, in Italian when one of two arbitrators did not know the language and the other had a very imperfect knowledge of it: *Rotheray* v. *Carlo* (1961)

(f) failure to make an award which can be enforced as a judgment of the court: *Margulies* v. *Dafnis* (1958).

(g) 'any failure to give a party a reasonable and proper opportunity to put forward his own case and to rebut that of the opposite party': *Moran* v. *Lloyd's* (1983).

In *Thomas Borthwick (Glasgow) Ltd* v. *Faure Fairclough Ltd* (1968), Mr Justice Donaldson said:

'Lawyers are well aware that arbitrators take it ill if they are accused of misconduct, perhaps because the word has acquired a technical meaning in a quite different realm which occupies so much of the time of the Probate, Divorce and Admiralty Division of the High Court.

It is therefore customary to add, in an apologetic parenthesis, that what is meant is technical misconduct. Whether or not "misconduct" is an appropriate term, "technical" is certainly inappropriate.

What is complained of here – I venture to think that the same can be said of all allegations of misconduct by arbitrators – is that the board was in breach of its duty to act fairly and to be seen to act fairly.'

It has been said, however, that if the parties agree expressly or impliedly on the procedure it will not be misconduct on the part of the arbitrator if he disregards any of the rules of natural justice: *Norman Hughes* v. *Ruthin Borough Council* (1972). *Contra* it has been held that if the agreed customary procedure violates natural justice, as where an umpire whose award was under appeal was allowed to confer in private with the appeal committee, the award would be set aside: *London Export* v. *Jubilee Coffee* (1958).

It can, however, be safely said that 'misconduct' must be related, however loosely, to the express or implied terms of the arbitration agreement. Mr Justice Atkin did define it in *Williams* v. *Wallis & Cox* (1914) as 'such a mishandling of the arbitration as is likely to amount to some substantial miscarriage of justice'. Had the courts confined themselves to this definition there would be no cause for complaint.

Where parties have chosen their own arbitrators and incurred expense of a hearing, a discretion to set aside the award and so render the expenditure nugatory should be sparingly exercised, it was said in *Kiril Mischeff Ltd* v. *Constant Smith* (1950) following *Hodgkinson* v. *Fernie* (1857).

'The approach that a court makes to an award has always been to support the validity of the award and to make every reasonable intendment and presumption in its favour,' said Lord Justice Parker in *Mayer* v. *Leanse* (1958). If only it were true!

'It is doubtful whether unconsistency between one part of an award and another can ever be misconduct,' said Sir John Donaldson MR in *Moran* v. *Lloyd's*, and *Halsbury's Laws of England*, 4th Edition, Vol 2 (1973), para. 622 is incorrect in so stating.

6.11 Time of application to set aside

Application to set aside or to remit the award is made by an originating motion in the Queen's Bench Division, and comes before a single judge in court. By Order 73 rule 5 there is a time limit of *six weeks* after the time when the award is made and *published to the parties.*

The notice of motion must state in general terms the grounds of the application and if the motion is based on evidence by affidavit, a copy of the affidavit must be served with the notice.

The arbitrator (or umpire) has no privilege in the proceedings and can be called as a witness. It would appear, however, that he can decline to answer questions designed to show that he exceeded his jurisdiction. It would also seem that he cannot be called to give evidence in chief about what factors he took into account in arriving at his award, but that he can be cross-examined about such matters by the party that does not call him. Admissions made by the parties before him can be given in evidence on either side.

6.12 Waiver of irregularities

A party may by conduct or words waive rights he may have to object to an award subsequently on the ground of irregularity. If, for example, he consents to the other party calling on the arbitrator alone and producing books of accounts, he cannot subsequently object to the award on the ground that there had been a private meeting between the arbitrator and the other party: *Hamilton* v. *Bankin* (1850).

So, too, if one arbitrator in a London arbitration [4.02] allows the umpire to inspect the other's file, without requiring its production to him, he cannot subsequently object to the award. If he admits inadmissible evidence without protest, he may have waived the right he would otherwise have to object to the award.

'But a waiver must be an intentional act with knowledge,' said Lord Chelmsford in *Darnley* v. *London, Chatham and Dover Railway* (1867). And when one party, not a lawyer and not represented, did not protest or reserve his rights when the arbitrator refused to show him a document which reflected seriously on his interests, he was held not to have waived his right to have the award set aside for misconduct of the arbitrator: *CMA Martin Engineering Ltd* v. *J. Donne Holdings Ltd* (1980). Where the iregularity is serious the courts look for a positive consent or direct proof of direct acquiescence.

6.13 Mistakes admitted by an arbitrator

The arbitrator is *functus officio* – that is, he has no powers left – as soon as he has made his award. He has power to correct minor clerical errors (section 17 of the 1950 Act) but if he realises he has made a mistake he has no power to correct it. This applies whether or not the award has been taken up. Even if he tears up one award before it has been taken up and makes a fresh one, the second award is invalid.

It is doubtful whether an award can be set aside for a mistake admitted by an arbitrator. Section 23(2) does not appear wide enough to cover it and the general rule at common law was expressed by Baron Parke in 1843:

> 'I think it better to adhere to the general principle of not allowing awards to be set aside for mistakes, although such principle may be productive of some injustice in the particular case, than go one step beyond it.'

However, there are recorded cases where, prior to 1854, the courts did set aside an award for a mistake notified by the arbitrator to the court but there is no principle discernible in them. Since 1854, when the courts acquired the power to remit, there do not seem to be any reported occasions, and remission is clearly the appropriate remedy.

Now that the courts have power to remit, it is obviously the more appropriate course to send it back, since it allows the arbitrator who has admitted a mistake to correct it by making a fresh award. But the court has to be satisfied not merely that the arbitrator has admitted it, but that in fact he has made a mistake in the sense that his award does not correctly represent the adjudication he arrived at. He cannot change his mind subsequent to his adjudication. If the award corresponds with what he intended, it is no mistake. The mistake must be that the award does not correspond with what he intended. The power contained in section 17 of the 1950 Act does not empower him to alter an award so as to correct errors in expressing his intention.

'In the present case, the arbitrator made an award and he included in his award certain costs incurred in a matter between one of the parties and a third party, and the question arose whether the words he had used included all those costs or only some of them.

The award was sent back to the arbitrator and he told Mr Lewis, of the firm of solicitors representing the respondents, that he certainly had made an error in writing his award, and he amended it so that it read, as he said, as he had originally intended that it should read.

That was not correcting a clerical mistake within the meaning of [Act] ...

What is meant there is something almost mechanical – a slip of the pen or something of that kind': *Sutherland & Co.* v. *Hannevig Bros Ltd* (1920).

6.14 Does removal invalidate interim awards?

Whether the removal of the arbitrator and the setting aside of his award under section 24(1) and 24(2) invalidated any interim award he may have made was discussed in *Fisher & Ors* v. *W. G. Wellfair Ltd* (1981) by Mr Justice Ackner when he said:

'I have to deal with a further new point which is the question as to whether the setting aside of the award of 12 April and ordering the removal of the arbitrator also has the effect of cancelling his interim award ... I do not think it does. It was a separate, self-contained decision given in a form designed to enable the applicants to challenge it if they were so minded and they chose not to do so. None of the deficiencies in procedure which are alleged in this case – that is, no suggestion of any breach of the rules of natural justice – were ever suggested so far as that interim award is concerned and I can see no reason in logic why that decision does not stand.'

The decision in the interim award cost the claimants £37,000 and was on the apparently erroneous ground that since the arbitration was taking place under the HB5 contract, the failure of the respondents to provide a specially strengthened roof capable of use as a roof garden was not a breach of the requirements of the NHBC even though it was in the contract plans.

6.15 Less than *Angelic Grace*

In addition to the power to interfere with an award either by setting it aside under section 23(2) of the 1950 Act or allowing an appeal under section 1(3) of the 1979 Act, in several cases in the late 1970s and early 1980s, a doctrine emerged from the courts that they were entitled to interfere at any stage in arbitral proceedings. One aspect of this has been dealt with already [6.02]. But another was contained in the case of *Japan Line* v. *Aggeliki Charis (The Angelic Grace)* (1980). In that, the Court of Appeal asserted that it had a general and inherent power to supervise and interfere with impending arbitrations, quite apart from the powers conferred by statute. It is to be hoped that the House of Lords has disposed of this doctrine by *Paal Wilson* (1982) but no doubt it will be revived in some other form.

It has been said that the courts also have power to intrude upon men's contractual obligations by means of declaratory judgments: see Mustill and Boyd's, *Commercial Arbitration*, page 468 and *Russell on Arbitration* 19th Edition, page 1979. No authority is quoted for this, no examples are given and no source for this jurisdiction is advanced by any of these learned authors. If in fact the courts have done this, which may in these circumstances be doubted, it must be, it is submitted, totally unauthorised by statute or common law. What is more, nothing is advanced to indicate what the consequences are if, as happened in the case of a local authority, a party choses to disregard a declaratory judgment; still less what power the courts have by declaration to bind parties not within the jurisdiction.

It is, however, undoubtedly true that the courts have on occasions issued injunctions to restrain arbitrators from acting as such in exercise of a claimed inherent jurisdiction: see *Malmesbury Railway* v. *Budd* (1876); *Beddow* v. *Beddow* (1878).

It is highly doubtful whether the courts ever had any such inherent jurisdiction, but in any event, after the 1889 Act it is clear from *Oakland Metal* v. *Benaim* (1953) that any such power must be entirely statutory, under section 23(1) or 24.

6.16 Summary of courts' powers to interfere

It may therefore be convenient to summarise at this point all the ways in which the courts in England are authorised by statute to interfere with arbitrations:

(a) apparently (although no statute expressly authorises it) to grant leave to one party to revoke the appointment of an arbitrator: section 1, 1950 Act

(b) to stay litigation in their discretion if there is an arbitration agreement in force in the case of domestic arbitration: section 4, 1950; there is no such power in the case of non-domestic proceedings: section 1

(c) to appoint a single arbitrator in circumstances set out in section 10(1), 10(2), 10(3) and 10(4)

(d) to order that anybody in prison shall appear to give evidence before an arbitrator: section 2(3)

(e) to order on application in arbitration cases:
    (1) security for costs
    (2) discovery of documents
    (3) giving of evidence on affidavit
    (4) examination of witnesses on commission
    (5) preservation or disposal of goods
    (6) securing amounts in dispute (possibly by a *Mareva* injunction)
    (7) preservation etc. of property
    (8) interim injunction
    provided that these orders do not prejudice powers vested in an arbitrator: section 12

(f) to remove an arbitrator who does not exercise reasonable dispatch: section 13

(g) to remit an award to the arbitrator: section 22

(h) to remove an arbitrator who has 'misconducted himself or the proceedings': section 23(1)

(i) in such cases, to set the award aside: section 23(2)

(j) to revoke the appointment of an arbitrator if he 'is not or may not be impartial': section 24

(k) to order that an arbitration agreement shall cease to have effect (and to revoke appointment of arbitrator) if
    (1) it deals with future disputes, and
    (2) the question arises whether any party has been guilty of fraud

(l) to appoint new arbitrator/s or umpire where these are removed or their appointment revoked: section 25

(m) to enrol an award as judgment of court: section 26

(n) to extend time for commencing arbitration proceedings: section 27, Arbitration Act 1979

(o) on appeal on a point of law only to confirm, vary, set aside or remit an award: section 1(2)

(p) to order an arbitrator to state reasons in certain circumstances: section 1(5)(b)

(q) to determine preliminary points of law: section 2

(r) to authorise an arbitrator to continue with reference: section 5(2).

These would appear to be the entire powers vested in the High Court with the authority of the legislature.

6.17 Exclusion agreements

The much heralded right to exclude judicial review, contained in section 3 of the 1979 Act, turns out on close examination to be of much less value than was claimed publicly.

To start with, it prohibits any agreement whether in a domestic or non-domestic arbitration which would:

(a) prohibit or restrict access to the High Court, or

(b) restrict the jurisdiction of that court, or

(c) prohibit or restrict the making of a reasoned award.

The section is far more restrictive of liberty to contract than under the former case stated procedure [6.06].

Secondly, all the sort of contracts where the parties are likely, for good reason, to want to exclude appeals to the High Court are termed 'Special Category' cases. These are barred from making valid exclusion agreements unless they come under section 4(2)(ii) Special Category cases:

(a) A question or claim falling within the Admirality jurisdiction of the High Court. It is outside the scope of this book to try to define Admiralty jurisdiction. Reference should be made to the section 20 of the Supreme Court Act 1981, which is considerably wider than questions about the collision of ships at sea. It may even be wide enough to include the collision of a ship with a jetty, which was the subject of a construction industry dispute under the terms of the government form of contract CC/Works/1 in *Farr* v. *The Admiralty* (1953).

(b) Disputes arising out of a contract of insurance.

(c) Disputes arising out of a commodity contract.

What is a commodity contract is set out in the section and in SI 1979 No. 754. These include:

The London Cocoa Terminal Market
The London Coffee Terminal Market
The London Grain Futures Market
The London Metal Exchange
The London Rubber Terminal Market
The Gafta Soya Bean Meal Futures Market
The London Sugar Terminal Market
The London Vegetable Oil Terminal Market
The London Wool Terminal Market
The Cocoa Association of London Ltd
The Coffee Trade Federation
The Combined Edible Nut Trade Association
Federation of Oils, Seeds and Fats Associations Ltd
The General Produce Brokers' Association of London
The Grain and Feed Trade Association Ltd
The Hull Seed, Oil and Cake Association
The Liverpool Cotton Association Ltd
London Jute Association
London Rice Brokers' Association
The National Federation of Fruit and Potato Trades Ltd
The Rubber Trade Association of London
Skin, Hide and Leather Traders' Association Ltd
The Sugar Association of London
The Refined Sugar Association
The Tea Brokers' Association of London
The British Wool Confederation

The 'Special Category' cases which are valid are those in which the exclusion agreement is either made after the commencement of the arbitration *or* 'the award or question relates to a contract expressed to be governed by a law other than the laws of England and Wales'.

In the latter connection it will be noted that the word used is *expressed* i.e. there has to be a contractual term to that effect. It does not apply to cases where the proper law of the contract is clearly foreign law by reason of an *implied* term.

Moreover, unlike the definition of a 'domestic arbitration agreement' in section 3(7) of the 1979 Act, which is itself different from the definition of 'domestic arbitration agreement' in section 1(4) of the 1975 Act, the words used are 'England and Wales' and not 'the United Kingdom'.

Section 3 is highly ambiguous and it is not clear whether the parties can simply exclude the right of appeal under section 1(2) or whether it is open to the parties to exclude also the powers in section 1(5) to order the arbitrator to state reasons, preliminary points of law under section 2 and the transfer to the High Court of issues of fraud under 25(2) of the 1950 Act and section 3(3) of the 1979 Act. The learned editors of the *Supreme Court Practice*, 1982 Edition, think it covers all the powers listed in sections 3(1) and 3(3) of the 1979 Act.

The result is that it is virtually impossible to draft a satisfactory exclusion agreement which will stand up in court. The wording probably to be preferred is to make it as wide as possible: 'The parties hereby agree that no provision of the Arbitration Act 1979 shall be applicable to their reference or the award therein.' Some provisions of the Act they cannot contract out of, some they can; but only the courts can sort out what can and cannot be validly excluded.

No doubt, as a judge once said of the RIBA contract, the statute was drafted with 'a calculated lack of clarity' in order to discourage exclusion agreements.

The present position appears to be that it would be possible to write in an exclusion clause in, for example the Standard Form of Building Contract, which would be valid if it were a 'domestic arbitration agreement' as defined in section 3(7) of the 1979 Act [1.07]. Otherwise the parties can make an exclusion agreement 'after the commencement of the arbitration'.

6.18 The EEC Commission and patent arbitrations

Perhaps the most extreme case of interference with arbitration is to be found in Article 4 of the proposal for an EEC Commission regulation concerning the application of Article 85(3) of the Treaty of Rome to certain patent licensing agreements. This stipulates that the Commission must be notified directly of arbitration awards because 'Articles 85 and 86 form part of the Community's public policy, and there is an inherent risk in the case of arbitration that patent licensing agreements may be given an interpretation which goes beyond the limits imposed by this regulation'.

As Mrs Advocate General Rozès of the European Court commented in her 1982 opinion in case 258/78: 'If it were adopted, such a provision might seriously impair the right to have recourse to arbitration in an important field.'

Appendix A
Relevant statutes: Selected sections

Arbitration Act 1950

Part 1 GENERAL PROVISIONS AS TO ARBITRATION

1 *Authority of arbitrators and umpires to be irrevocable.*
The authority of an arbitrator or umpire appointed by or by virtue of an arbitration agreement shall, unless a contrary intention is expressed in the agreement, be irrevocable except by leave of the High Court or a judge thereof.

2 *Death of party*
(1) An arbitration agreement shall not be discharged by the death of any party thereto, either as respects the deceased or any other party, but shall in such an event be enforceable by or against the personal representative of the deceased.

(2) The authority of an arbitrator shall not be revoked by the death of any party by whom he was appointed.

(3) Nothing in this section shall be taken to affect the operation of any enactment or rule of law by virtue of which any right of action is extinguished by the death of a person.

3 *Bankruptcy*
(1) Where it is provided by a term in a contract to which a bankrupt is a party that any differences arising thereout or in connection therewith shall be referred to arbitration, the said term shall, if the trustee in bankruptcy adopts the contract, be enforceable by or against him so far as relates to any such differences.

(2) Where a person who has been adjudged bankrupt had, before the commencement of the bankruptcy, become a party to an

arbitration agreement, and any matter to which the agreement applies requires to be determined in connection with or for the purposes of the bankruptcy proceedings, then, if the case is one to which subsection (1) of this section does not apply, any other party to the agreement or, with the consent of the committee of inspection, the trustee in bankruptcy, may apply to the court having jurisdiction in the bankruptcy proceedings for an order directing that the matter in question shall be referred to arbitration in accordance with the agreement, and that court may, if it is of opinion that, having regard to all the circumstances of the case, the matter ought to be determined by arbitration, make an order accordingly.

4 *Staying court proceedings where there is submission to arbitration* (1) If any party to an arbitration agreement, or any person claiming through or under him, commences any legal proceedings in any court against any other party to the agreement, or any person claiming through or under him, in respect of any matter agreed to be referred, any party to those legal proceedings may at any time after appearance, and before delivering any pleadings or taking any other steps in the proceedings, apply to that court to stay the proceedings, and that court or a judge thereof, if satisfied that there is no sufficient reason why the matter should not be referred in accordance with the agreement, and that the applicant was, at the time when the proceedings were commenced, and still remains, ready and willing to do all things necessary to the proper conduct of the arbitration, may make an order staying the proceedings.

[(2) Notwithstanding anything in this Part of this Act, if any party to a submission to arbitration made in pursuance of an agreement to which the protocol set out in the First Schedule to this Act applies, or any person claiming through or under him, commences any legal proceedings in any court against any other party to the submission, or any person claiming through or under him, in respect of any matter agreed to be referred, any party to those legal proceedings may at any time after appearance, and before delivering any pleadings or taking any other steps in the proceedings, apply to that court to stay the proceedings, and that court or a judge thereof, unless satisfied that the agreement or arbitration has become inoperative or cannot proceed or that there is not in fact any dispute between the parties with regard to the matter agreed to be referred, shall make an order staying the proceedings.]

5 *Reference of interpleader issues to arbitration*

Where relief by way of interpleader is granted and it appears to the High Court that the claims in question are matters to which an arbitration agreement, to which the claimants are parties, applies, the High Court may direct the issue between the claimants to be determined in accordance with the agreement.

6 *When reference is to a single arbitrator*

Unless a contrary intention is expressed therein, every arbitration agreement shall, if no other mode of reference be provided, be deemed to include a provision that the reference shall be to a single arbitrator.

7 *Power of parties in certain cases to supply vacancy*

Where an arbitration agreement provides that the reference shall be to two arbitrators, one to be appointed by each party then, unless a contrary intention is expressed therein —

(a) if either of the appointed arbitrators refuses to act, or is incapable of acting, or dies, the party who appointed him may appoint a new arbitrator in his place;

(b) if, on such a reference, one party fails to appoint an arbitrator, either originally, or by way of substitution as aforesaid, for seven clear days after the other party having appointed his arbitrator, has served the party making default with notice to make the appointment, the party who has appointed an arbitrator may appoint that arbitrator to act as sole arbitrator in the reference and his award shall be binding on both parties as if he had been appointed by consent:

Provided that the High Court or a judge thereof may set aside any appointment made in pursuance of this section.

8 *Umpires*

(1) Unless a contrary intention is expressed therein, every arbitration agreement shall, where the reference is to two arbitrators, be deemed to include a provision that the two arbitrators may appoint an umpire at any time after they are themselves appointed, and shall do so forthwith if they cannot agree.

(2) Unless a contrary intention is expressed therein, every arbitration agreement shall, where such a provision is applicable to the reference, be deemed to include a provision that if the arbitrators have delivered to any party to the arbitration agreement, or to the umpire, a notice in writing stating that they cannot agree, the umpire may

forthwith enter on the reference in lieu of the arbitrators.

(3) At any time after the appointment of an umpire, however appointed, the High Court may, on the application of any party to the reference and notwithstanding anything to the contrary in the arbitration agreement, order that the umpire shall enter upon the reference in lieu of the arbitrators and as if he were a sole arbitrator.

10 *Power of court in certain cases to appoint an arbitrator or umpire*
(1) In any of the following cases —

  (a) where an arbitration agreement provides that the reference shall be to a single arbitrator, and all the parties do not, after differences have arisen, concur in the appointment of an arbitrator;
  (b) if an appointed arbitrator refuses to act, or is incapable of acting, or dies, and the arbitration agreement does not show that it was intended that the vacancy should not be supplied and the parties do not supply the vacancy;
  (c) where the parties or two arbitrators are required or are at liberty to appoint an umpire or third arbitrator and do not appoint him;
  (d) where an appointed umpire or third arbitrator refuses to act, or is incapable of acting, or dies, and the arbitration agreement does not show that it was intended that the vacancy should not be supplied, and the parties or arbitrators do not supply the vacancy;

any party may serve the other parties or the arbitrators, as the case may be, with a written notice to appoint or, as the case may be, concur in appointing, an arbitrator, umpire or third arbitrator, and if the appointment is not made within seven clear days after the service of the notice, the High Court or a judge thereof may, on application by the party who gave the notice, appoint an arbitrator, umpire or third arbitrator who shall have the like powers to act in the reference and make an award as if he had been appointed by consent of all parties.

(2) In any case where —

  (a) an arbitration agreement provides for the appointment of an arbitrator or umpire by a person who is neither one of the parties nor an existing arbitrator (whether the provision applies directly or in default of agreement by the parties or otherwise), and
  (b) that person refuses to make the appointment or does not make it within the time specified in the agreement or, if no time is so specified, within a reasonable time
    any party to the agreement may serve the person in question

with a written notice to appoint an arbitrator or umpire and, if the appointment is not made within seven clear days after the service of the notice, the High Court or a judge thereof may, on the application of the party who gave the notice, appoint an arbitrator or umpire who shall have the like powers to act in the reference and make an award as if he had been appointed in accordance with the terms of the agreement.

11 *Reference to official referee*

Where an arbitration agreement provides that the reference shall be to an official referee, any official referee to whom application is made shall, subject to any order of the High Court or a judge thereof as to transfer or otherwise, hear and determine the matters agreed to be referred.

12 *Conduct of proceedings, witnesses, etc*

(1) Unless a contrary intention is expressed therein, every arbitration agreement shall, where such a provision is applicable to the reference, be deemed to contain a provision that the parties to the reference, and all persons claiming through them respectively, shall, subject to any legal objection, *submit to be examined by the arbitrator* or umpire, *on oath or affirmation, in relation to the matters in dispute*, and shall, subject as aforesaid, produce before the arbitrator or umpire all documents within their possession or power respectively which may be required or called for, and do all other things which during the proceedings on the reference the arbitrator or umpire may require.

(2) Unless a contrary intention is expressed therein, every arbitration agreement shall, where such a provision is applicable to the reference, be deemed to contain a provision that the witnesses on the reference shall, if the arbitrator or umpire thinks fit, be examined on oath or affirmation.

(3) An arbitrator or umpire shall, unless a contrary intention is expressed in the arbitration agreement, *have power* to administer oaths to, or take the affirmations of, the parties to and witnesses on a reference under the agreement.

(4) Any party to a reference under an arbitration agreement may sue out a writ of subpoena ad testificandum or a writ of subpoena duces tecum, but no person shall be compelled under any such writ to produce any document which he could not be compelled to produce on the trial of an action, and the High Court or a judge thereof may order that a writ of subpoena ad testificandum or of subpoena duces tecum

shall issue to compel the attendance before an arbitrator or umpire of a witness wherever he may be within the United Kingdom.

(5) The High Court or a judge thereof may also order that a writ of habeas corpus and testificandum shall issue to bring up a prisoner for examination before an arbitrator or umpire.

(6) The High Court shall have, for the purpose of and in relation to a reference, the same power of making orders in respect of —

(a) security for costs;

(b) discovery of documents and interrogatories;

(c) the giving of evidence by affidavit;

(d) examination on oath of any witness before an officer of the High Court or any other person, and the issue of a commission or request for the examination of a witness out of the jurisdiction.

(e) the preservation, interim custody or sale of any goods which are the subject matter of the reference;

(f) securing the amount in dispute in the reference;

(g) the detention, preservation or inspection of any property or thing which is the subject of the reference or as to which any question may arise therein, and authorising for any of the purposes aforesaid any persons to enter upon or into any land or building in the possession of any party to the reference, or authorising any samples to be taken or any observation to be made or experiment to be tried which may be necessary or expedient for the purpose of obtaining full information or evidence; and

(h) interim injunctions or the appointment of a receiver;

as it has for the purpose of and in relation to an action or matter in the High Court:

Provided that nothing in this subsection shall be taken to prejudice any power which may be vested in an arbitrator or umpire of making orders with respect to any of the matters aforesaid.

13 *Time for making award*

(1) Subject to the provisions of subsection (2) of section twenty-two of this Act, and anything to the contrary in the arbitration agreement, an arbitrator or umpire shall have power to make an award at any time.

(2) The time, if any, limited for making an award, whether under this Act or otherwise, may from time to time be enlarged by order of the High Court or a judge thereof, whether that time has expired or not.

(3) The High Court may, on the application of any party to a reference, remove an arbitrator or umpire who fails to use all

reasonable dispatch in entering on and proceeding with the reference and making an award, and an arbitrator or umpire who is removed by the High Court under this subsection shall not be entitled to receive any remuneration in respect of his services.

For the purposes of this subsection, the expression 'proceeding with a reference' includes, in a case where two arbitrators are unable to agree, giving notice of that fact to the parties and to the umpire.

14 *Interim awards*

Unless a contrary intention is expressed therein, every arbitration agreement shall, where such a provision is applicable to the reference, be deemed to contain a provision that the arbitrator or umpire may, if he thinks fit, make an interim award, and any reference in this Part of this Act to an award includes a reference to an interim award.

15 *Specific performance*

Unless a contrary intention is expressed therein, every arbitration agreement shall, where such a provision is applicable to the reference, be deemed to contain a provision that the arbitrator or umpire shall have the same power as the High Court to order specific performance of any contract other than a contract relating to land or any interest in land.

16 *Awards to be final*

Unless a contrary intention is expressed therein, every arbitration agreement shall, where such a provision is applicable to the reference, be deemed to contain a provision that the award to be made by the arbitrator or umpire shall be final and binding on the parties and the persons claiming under them respectively.

17 *Power to correct slips*

Unless a contrary intention is expressed in the arbitration agreement, the arbitrator or umpire shall have power to correct in an award any clerical mistake or error arising from any accidental slip or omission.

18 *Costs*

(1) Unless a contrary intention is expressed therein, every arbitration agreement shall be deemed to include a provision that the costs of the reference and award shall be in the discretion of the arbitrator or umpire, who may direct to and by whom and in what manner those costs or any part thereof shall be paid, and may tax or settle the amount of costs to be so paid or any part thereof, and may award costs to be

paid as between solicitor and client.

(2) Any costs directed by an award to be paid shall, unless the award otherwise directs, be taxable in the High Court.

(3) Any provision in an arbitration agreement to the effect that the parties or any party thereto shall in any event pay their or his own costs of the reference or award or any part thereof shall be void, and this Part of this Act shall, in the case of an arbitration agreement containing any such provision, have effect as if that provision were not contained therein:

Provided that nothing in this subsection shall invalidate such a provision when it is a part of an agreement to submit to arbitration a dispute which has arisen before the making of that agreement.

(4) If no provision is made by an award with respect to the costs of the reference, any party to the reference may, within fourteen days of the publication of the award or such further time as the High Court or a judge thereof may direct, apply to the arbitrator for an order directing by and to whom those costs shall be paid, and thereupon the arbitrator shall, after hearing any party who may desire to be heard, amend his award by adding thereto such directions as he may think proper with respect to the payment of the costs of the reference.

(5) Section sixty-nine of the Solicitors Act 1932 (which empowers a court before which any proceeding is being heard or is pending to charge property recovered or preserved in the proceeding with the payment of solicitors' costs) shall apply as if an arbitration were a proceeding in the High Court, and the High Court may make declarations and orders accordingly.

19 *Taxation of arbitrator's or umpire's fees*

(1) If in any case an arbitrator or umpire refuses to deliver his award except on payment of the fees demanded by him, the High Court may, on an application for the purpose, order that the arbitrator or umpire shall deliver the award to the applicant on payment into court by the applicant of the fees demanded, and further that the fees demanded shall be taxed by the taxing officer and that out of the money paid into court there shall be paid out to the arbitrator or umpire by way of fees such sum as may be found reasonable on taxation and that the balance of the money, if any, shall be paid out to the applicant.

(2) An application for the purposes of this section may be made by any party to the reference unless the fees demanded have been fixed by a written agreement between him and the arbitrator or umpire.

(3) A taxation of fees under this section may be reviewed in the same

manner as a taxation of costs.

(4) The arbitrator or umpire shall be entitled to appear and be heard on any taxation or review of taxation under this section.

20 *Interest on awards*

A sum directed to be paid by an award shall, unless the award otherwise directs, carry interest as from the date of the award and at the same rate as a judgment debt.

21 *Statement of Case:* Repealed by section 8(3)(b) of the 1979 Act.

22 *Power to remit award*

(1) In all cases of reference to arbitration the High Court or a judge thereof may from time to time remit the matters referred, or any of them, to the reconsideration of the arbitrator or umpire.

(2) Where an award is remitted, the arbitrator or umpire shall, unless the order otherwise directs, make his award within three months after the date of the order.

23 *Removal of arbitrator and setting aside of award*

(1) Where an arbitrator or umpire has misconducted himself or the proceedings, the High Court may remove him.

(2) Where an arbitrator or umpire has misconducted himself or the proceedings, or an arbitration or award has been improperly procured, the High Court may set the award aside.

(3) Where an application is made to set aside an award, the High Court may order that any money made payable by the award shall be brought into court or otherwise secured pending the determination of the application.

24 *Power of court to give relief where arbitrator is not impartial or the dispute involves question of fraud*

(1) Where an agreement between any parties provided that disputes which may arise in the future between them shall be referred to an arbitrator named or designated in the agreement, and after a dispute has arisen any party applies, on the ground that the arbitrator so named or designated is not or may not be impartial, for leave to revoke the authority of the arbitrator or for an injunction to restrain any other party or the arbitrator from proceeding with the arbitration, it shall not be a ground for refusing the application that the said party at the time when he made the agreement knew, or ought to have known, that

the arbitrator, by reason of his relation towards any other party to the agreement or of his connection with the subject referred, might not be capable of impartiality.

(2) Where an agreement between any parties provides that disputes which may arise in the future between them shall be referred to arbitration, and a dispute which so arises involves the question whether any such party has been guilty of fraud, the High Court shall, so far as may be necessary to enable that question to be determined by the High Court, have power to order that the agreement shall cease to have effect and power to give leave to revoke the authority of any arbitrator or umpire appointed by or by virtue of the agreement.

(3) In any case where by virtue of this section the High Court has power to order that an arbitration agreement shall cease to have effect or to give leave to revoke the authority of an arbitrator or umpire, the High Court may refuse to stay any action brought in breach of the argument.

25 *Power of court where arbitrator is removed or authority of arbitrator is revoked*

(1) Where an arbitrator (not being a sole arbitrator), or two or more arbitrators (not being all the arbitrators) or an umpire who has not entered on the reference is or are removed by the High Court or the Court of Appeal, the High Court may, on the application of any party to the arbitration agreement, appoint a person or persons to act as arbitrator or arbitrators or umpire in place of the person or persons so removed.

(2) Where the authority of an arbitrator or arbitrators or umpire is revoked by leave of the High Court or the Court of Appeal, or a sole arbitrator or all the arbitrators or an umpire who has entered on the reference is or are removed by the High Court or the Court of Appeal, the High Court may, on the application of any party to the arbitration agreement, either —

- (a) appoint a person to act as sole arbitrator in place of the person or persons removed; or
- (b) order that the arbitration agreement shall cease to have effect with respect to the dispute referred.

(3) A person appointed under this section by the High Court or the Court of Appeal, as an arbitrator or umpire shall have the like power to act in the reference and to make an award as if he had been appointed in accordance with the terms of the arbitration agreement.

(4) Where it is provided (whether by means of a provision in the

arbitration agreement or otherwise) that an award under an arbitration agreement shall be a condition precedent to the bringing of an action with respect to any matter to which the agreement applies, the High Court or the Court of Appeal, if it orders (whether under this section or under any other enactment) that the agreement shall cease to have effect as regards any particular dispute, may further order that the provision making an award a condition precedent to the bringing of an action shall also cease to have effect as regards that dispute.

26 *Enforcement of award*

(1) An award on an arbitration agreement may, by leave of the High Court or a judge thereof, be enforced in the same manner as a judgment or order to the same effect, and where leave is so given, judgment may be entered in terms of the award.

(2) If —

(a) the amount sought to be recovered does not exceed the current limit on jurisdiction in s. 40 of the County Courts Act 1959, and

(b) a county court so orders,

it shall be recoverable (by exceccution issued from the county court or otherwise) as if payable under an order of that court and shall not be enforceable under subsection (1) above.

(3) An application to the High Court under this section shall preclude an application to a county court, and an application to a county court under this section shall preclude an application to the High Court.

27 *Power of court to extend time for commencing arbitration proceedings*

Where the terms of an agreement to refer future disputes to arbitration provide that any claims to which the agreement applies shall be barred unless notice to appoint an arbitrator is given or an arbitrator is appointed or some other step to commence arbitration proceedings is taken within a time fixed by the agreement, and a dispute arises to which the agreement applies, the High Court, if it is of opinion that in the circumstances of the case undue hardship would otherwise be caused, and notwithstanding that the time so fixed has expired, may, on such terms, if any, as the justice of the case may require, but without prejudice to the provisions of any enactment limiting the time for the commencement of arbitration proceedings, extend the time for such period as it thinks proper.

28 *Terms as to costs, etc.*
Any order made under this Part of this Act may be made on such terms as to costs or otherwise as the authority making the order thinks just:
  [Provided that this section shall not apply to any order made under subsection (2) of section four of this Act.]

30 *Crown to be bound*
This Part of this Act [(except the provisions of subsection (2) of section four thereof)] shall apply to any arbitration to which His Majesty, either in right of the Crown or of the Duchy of Lancaster or otherwise, or the Duke of Cornwall, is a party.

31 *Application of Part I to statutory arbitrations*
(1) Subject to the provisions of section thirty-three of this Act, this Part of this Act, except the provisions thereof specified in subsection (2) of this section, shall apply to every arbitration under any other Act (whether passed before or after the commencement of this Act) as if the arbitration were pursuant to an arbitration agreement and as if that other Act were an arbitration agreement, except in so far as this Act is inconsistent with that other Act or with any rules or procedure authorised or recognised thereby.
  (2) The provisions referred to in subsection (1) of this section are subsection (1) of section two, section three, [subsection (2) of section four,] section five, subsection (3) of section eighteen and sections twenty-four, twenty-five, twenty-seven and twenty-nine.

32 *Meaning of 'arbitration agreement'*
In this Part of this Act, unless the context otherwise requires, the expression 'arbitration agreement' means a written agreement to submit present or future differences to arbitration, whether an arbitrator is named therein or not.

Arbitration Act 1975
1 *Staying court proceedings where party proves arbitration agreement*
(1) If any party to an arbitration agreement to which this section applies, or any person claiming through or under him, commences any legal proceedings in any court against any other party to the agreement, or any person claiming through or under him, in respect of any matter agreed to be referred, any party to the proceedings may at any time after appearance, and before delivering any pleadings or taking any other steps in the proceedings, apply to the court to stay the

proceedings; and the court, unless satisfied that the arbitration agreement is null and void, inoperative or incapable of being performed or that there is not in fact any dispute between the parties with regard to the matter agreed to be referred, shall make an order staying the proceedings.

(2) This section applies to any arbitration agreement which is not a domestic arbitration agreement; and neither section 4(1) of the Arbitration Act 1950 nor section 4 of the Arbitration Act (Northern Ireland) 1937 shall apply to an arbitration agreement to which this section applies.

(3) In the application of this section to Scotland, for the references to staying proceedings there shall be substituted references to sisting proceedings.

(4) In this section 'domestic arbitration agreement' means an arbitration agreement which does not provide, expressly or by implication, for arbitration in a State other than the United Kingdom and to which neither —

(a) an individual who is a national of, or habitually resident in, any State other than the United Kingdom; nor

(b) a body corporate which is incorporated in, or whose central management and control is exercised in, any State other than the United Kingdom;

is a party at the time the proceedings are commenced.

Arbitration Act 1979

1 *Judicial review of arbitration awards*

(1) In the Arbitration Act 1950 (in this Act referred to as 'the principal Act') section 21 (statement of case for a decision of the High Court) shall cease to have effect and, without prejudice to the right of appeal conferred by subsection (2) below, the High Court shall not have jurisdiction to set aside or remit an award on an arbitration agreement on the ground of errors of fact or law on the face of the award.

(2) Subject to subsection (3) below, an appeal shall lie to the High Court on any question of law arising out of an award made on an arbitration agreement; and on the determination of such an appeal the High Court may by order —

(a) confirm, vary or set aside the award; or

(b) remit the award to the reconsideration of the arbitrator or umpire together with the court's opinion on the question of law which was the subject of the appeal;

and where the award is remitted under paragraph (b) above the arbitrator or umpire shall, unless the order otherwise directs, make his award within three months after the date of the order.

(3) An appeal under this section may be brought by any of the parties to the reference —

    (a) with the consent of all the other parties to the reference; or

    (b) subject to section 3 below, with the leave of the court.

(4) The High Court shall not grant leave under subsection (3)(b) above unless it considers that, having regard to all the circumstances, the determination of the question of law concerned could substantially affect the rights of one or more of the parties to the arbitration agreement; and the court may make any leave which it gives conditional upon the applicant complying with such conditions as it considers appropriate.

(5) Subject to subsection (6) below, if an award is made and, on an application made by any of the parties to the reference —

    (a) with the consent of all the other parties to the reference, or

    (b) subject to section 3 below, with the leave of the court,

it appears to the High Court that the award does not or does not sufficiently set out the reasons for the award, the court may order the arbitrator or umpire concerned to state the reasons for his award in sufficient detail to enable the court, should an appeal be brought under this section, to consider any question of law arising out of the award.

(6) In any case where an award is made without any reason being given, the High Court shall not make an order under subsection (5) above unless it is satisfied —

    (a) that before the award was made *one* of the parties to the reference gave notice to the arbitrator or umpire concerned that a reasoned award would be required; or

    (b) that there is some special reason why such a notice was not given.

*(6A) Unless the High Court gives leave, no appeal shall lie to the Court of Appeal from a decision of the High Court —

    (a) to grant or refuse leave under subsection 3(b) or 5(b) above; or

    (b) to make or not to make an order under subsection (5) above.

(7) No appeal shall lie to the Court of Appeal from a decision of the High Court on an appeal under this section unless —

    (a) the High Court or the Court of Appeal gives leave; and

    (b) it is certified by the High Court that the question of law to which its decision relates either is one of general public importance or is one which for some other special reason should be considered

*Added by section 148(2) of the Supreme Court Act 1981

by the Court of Appeal.

(8) Where the award of an arbitrator or umpire is varied on appeal, the award as varied shall have effect (except for the purposes of this section) as if it were the award of the arbitrator or umpire.

2 *Determination of preliminary point of law by court*

(1) Subject to subsection (2) and section 3 below, on an application to the High Court made by any of the parties to a reference —

(a) with the consent of an arbitrator who has entered on the reference or, if an umpire has entered on the reference, with his consent, or

(b) with the consent of all the other parties,

the High Court shall have jurisdiction to determine any question of law arising in the course of the reference.

(2) The High Court shall not entertain an application under subsection (1)(a) above with respect to any question of law unless it is satisfied that —

(a) the determination of the application might produce substantial savings in costs to the parties; and

(b) the question of law is one in respect of which leave to appeal would be likely to be given under section 1(3)(b) above.

**(2A) Unless the High Court gives leave, no appeal shall lie to the Court of Appeal from a decision of the High Court to entertain or not to entertain an application under subsection 1(a) above.

(3) A decision of the High Court under †[sub-section (1) above] shall be deemed to be a judgment of the court within the meaning of section [16 of the Supreme Court Act 1981] (appeals to the Court of Appeal), but no appeal shall lie from such a decision unless —

(a) the High Court or the Court of Appeal gives leave; and

(b) it is certified by the High Court that the question of law to which its decision relates either is one of general public importance or is one which for some other special reason should be considered by the Court of Appeal.

3 *Exclusion agreements affecting rights under sections 1 and 2*

(1) Subject to the following provisions of this section and section 4 below —

(a) the High Court shall not, under section 1(3)(b) above, grant leave to appeal with respect to a question of law arising out of an award, and

** Added by Schedule 5, section 148 of the Supreme Court Act 1981.
† Substituted by section 148(3) of the Supreme Court Act 1981.

(b) the High Court shall not, under section 1(5)(b) above, grant leave to make an application with respect to an award, and

(c) no application may be made under section 2(1)(a) above with respect to a question of law.

if the parties to the reference in question have entered into an agreement in writing (in this section referred to as an 'exclusion agreement') which excludes the right of appeal under section 1 above in relation to that award or, in a case falling within paragraph (c) above, in relation to an award to which the determination of the question of law is material.

(2) An exclusion agreement may be expressed so as to relate to a particular award, to awards under a particular reference or to any other description of awards, whether arising out of the same reference or not; and an agreement may be an exclusion agreement for the purposes of this section whether it is entered into before or after the passing of this Act and whether or not it forms part of an arbitration agreement.

(3) In any case where —

(a) an arbitration agreement, other than a domestic arbitration agreement, provides for disputes between the parties to be referred to arbitration, and

(b) a dispute to which the agreement relates involves the question whether a party has been guilty of fraud, and

(c) the parties have entered into an exclusion agreement which is applicable to any award made on the reference of that dispute,

then, except in so far as the exclusion agreement otherwise provides, the High Court shall not exercise its powers under section 24(2) of the principal Act (to take steps necessary to enable the question to be determined by the High Court) in relation to that dispute.

(4) Except as provided by subsection (1) above, sections 1 and 2 above shall have effect notwithstanding anything in any agreement purporting —

(a) to prohibit or restrict access to the High Court; or

(b) to restrict the jurisdiction of that court; or

(c) to prohibit or restrict the making of a reasoned award.

(5) An exclusion agreement shall be of no effect in relation to an award made on, or a question of law arising in the course of a reference under, a statutory arbitration, that is to say, such an arbitration as is referred to in subsection (1) of section 31 of the principal Act.

(6) An exclusion agreement shall be of no effect in relation to an

award made on, or a question of law arising in the course of a reference under, an arbitration agreement which is a domestic arbitration agreement unless the exclusion agreement is entered into after the commencement of the arbitration in which the award is made or, as the case may be, in which the question of law arises.

(7) In this section 'domestic arbitration agreement' means an arbitration agreement which does not provide, expressly or by implication, for arbitration in a State other than the United Kingdom and to which neither —

    (a) an individual who is a national of, or habitually resident in, any State other than the United Kingdom, nor

    (b) a body corporate which is incorporated in, or whose central management and control is exercised in, any State other than the United Kingdom,

is a party at the time the arbitration agreement is entered into.

4 *Exclusion agreements not to apply in certain cases*

(1) Subject to subsection (3) below, if an arbitration award or a question of law arising in the course of a reference relates, in whole or in part, to —

    (a) a question or claim falling within the Admiralty jurisdiction of the High Court, or

    (b) a dispute arising out of a contract of insurance, or

    (c) a dispute arising out of a commodity contract,

an exclusion agreement shall have no effect in relation to the award or question unless either —

    (i) the exclusion agreement is entered into after the commencement of the arbitration in which the award is made or, as the case may be, in which the question of law arises, or

  (ii) the award or question relates to a contract which is expressed to be governed by a law other than the law of England and Wales.

    (2) In subscription (1)(c) above 'commodity contract' means a contract —

  (a) for the sale of goods regularly dealt with on a commodity market or exchange in England or Wales which is specified for the purposes of this section by an order made by the Secretary of State; and

(b) of a description so specified.

    (3) The Secretary of State may by order provide that subsection (1) above —

  (a) shall cease to have effect; or

(b) subject to such conditions as may be specified in the order, shall not apply to any exclusion agreement made in relation to an arbitration award of a description so specified;

and an order under this subsection may contain such supplementary, incidental and transitional provisions as appear to the Secretary of State to be necessary or expedient.

(4) The power to make an order under subsection (2) or subsection (3) above shall be exercisable by statutory instrument which shall be subject to annulment in pursuance of a resolution of either House of Parliament.

(5) In this section 'exclusion agreement' has the same meaning as in section 3 above.

5 *Interlocutory orders*

(1) If any party to a reference under an arbitration agreement fails within the time specified in the order or, if no time is so specified, within a reasonable time to comply with an order made by the arbitrator or umpire in the course of the reference, then, on the application of the arbitrator or umpire or of any party to the reference, the High Court may make an order extending the powers of the arbitrator or umpire as mentioned in subsection (2) below.

(2) If an order is made by the High Court under this section, the arbitrator or umpire shall have power, to the extent and subject to any conditions specified in that order, to continue with the reference in default of appearance or of any other act by one of the parties in like manner as a judge of the High Court might continue with proceedings in that court where a party fails to comply with an order of that court or a requirement of rules of court.

(3) Section 4(5) of the Administration of Justice Act 1970 (jurisdiction of the High Court to be exercisable by the Court of Appeal in relation to judge arbitrators and judge-umpires) shall not apply in relation to the power of the High Court to make an order under this section, but in the case of a reference to a judge-arbitrator or judge-umpire that power shall be exercisable as in the case of any other reference to arbitration and also by the judge-arbitrator or judge-umpire himself.

(4) Anything done by a judge-arbitrator or judge-umpire in the exercise of the power conferred by subsection (3) above shall be done by him in his capacity as judge of the High Court and have effect as if done by that court.

(5) The preceding provisions of this section have effect notwith-

standing anything in any agreement but do not derogate from any powers conferred on an arbitrator or umpire, whether by an arbitration agreement or otherwise.

(6) In this section 'judge-arbitrator' and 'judge-umpire' have the same meaning as in Schedule 3 to the Administration of Justice Act 1970.

6 *Minor amendments relating to awards and appointment of arbitrators and umpires* (1) In subsection (1) of section 8 of the principal Act (agreements where reference is to two arbitrators deemed to include provision that the arbitrators shall appoint an umpire immediately after their own appointment) —

    (a) for the words 'shall appoint an umpire immediately' there shall be substituted the words 'may appoint an umpire at any time'; and

    (b) at the end there shall be added the words 'and shall do so forthwith if they cannot agree'.

(2) For section 9 of the principal Act (agreements for reference to three arbitrators) there shall be substituted the following section: —

9 '*Majority award of three arbitrators*
Unless the contrary intention is expressed in the arbitration agreement, in any case where there is a reference to three arbitrators, the award of any two of the arbitrators shall be binding'.

(3) In section 10 of the principal Act (power of court in certain cases to appoint an arbitrator or umpire) in paragraph (c) after the word 'are', in the first place where it occurs, there shall be inserted the words 'required or are' and the words from 'or where' to the end of the paragraph shall be omitted.

(4) At the end of section 10 of the principal Act there shall be added the following subsection: —

    '(2) In any case where —

        (a) an arbitration agreement provides for the appointment of an arbitrator or umpire by a person who is neither one of the parties nor an existing arbitrator (whether the provision applies directly or in default of agreement by the parties or otherwise), and

        (b) that person refuses to make the appointment or does not make it within the time specified in the agreement or, if no time is so specified, within a reasonable time, any party to the agreement may serve the person in question with a written notice to appoint an arbitrator or umpire and, if the appointment is not made within seven clear days after the service of the notice, the High Court or a judge thereof may, on the application of the party who gave the notice, appoint an arbitrator or umpire who shall have the like powers to act in the reference and make an award as if he had been appointed in accordance with the terms of the agreement'.

7 Application and interpretation of certain provisions of Part I of principal Act

(1) References in the following provisions of Part I of the principal Act to that part of that Act shall have effect as if the preceding provisions of this Act were included in that Part, namely, —

(a) section 14 (interim awards);

(b) section 28 (terms as to costs of orders);

(c) section 30 (Crown to be bound);

(d) section 31 (application to statutory arbitrations); and

(e) section 32 (meaning of 'arbitration agreement').

(2) Subsections (2) and (3) of section 29 of the principal Act shall apply to determine when an arbitration is deemed to be commenced for the purposes of this Act.

(3) For the avoidance of doubt, it is hereby declared that the reference in subsection (1) of section 31 of the principal Act (statutory arbitrations) to arbitration order any other Act does not extend to arbitration under section 92 of the County Courts Act 1959 (cases in which proceedings are to be or may be referred to arbitration) and accordingly nothing in this Act or in Part I of the principal Act applies to arbitration under the said section 92.

Limitation Act 1980

34 Application of Act and other limitation enactments to arbitrations
(1) This Act and any other limitation enactment shall apply to arbitrations as they apply to actions in the High Court.

(2) Notwithstanding any term in an arbitration agreement to the effect that no cause of action shall accrue in respect of any matter required by the agreement to be referred until an award is made under the agreement, the cause of action shall, for the purposes of this Act

and any other limitation enactment (whether in their application to arbitrations or to other proceedings), be deemed to have accrued in respect of any such matter at the time when it would have accrued but for that term in the agreement.

(3) For the purposes of this Act and of any other limitation enactment an arbitration shall be treated as being commenced —

(a) when one party to the arbitration serves on the other party or parties a *notice* requiring him or them to appoint an arbitrator or to agree to the appointment of an arbitrator; or

(b) where the arbitration agreement provides that the reference shall be to a person named or designated in the agreement, when one party to the arbitration serves on the other party or *parties* a *notice* requiring him or them to submit the dispute to the person so named or designated.

(4) Any such notice may be served either —

(a) by delivering it to the person on whom it is to be served; or

(b) by leaving it at the usual or last-known place of abode in England and Wales of that person; or

(c) by sending it by post in a registered letter addressed to that person at his usual or last-known place of abode in England and Wales:

as well as in any other manner provided in the arbitration agreement.

(5) Where the High Court —

(a) orders that an award be set aside; or

(b) orders, after the commencement of an arbitration, that the arbitration agreement shall cease to have effect with respect to the dispute referred;

the court may further order that the period between the commencement of the arbitration and the date of the order of the court shall be excluded in computing the time prescribed by this Act or by any other limitation enactment for the commencement of proceedings (including arbitration) with respect to the dispute referred.

(6) This section shall apply to an arbitration under an Act of Parliament as well as to an arbitration pursuant to an arbitration agreement.

Administration of Justice Act 1970

4 *Power of judges of Commercial Court to take arbitrations*
(1) A judge of the Commercial Court may, if in all the circumstances he thinks fit, accept appointment as sole arbitrator, or as umpire, by or

by virtue of an arbitration agreement within the meaning of the Arbitration Act 1950, where the dispute appears to him to be of a commercial character.

(2) A judge of the Commercial Court shall not accept appointment as arbitrator or umpire unless the Lord Chief Justice has informed him that, having regard to the state of business in the High Court and [in the Crown Court], he can be made available to do so.

Appendix B

Arbitration terms in construction contracts

Joint Contracts Tribunal
Standard Form of Building Contract, Private Edition with Quantities
1963 Edition (July 1977 revision)

35* (1) Provided always that in case any dispute or difference shall arise between the Employer or the Architect on his behalf and the Contractor, either during the progress or after the completion or abandonment of the Works, as to the construction of this Contract or as to any matter or thing of whatsoever nature arising thereunder or in connection therewith (including any matter or thing left by this Contract to the discretion of the Architect or the withholding by the Architect of any certificate to which the Contractor may claim to be entitled or the measurement and valuation mentioned in clause 30(5) (a) of these Conditions or the rights and liabilities of the parties under clauses 25, 26, 32 or 33 of these Conditions), then such dispute of difference shall be and is hereby referred to the arbitration and final decision of a person to be agreed between the parties, or, failing agreement within 14 days after either party has given to the other a written request to concur in the appointment of an Arbitrator, a person to be appointed on the request of either party by the President or a Vice-President for the time being of the Royal Institute of British Architects.

(2) Such reference, except on article 3 or article 4 of the Articles of Agreement, or on the questions whether or not the issue of an instruction is empowered by these Conditions, whether or not a certificate has been improperly withheld or is not in accordance with

---

*The provisions of this Condition do not apply to any dispute that may arise between the Employer and the Contractor as referred to in clause 3 of the Supplemental Agreement annexed to these Conditions (the VAT Agreement).

these Conditions, or on any dispute or difference under clauses 32 and 33 of these Conditions, shall not be opened until after Practical Completion or alleged Practical Completion of the Works or termination or alleged termination of the Contractor's employment under this Contract, or abandonment of the Works, unless with the written consent of the Employer or the Architect on his behalf and the Contractor.

(3) Subject to the provisions of clauses 2 (2), 30 (7) and 31 D (3) of these Conditions, the Arbitrator shall, without prejudice to the generality of his powers, have power to direct such measurements and/or valuations as may in his opinion be desirable in order to determine the rights of the parties and to ascertain and award any sum which ought to have been the subject of or included in any certificate and to open up, review and revise any certificate, opinion, decision, requirement or notice and to determine all matters in dispute which shall be submitted to him in the same manner as if no such certificate, opinion, decision, requirement or notice had been given.

(4) The award of such Arbitrator shall be final and binding on the parties.

(5) *Whatever the nationality, residence or domicile of the Employer, the Contractor, any subcontractor or supplier or the Arbitrator, and wherever the Works, or any part thereof, are situated, the law of England shall be the proper law of this Contract and in particular (but not so as to derogate from the generality of the foregoing) the provisions of the Arbitration Act, 1950 (notwithstanding anything in section 34 thereof) shall apply to any arbitration under this Contract wherever the same, or any part of it, shall be conducted.

Joint Contracts Tribunal
Standard Form of Building Contract, Local Authorities
Edition with Quantities
1980 Edition

Article 5

5.1   In case any dispute or difference shall arise between the Employer or the Architect/Supervising Officer on his behalf and the

---

*Where the parties do not wish the proper law of the contract to be the law of England and/or do not wish the provisions of the Arbitration Act, 1950 to apply to any arbitration under the contract held under Scottish procedural law or other country appropriate amendments to this sub-clause should be made.

Contractor, either during the progress or after the completion or abandonment of the Works, as to

5.1   .1   the construction of this Contract, or

5.1   .2   any matter or thing of whatsoever nature arising hereunder or in connection herewith including any matter or thing left by this Contract to the discretion of the Architect/Supervising Officer or the withholding by the Architect/Supervising Officer of any certificate to which the Contractor may claim to be entitled or the adjustment of the Contract Sum under clause 30.6.2 or the rights and liabilities of the parties under clauses 27, 28, 32 or 33 or unreasonable withholding of consent or agreement by the Employer or the Architect/Supervising Officer on his behalf or by the Contractor, but

5.1   .3   excluding any dispute or difference under clause 19A, under clause 31 to the extent provided in clause 31.9 and under clause 3 of the VAT Agreement,

then such dispute or difference shall be and is hereby referred to the arbitration and final decision of a person to be agreed between the parties to act as Arbitrator, or, failing agreement within 14 days after either party has given to the other a written request to concur in the appointment of an Arbitrator, a person to be appointed on the request of either party by the President or a Vice-President for the time being of the Royal Institute of British Architects.

5.1   .4   Provided that if the dispute or difference to be referred to arbitration under this Contract raises issues which are substantially the same as or connected with issues raised in a related dispute between

the Employer and a Nominated Sub-Contractor under Agreement NSC/2 or NSC/2a as applicable or

the Contractor and any Nominated Sub-Contractor under Sub-Contract NSC/4 or NSC/4a as applicable or

the Contractor and/or the Employer and any Nominated Supplier whose contract of sale with the Contractor provides for the matters referred to in clause 36.4.8,

and if the related dispute has already been referred for determination to an Arbitrator, the Employer and Contractor hereby agree that the dispute or difference under this Contract shall be referred to the Arbitrator appointed to determine the related dispute; and such Arbitrator shall have power to make such directions and all necessary awards in the same way as if the procedure of the High Court as to joining one or more defendants or joining co-defendants or third parties was available to the parties and to him;

5.1 .5 save that the Employer or the Contractor may require the dispute or difference under this Contract to be referred to a different Arbitrator (to be appointed under this Contract) if either of them reasonably considers that the Arbitrator appointed to determine the related dispute is not appropriately qualified to determine the dispute or difference under this Contract.

5.1 .6 Articles 5.1.4 and 5.1.5 shall apply unless in the Appendix the words "Articles 5.1.4 and 5.1.5 apply" have been deleted.

5.2 Such reference, except

.1 on article 3 or article 4; or

.2 on the questions
whether or not the issue of an instruction is empowered by the Conditions or
whether or not a certificate has been improperly withheld; or
whether a certificate is not in accordance with the Conditions; or

.3 on any dispute or difference under clause 4.1 in regard to a reasonable objection by the Contractor, and clauses 25, 32 and 33,
shall not be opened until after Practical Completion or alleged Practical Completion of the Works or termination or alleged termination of the Contractor's employment under this Contract or abandonment of the Works, unless with the written consent of the Employer or the Architect/Supervising Officer on his behalf and the Contractor.

5.3 Subject to the provisions of clauses 4.2, 30.9, 38.4.3, 39.5.3 and 40.5 the Arbitrator shall, without prejudice to the generality of his powers, have power to direct such measurements and/or valuations as may in his opinion be desirable in order to determine the rights of the parties and to ascertain and award any sum which ought to have been the subject of or included in any certificate and to open up, review and revise any certificate, opinion, decision, requirement or notice and to determine all matters in dispute which shall be submitted to him in the same manner as if no such certificate, opinion, decision, requirement or notice had been given.

5.4   The award of such Arbitrator shall be final and binding on the parties.

5.5   Whatever the nationality, residence or domicile of the Employer, the Contractor, any subcontractor or supplier or the Arbitrator, and wherever the Works or any part thereof are situated, the law of England shall be the proper law of this Contract and in particular (but not so as to derogate from the generality of the foregoing) the provisions of the Arbitration Acts 1950 (notwithstanding anything in S.34 thereof) to 1979 shall apply to any arbitration under this Contract wherever the same, or any part of it, shall be conducted[f].

Form GC/Works/1
General Conditions of Government Contract
for Building and Civil Engineering Works
Edition 2 – September 1977

61   (1) All disputes, differences or questions between the parties to the Contract with respect to any matter or thing arising out of or relating to the Contract other than a matter or thing arising out of or relating to Condition 51 or as to which the decision or report of the Authority or of any other person is by the Contract expressed to be final and conclusive shall after notice by either party to the Contract to the other of them be referred to a single Arbitrator agreed for that purpose, or in default of such agreement to be appointed at the request of the Authority by the President of such one of the undermentioned as the Authority may decide, viz, the Law Society (or, when appropriate, the Law Society of Scotland), the Royal Institute of British Architects, the Royal Institution of Chartered Surveyors, the Royal Incorporation of Architects in Scotland, the Institutions of Civil Engineers, Mechanical Engineers, Heating and Ventilating Engineers, Electrical Engineers or Structural Engineers.

[f] Where the parties do not wish the proper law of the Contract to be the law of England and/or do not wish the provisions of the Arbitration Acts 1950 to 1979 to apply to any arbitration under the Contract held under the procedural law of Scotland (or other country) appropriate amendments to article 5.5 should be made.

(2) Unless the parties otherwise agree, such reference shall not take place until after the completion, alleged completion or abandonment of the Works or the determination of the Contract.

(3) In the case of the Contract being subject to English Law such reference shall be deemed to be a submission to arbitration under the Arbitration Act 1950, or any statutory modification or re-enactment thereof.

(4) In the case of the Contract being subject to Scots Law, the Law of Scotland shall apply to the arbitration and the award of the Arbiter, including any award as to the amount of any compensation, damages and expenses to or against any of the parties to the arbitration, shall be final and binding on the parties, provided that at any stage of the arbitration the Arbiter may, and if so requested by either of the parties shall, prepare a statement of facts in a special case for the opinion and judgment of the Court of Session on any question or questions of Law arising in the arbitration, and both parties to the arbitration shall be bound to concur in presenting to the Court a special case in the terms prepared by the Arbiter and in which the statement of facts prepared by him is agreed to by the parties, with such contentions as the parties or either of them may desire to add thereto for the opinion and judgment of the Court; and the Arbiter and the parties to the arbitration shall be bound by the answer or answers returned by the Court of Session, or if the case is appealed to the House of Lords, by the House, to the question or questions of Law stated in the case.

**Association of Consultant Architects
Form of Building Agreement 1982**

25.   DISPUTES

25.1   Alternative 1 – ADJUDICATOR – Delete as appropriate

The term "the Adjudicator" in this Agreement shall mean _____ of _____ _____ or such other person as may be appointed from time to time under Clause 25.4 to act as Adjudicator in place of the Adjudicator so appointed.

25.2   If any dispute or difference of any kind whatsoever shall arise between the Employer or the Architect and the Contractor at any time prior to the Taking-Over of the Works arising out of or in connection with this Agreement or the construction of the Works (either during the progress or after the completion or abandonment of the Works) as to: —

(a) any adjustment or alteration of the Contract Sum; or

(b) the Contractor's entitlement to and the length of any extension of time for the Taking-Over of the Works or any Section under Clause 11.5; or

(c) whether the Works are being executed in accordance with the Contract Documents; or

(d) either party's entitlement to terminate the Contractor's employment under Clause 20.1 or 20.2;

then such dispute or difference shall in the first place be referred to and settled by the Adjudicator who, within a period of 7 days after being requested by either party to do so, shall give written notice of his decision to the Employer and the Contractor. Such reference shall not relieve either party from any liability for the due and punctual performance of his obligations under this Agreement. The Adjudicator shall determine which party shall bear the costs of any reference to him and such costs shall be paid within 30 days of the date of his decision.

25.3 In giving a decision under Clause 25.2, the Adjudicator shall be deemed to be acting as expert and not as arbitrator and his decision under Clause 25.2 shall be final and binding upon the parties until the Taking-Over of the Works and shall forthwith be given effect to by the Contractor who shall proceed with the Works with all due diligence whether or not either party requires arbitration as provided in Clause 25.5.

25.4 If the Adjudicator fails to give his decision in accordance with the provisions of Clause 25.2 or if he shall be unable or refuse to act, all disputes or differences under Clause 25.2 shall be referred to and settled by a person to be agreed between the parties or, failing agreement within 7 days after either party has given to the other a written request to concur in the appointment of an Adjudicator, a person to be appointed upon the application of either party by the Chairman for the time being of the Association of Consultant Architects to act as Adjudicator for all the purposes of this Agreement.

25.5 If the Adjudicator appointed under Clause 25.4 of this Agreement refuses or neglects to give a decision or if, upon receipt of the Adjudicator's notice of his decision under Clause 25.2, either party is dissatisfied with the same such party may, subject to the provisions of Clauses 20.1 and 20.2, within 28 days after receiving the Adjudicator's notice of his decision, give notice to the Architect requiring that the matter should be referred to the arbitration of a person to be appointed under Clause 25.6. If no claim to arbitration has been notified to the Architect by either party within 28 days from receipt of notice of the Adjudicator's decision, such decision shall remain final and binding upon the parties.

25.6   All disputes or differences in respect of which a decision (if any) of the Adjudicator has not become final and binding under Clause 25.5 and all disputes or differences arising out of or in connection with this Agreement or the carrying out of the Works as to any matter or thing of whatsoever nature (including any matter or thing left to the discretion of the Architect or to the withholding by the Architect of any certificate to which the Contractor may claim to be entitled or any issue as to whether or not any certificate is in accordance with the provisions of this Agreement) which are not referable to the Adjudicator under Clause 25.2 shall, unless the parties agree to the contrary, be referred to the arbitration and final decision of the Adjudicator. Such reference shall not be opened until after the Taking-Over or alleged Taking-over of the Works or termination or alleged termination of the Contractor's employment except with the written consent of the Employer and the Contractor: Provided always that if, in the Employer's opinion, any dispute or difference to be referred to arbitration under this Agreement raises matters which are connected with matters raised in another dispute between the Contractor and any of his sub-contractors or suppliers and provided that such other dispute has not already been referred to an arbitrator, the Employer and the Contractor agree that such other dispute shall be referred to the arbitrator appointed under this Agreement and such arbitrator shall have power to deal with both such disputes as he thinks most just and convenient.

25.7   The arbitrator appointed under Clause 25.6 (whether he be the Adjudicator or otherwise) shall have full power to open up review and revise any decision, opinion, direction, certificate or valuation of the Architect or of the Adjudicator and the award of such arbitrator shall be final and binding on the parties. Where the Adjudicator is not the arbitrator appointed under Clause 25.6, no decision given by the Adjudicator under this Agreement shall disqualify him from being called as a witness and giving evidence before the arbitrator on any matter whatsoever.

English Law – Delete as appropriate

25.8 The law of England shall be the proper law of this Agreement and the provisions of the Arbitration Acts, 1950 to 1979 or any statutory modification or re-enactment thereof shall apply to any arbitration under this Agreement and such arbitration shall take place in England.

Scottish Law – Delete as appropriate

The law of Scotland shall be the proper law of this Agreement and the provisions of the Arbitration (Scotland) Act, 1894 or any statutory modification or re-enactment thereof shall apply to any arbitration under this Agreement and such arbitration shall take place in Scotland.

The parties hereby agree that the procedures contained in Administration of Justice (Scotland) Act, 1972 Section 3 shall not apply to any arbitration under this Agreement.

25.   DISPUTES
Alternative 2 – ARBITRATION – Delete as appropriate

25.1 If any dispute or difference of any kind whatsoever shall arise between the Employer or the Architect and the Contractor at any time prior to the Taking-Over of the Works arising out of or in connection with this Agreement or the carrying out of the Works, (either during the progress or after the completion or abandonment of the Works) as to:

(a)   the construction of this Agreement; or

(b)   any adjustment or alteration of the Contract Sum; or

(c)   the Contractor's entitlement to and the length of any extension of time for the Taking-Over of the Works or any Section under Clause 11.5; or

(d)   whether the Works are being executed in accordance with this Agreement; or

(e)   any other matter or thing of whatsoever nature (including any matter or thing left by this Agreement to the discretion of the Architect the withholding by the Architect of any certificate to which the Contractor may claim to be entitled or any issue as to whether or not any certificate is in

accordance with the provisions of this Agreement);
then such dispute or difference shall in the first place be referred to
and settled by the Architect who within a period of 7 days after
being requested by either party to do so shall give written notice of
his decision to the Employer and the Contractor. Such reference
shall not relieve either party from any liability for the due and
punctual performance of his obligations under this Agreement.

25.2　In giving a decision under Clause 25.1, the Architect shall be
deemed to be acting as expert and not as arbitrator and his decision
under Clause 25.1 shall be final and binding upon the parties until
the Taking-Over of the Works and shall forthwith be given effect
to by the Contractor who shall proceed with the Works with all due
diligence whether or not either party requires arbitration as
provided in Clause 25.4.

25.3　Upon receipt of the Architect's notice of his decision under Clause
25.1, if either party is dissatisfied with the same or if the Architect
shall fail to give notice of his decision within the time or in the
manner required by Clause 25.1, then either party may within 28
days after receiving the Architect's notice of his decision or of the
expiry of the time within which it should have been given, give
notice to the Architect requiring that the matter should be referred
to the arbitration of a person to be appointed under Clause 25.4. If
no claim to arbitration has been notified to the Architect by either
party within 28 days from receipt of such notice, the Architect's
decision shall remain final and binding upon the parties.

25.4　All disputes or differences in respect of which a decision (if any) of
the Architect has not become final and binding under Clause 25.3
shall be referred to the arbitration and final decision of a person to
be agreed between the parties, or, failing agreement within 14 days
after either party has given to the other a written request to concur
in the appointment of an arbitrator, a person to be appointed on the
request of either party by the Chairman for the time being of the
Association of Consultant Architects. The arbitrator so appointed
shall have full power to open up review and revise any decision
opinion direction certificate or valuation of the Architect.

25.5　Such reference shall not be opened until after the Taking-over or
alleged Taking-Over of the Works or termination or alleged
termination of the Contractor's employment, except with the
written consent of the Employer and the Contractor: Provided

always that if, in the Employer's opinion, any dispute or difference to be referred to arbitration under this Agreement raises matters which are connected with matters raised in another dispute between the Contractor and any of his sub-contractors or suppliers and provided that such other dispute has not already been referred to an arbitrator, the Employer and the Contractor agree that such other dispute shall be referred to the arbitrator appointed under this Agreement and such arbitrator shall have power to deal with both such disputes as he thinks most just and convenient.

English Law – Delete as appropriate

25.6 The law of England shall be the proper law of this Agreement and the provisions of Arbitration Acts 1950 to 1979 or any statutory modification or re-enactment thereof shall apply to any arbitration under this Agreement and such arbitration shall take place in England.

Scottish Law – Delete as appropriate

The law of Scotland shall be the proper law of this Agreement and the provisions of the Arbitration (Scotland) Act, 1894 or any statutory modification or re-enactment thereof shall apply to any arbitration under this Agreement and such arbitration shall take place in Scotland.
The parties hereby agree that the procedures contained in Administration of Justice (Scotland) Act, 1972 Section 3 shall not apply to any arbitration under this Agreement.

25. DISPUTES
Alternative 3 – LITIGATION – Delete as appropriate
English Law – Delete as appropriate

The English courts shall have jurisdiction over any dispute or difference which shall arise between the Employer or the Architect and the Contractor arising out of or in connection with this Agreement or the carrying out of the Works. The law of England shall be the proper law of this Agreement.

Scottish Law – Delete as appropriate

The Scottish courts shall have jurisdiction over any dispute or difference which shall arise between the Employer or the Architect and the Contractor arising out of or in connection with this Agreement or the carrying out of the Works. The law of Scotland shall be the proper law of this Agreement.

Institution of Civil Engineers
Conditions of Contract for Use in Connection
with Civil Engineering Construction
Fifth Edition

66. (1) If any dispute or difference of any kind whatsoever shall arise between the Employer and the Contractor in connection with or arising out of the Contract or the carrying out of the Works including any dispute as to any decision opinion instruction direction certificate or valuation of the Engineer (whether during the progress of the Works or after their completion and whether before or after the determination abandonment or breach of the Contract) it shall be referred to and settled by the Engineer who shall state his decision in writing and give *notice* of the same to *the Employer and the Contractor.* Unless the Contract shall have been already determined or abandoned the Contractor shall in every case continue to proceed with the Works with all due diligence and he shall give effect forthwith to every such decision of the Engineer unless and until the same shall be revised by an arbitrator as hereinafter provided. Such decisions shall be final and binding upon the Contractor and the Employer unless either of them shall require that the matter be referred to arbitration as hereinafter provided. If the Engineer shall fail to give such decision for a period of 3 calendar months after being requested to do so or if either the Employer or the Contractor be dissatisfied with any such decision of the Engineer then and in any such case either the Employer or the Contractor may within 3 calendar months after receiving notice of such decision or within *3 calendar months* after the expiration of the said period of 3 months (as the case may be) require that the matter shall be referred to the arbitration of a person to be agreed upon between the parties or (if the parties fail to appoint an arbitrator within one calendar month of either party serving on the other party a written notice to concur in the appointment of an arbitrator) a person to be appointed on the application of either party by the President for the time being of the Institution of Civil Engineers. If an arbitrator declines the appointment or after appointment is removed by order of a competent court or is incapable of acting or dies and the parties do not within one calendar month of the vacancy arising fill the vacancy then the President for the time being of the Institution of Civil Engineers may on the application of either party appoint an arbitrator to fill the vacancy. Any such reference to arbitration shall be deemed to be a submission to arbitration within the meaning of the Arbitration Act 1950 or the Arbitration (Scotland) Act 1894 as the case may be or any statutory re-enactment or amendment thereof for the time being in force. Any such reference to arbitration may be conducted in accordance with the Institution of Civil Engineer's Arbitration Procedure (1973) or any amendment or modification thereof being in force at the time of the appointment of the arbitrator and in cases where the President of the Institution of Civil Engineers is requested to appoint the arbitrator he may direct that the arbitration is conducted in accordance with the aforementioned Procedure or any amendment or modification thereof. Such arbitrator shall have full power to open up review and revise any decision opinion instruction direction certificate or valuation of the Engineer and neither party shall be limited in the proceedings before such arbitrator to the evidence or arguments put before the Engineer for the purpose of obtaining his decision above referred to. The award of the arbitrator shall be final and binding on the parties. Save as provided for in sub-clause (2) of this Clause no steps shall be taken in the reference to the arbitrator until after the completion or alleged completion of the Works unless with the written consent of the Employer and the Contractor. Provided always: —

(a) that the giving of a Certificate of Completion under Clause 48 shall not be a condition precedent to the taking of any step in such reference;

(b) that no decision given by the Engineer in accordance with the foregoing provisions shall disqualify him from being called as a witness and giving evidence before the arbitrator on any matter whatsoever relevant to the dispute or difference so referred to the arbitrator as aforesaid.

(2) In the case of any dispute or difference as to any matter arising under Clause 12 or the withholding by the Engineer of

any certificate or the withholding of any portion of the retention money under Clause 60 to which the Contractor claims to be entitled or as to the exercise of the Engineer's power to give a certificate under Clause 63(1) the reference to the arbitrator may proceed notwithstanding that the Works shall not then be or be alleged to be complete.

(3) In any case where the President for the time being of the Institution of Civil Engineers is not able to exercise the functions conferred on him by this Clause the said functions may be exercised on his behalf by a Vice-President for the time being of the said Institution.

APPLICATION TO SCOTLAND

67. If the Works are situated in Scotland the Contract shall in all respects be construed and operate as a Scottish contract and shall be interpreted in accordance with Scots law.

Fédération Internationale des Ingénieurs –Conseils and Fédération Internationale Européenne de la Construction Conditions of Contract (International) for Works of Civil Engineering Third Edition

67. If any *dispute* or *difference* of any kind whatsoever shall arise between the Employer and the Contractor or the Engineer and the Contractor in connection with, or arising out of the contract, or the execution of the Works, whether during the progress of the Works or after their completion and whether before or after the termination, abandonment or breach of the Contract, it shall, in the *first place*, be referred to and settled by the Engineer who shall, within a period of *ninety days* after being requested by either party to do so, give *written notice* of his decision to the Employer and the Contractor.

Subject to *arbitration*, as hereinafter provided, such decision in respect of every matter so referred shall be *final and binding* upon the Employer and the Contractor and shall forthwith be given effect to by the Employer and by the Contractor, who shall proceed with the execution of the Works with all due diligence whether he or the Employer requires arbitration, as hereinafter provided, or not.

If the Engineer has given written notice of his decision to the

Employer and the Contractor and no claim to arbitration has been communicated to him by either the Employer or the Contractor within a period of ninety days from receipt of such notice, the said decision shall remain final and binding upon the Employer and the Contractor. If the Engineer shall fail to give notice of his decision, as aforesaid, within a period of ninety days after being requested as aforesaid, or if either the Employer or the Contractor be dissatisfied with any such decision, then and in any such case either the Employer or the Contractor may within ninety days after receiving notice of such decision, or within ninety days after the expiration of the first-named period of ninety days, as the case may be, require that the matter or matters in dispute be referred to arbitration as hereinafter provided.

All disputes or differences in respect of which the decision, if any, of the Engineer has not become final and binding as aforesaid shall be finally settled under the Rules of Conciliation and Arbitration of the International Chamber of Commerce by one or more arbitrators appointed under such Rules. The said arbitrator/s shall have full power to open up, revise and review any decision, opinion, direction, certificate or valuation of the Engineer. Neither party shall be limited in the proceedings before such arbitrator/s to the evidence or arguments put before the Engineer for the purpose of obtaining his said decision. No decision given by the Engineer in accordance with the foregoing provisions shall disqualify him from being called as a witness and giving evidence before the arbitrator/s on any matter whatsoever relevant to the dispute or difference referred to the arbitrator/s as aforesaid. The reference to arbitration may proceed notwithstanding that the Works shall not then be or be alleged to be complete, provided always that the obligations of the Employer, the Engineer and the Contractor shall not be altered by reason of the arbitration being conducted during the progress of the Works.

IMechE/IEE
Model Form of General Conditions 'A' 1976

37.— (i) If at any time any question, dispute, or difference shall arise between the Purchaser and the Contractor, either party shall, as soon as reasonably practicable, give to the other notice in writing of the existence of such question, dispute or difference specifying its nature and the point at issue, and the same shall be referred to the arbitration of a person to be agreed upon, or failing such agreement within six weeks, to some person appointed on the application of either of the parties hereto by the President for the time being of the Institution named in the Appendix, provided that a question, dispute or difference relating to a decision, instruction, or order of the Engineer shall not be referred to arbitration unless notice has been given by the Contractor in accordance with Clause 19(*b*) (*Engineer's Decisions*).

(ii) Performance of the Contract shall continue during arbitration proceedings unless the Engineer shall order the suspension thereof or of any part thereof, and if any such suspension shall be ordered the reasonable expenses of the Contractor occasioned by such suspension shall be added to the Contract Price. No payments due or payable by the Purchaser shall be withheld on account of pending reference to arbitration.

38.— The Contract shall in all respects be construed and operate as an English Contract and in conformity with English law, and all payments thereunder shall be made in sterling money. The marginal notes hereto shall not affect the construction hereof.

19.— The Contractor shall proceed with the Works in accordance with decisions, instructions, and orders given by the Engineer in accordance with these Conditions, provided always that —

(*a*) if the Contractor shall, without undue delay after being given any decision, instruction, or order otherwise than in writing, require it to be confirmed in writing, such decision, instruction, or order shall not be effective until written confirmation thereof has been received by the Contractor, and

(*b*) if the Contractor shall, by written notice to the Engineer within 14 days after receiving any decision, or order of the Engineer in writing or written confirmation thereof, intimate that he disputes or questions the decision, instruction, or order, giving his reasons for so doing, either party to the Contract shall be at liberty to refer the matter to arbitration pursuant to Clause 37 (*Arbitration*), but such an intimation shall not relieve the Contractor of his obligation to proceed with the Works in accordance with the decision, instructions, or order in respect of which the intimation has been given. The Contractor shall be at liberty in any such arbitration to rely on reasons additional to the reasons stated in the said intimation.

Table of Cases

Note

The following abbreviations of references to Reports are used:

AC – Law Reports Appeal Cases Series
All ER – All England Law Reports
Ch – Law Reports Chancery Series
ER – English Reports
KB – Law Reports King's Bench Series
Ll.L.R – Lloyd's List Law Reports
Lloyd's Rep – Lloyd's Law Reports
QB – Law Reports Queen's Bench Series
WLR – Weekly Law Reports

Other reports cited are listed without abbreviation.
Where extracts from judgments appear in the text, these are denoted by references in **bold type**.

Table of Statutes

Where extracts from statutes or sections of statutes appear in the text, these are denoted by references in **bold type**.

Subject Index

Appendix C
The Arbitration Procedure of the Institution of Civil Engineers 1983 (replacing the I.C.E. Arbitration Procedure 1973, issued in 1976)

PART A Rule 1 Notice to Refer. The arbitration commences with a *Notice to Refer* served by one party on the other, which has to contain reference to the matters in dispute. If taking place under I.C.E. Clause 66, it must also specify: (a) date when the matters were referred to Engineer under Clause 66 (1) (b): date when he gave his decision on them. This is required, of course, for the purpose of determining whether the reference to arbitration is within the 3 months time limit, allowed by that clause. As to what is a decision by the Engineer see *Monmouth CC v Costelloe & Kemple Ltd (1965)*.

Rule 2. Appointment of Sole Arbitrator. Either party may serve on the other a *Notice to Concur* in the appointment of an arbitrator, with a list of suggested suitable arbitrators. In 14 days, the other may agree on one on the list or may submit an alternative list. If the parties agree, the person selected has to be advised. The date of appointment is the date when the arbitrator *posts* notice of acceptance.

Rule 3. Appointments by President. If the parties have not agreed upon an arbitrator within one month of service of Notice to concur, either party can apply to President of the I.C.E., with the appropriate fee. The procedure the Institution will follow is laid down.

Rule 4. Further Disputes. Either party may put forward other disputes before arbitrator's appointment. Once appointed, he is empowered to determine any issue 'connected with and necessary' to the determination of any dispute referred. This wording is presumably intended to make it clear that he has power to deal with issues arising from tort, such as negligence or breach of statutory duty, raised in connection with the same facts, and is not restricted to issues arising out of, or for breach of the contract.

PART B. Rule 4. Power to control Proceedings. Nothing new.

Rule 6. Power to order Protective Measures. Under section 12(1) of the Arbitration Act 1950, every arbitration agreement is deemed to contain a provision that the parties will 'do *all . . . things* during the proceedings on the reference the arbitrator . . . may require'. In spite of this wide wording, the width of which has been emphasised in *The Vasso* (1983), some limitations have been placed upon an arbitrator's powers by the courts. *In re Unione Stearinerie Lanza and Wiener* 1917 2 KB 558, in spite of the wording of the statute, it was held that an arbitrator, in the absence of express authorisation, could not order either party to give security for costs. The new rules expressly authorise him to do so, and also to order his own costs to be secured. He is also given power to order deposit of money or other security up to the amount in dispute. Also, he is expressly empowered to give directions for the detention or sale of any part of 'the subject matter of the dispute', and the preservation of evidence.

Rule 7. Power to order concurrent hearings. Where disputes have arisen under two or more different contracts (e.g. the I.C.E. main contract between employer and contractor, and that between contractor and sub-contractor) arising from the same subject matter, the arbitrator may *with the agreement of all the parties* order that the matters in issue shall be heard together. That is so self evident that it is surprising to find it stated. What is surprising, however, are the words authorising him to do so 'upon the application of one of the parties to all the contracts involved'. This appears to be unenforceable for the reasons set out in Parris *Standard Form of Building Contract: JCT 80* [2.02], since there is no privity of contract. In any event, it could only apply in the unlikely event of the same arbitrator being appointed to the two different arbitrations. The courts have no power to order concurrent hearings without the consent of the parties: *Abu Dhabi Gas v Eastern Bechtel* (1982) 1-CLD-10-27; even though they have power to appoint the same arbitrator to two references arising out of the same work.

Rule 8. Powers at Hearing. Contains nothing which is not within the arbitrator's ordinary powers.

PART C. Rule 10. Preliminary Meeting. Provides that a preliminary meeting shall be held 'as soon as possible' and there the arbitrator shall decide whether the Short Procedure (Part F below) or Special Procedure (Part G below) shall be followed.

Rule 11. Pleadings and Discovery. Confirms arbitrator's existing powers but expressly authorises him to debar a party in default 'from relying on the matters in respect of which he is in default'.

Rule 12. Procedural Meetings. Authorises these at any time.

Rule 13. Preparations for Hearing. Empowers arbitrator to order parties to agree facts and figures and produce agreed documents.

Rule 14. Summary Award. This is a major departure, at least in terminology, and is based on the (dubious) view that any Interim Award empowered by section 14 Arbitration Act 1950 must be 'final and binding'. The Act does not say so, and in view of the observations of Mr. Justice Lloyd in *The Vasso* (1983) to the effect that all interlocutory orders by the arbitrator are interim awards, this view appears unlikely to be correct. However, the arbitrator may order what is now termed a Summary Award of 'a reasonable proportion of the final nett amount which in his opinion that party is likely to be ordered to pay', but only after taking into account defence and counter-claims. The Summary Award can be made to a stakeholder. It is to be 'final and binding on the parties', unless varied by any subsequent award. If in fact it is an interim award for the purpose of s.14 of the 1950 Act, as it is submitted it is, it could be appealed under s.7(1)(a) of the 1979 Act; in which case, there will be no need to show 'a substantial saving on costs'.

PART D. Rule 15. Procedure. Empowers arbitrator to order that any submissions shall be put in writing etc., but all well within powers already conferred by section 12(1) *supra*.

Rule 16. Evidence. Little new, except that (a) no expert evidence to be admissible without the consent of the arbitrator, (b) he can order proofs of evidence on facts to be put in writing and delivered to the other side, and allow this instead of oral evidence (c) any party can be ordered to submit in advance questions he intends to put in cross-examination (d) allows arbitrator to adopt inquisitorial procedure.

PART E Rule 17. The Award. Nothing new.

Rule 18. Reasons for Award. Provides that if a party asks for reasons he must state why he wants them. If for appeal under s.1 of Arbitration Act 1979, he must specify the points of law with which he wishes the reasons to deal. The arbitrator is not obliged to give reasons, even if so requested.

Rule 19. Appeals. Obliges parties making appeal or application to court to notify arbitrator.

PART F Rule 20. Short Procedure. Provides for arbitration on documents alone plus view, if arbitrator deems it necessary, subject to an oral hearing for the purpose of receiving oral submissions or questions; obliges the arbitrator to publish award one month thereafter.

Rule 21. Other Matters. Costs: no power to award costs in short procedure; fees to be paid in equal shares. Short Procedure can be terminated at any point before award by either party, subject to conditions.

PART G Rule 22. Special Procedure for Experts. If parties agree, any issue of fact dependent on evidence of experts to be conducted on documents specified, and a subsequent meeting of the arbitrator with the experts – in the absence of the parties and with the exclusion of lawyers: 'No other person shall be entitled to address the Arbitrator or question any expert unless the parties *and* the Arbitrator agree'.

Rule 23. Costs. Arbitrator can award costs, *excluding* 'legal representation, assistance or other legal work' unless otherwise agreed.

PART H Rule 24. Interim Arbitrations. Provides for arbitration before completion of works, for award to be made 'as soon as possible and published within 14 days'. 'Interim Decision' to be final and binding, but may be re-opened by another arbitrator subsequently appointed.

PART J Rules 25, 26, 27 deal with definitions etc and purport to exclude liability of the Institution for 'any act, omission or misconduct'. Procedure does not apply to Scotland, for which a separate agreement is available.